THE ANGUISH OF DISPLACEMENT

The anguish
OF DISPLACEMENT

The Politics of Literacy in the
Letters of Mountain Families in
Shenandoah National Park

Katrina M. Powell

*To Jeff and Angela –
with fond memories,
Katy Powell*

University of Virginia Press | Charlottesville and London

University of Virginia Press
© 2007 by the Rector and Visitors of the University of Virginia
All rights reserved
Printed in the United States of America on acid-free paper

First published 2007

9 8 7 6 5 4 3 2 1

LIBRARY OF CONGRESS CATALOGING-IN-PUBLICATION DATA
Powell, Katrina M., 1967–
    The anguish of displacement : the politics of literacy in the letters of mountain
families in Shenandoah National Park / Katrina M. Powell.
        p. cm.
    Includes bibliographical references and index.
    ISBN 978-0-8139-2628-5 (cloth : alk. paper)
        1. Power (Social sciences)—Virginia. 2. Sociolinguistics—Virginia.
3. Appalachians (People)—Correspondence. 4. Internally displaced persons—
Virginia—History. 5. Shenandoah National Park (Va.)—History. I. Title.
HN 79. V 8 P 67 2007
307.209755'909043—dc22

                                                                2007014966

To the people who once had their homes
in Shenandoah National Park

and to Polly Powell, 1920–1998,
my grandmother, my inspiration

Contents

Preface

Over the Blue Ridge, the whisperer starts to whisper in tongues.
Remembered landscapes are left in me
The way a bee leaves its sting,
        hopelessly, passion-placed,
Untranslatable language.
Non-mystical, insoluble in blood, they act as an opposite
To the absolute, whose words are a solitude, and set to music.
All forms of landscape are autobiographical.
—Charles Wright, *Appalachia*

In the old mountain home
For six months more
Where then shall I go
Down in the valley
To perish and die
To leave my mountain home
Is such a loss and grief . . .
I would rather go to my grave
Than to leave my mountain home.
—From John T. Nicholson's poem "The Old Mountain Home,"
published in the *Madison County Eagle*, June 1, 1934

Shenandoah National Park of Virginia inspires stories. Some describe hiking its many trails, avoiding stinging nettles, crossing waterfalls, and gazing across the mountain range that reflects blue throughout the day. Few would dispute its beauty and the pleasure of seeing (or climbing over) the jagged rocks of Stony Man or Old Rag mountains. But underneath the beauty and preservation of the park is a cultural history that many do not know. For those who *do* know the park's history, telling stories about how the park was formed, particularly about the people who had lived there and been displaced, is an important part of the region's identity.

The collection of the nearly three hundred letters discussed in this book is housed at Shenandoah National Park's small archives in Luray, Virginia. I grew up in Madison County, Virginia, one of the eight counties affected by the formation of Shenandoah National Park (SNP) and across the mountain from the park's headquarters. While growing up I had heard stories about the park, but I became aware of the letters only recently while reading in my family's local newspaper about a controversy regarding the artifacts held by the park. Less than five years ago, the letters were not available to the public because they had not been cataloged. However, many family historians in the area were interested in viewing the letters and other artifacts collected from the homes of displaced families. Several people felt the park was "railroading" their efforts to view the various materials. Local newspapers covered the story, and subsequent letters to the editor insisted the items be made available for public access. The cultural historians at SNP, in fact, *were* in the process of cataloging the artifacts, and they became available to the public in 2001.

That same year, I was a new assistant professor in Louisiana. I was home visiting my family and decided to go to the archive to see what all the fuss was about. The small beige building tucked away in the woods at SNP's headquarters contained several kinds of valuable information about the park and its inhabitants, including land records, geological records, descriptions of plant and animal life, historical maps, and administrative correspondence. One of the archive's employees showed me the files housing information about the various families displaced when the park was formed. Among government documents in these files were also hand-penciled letters, written by mountain residents to government officials. As I sat at an antique table reading the small notepaper with penciled prose, I became overwhelmed by the stories contained in the letters. The letters documented what I had heard about the park and the people who had been "kicked out" of their homes so that a national park could be formed. The many stories I had heard growing up mingled with the stories in the letters, crafting new stories and perspectives about an old tension between some area residents and park officials.

As I read more and more letters, excitedly scribbling notes about particularly beautiful phrasings and phonetic spellings, I wondered how I might write about these letters so that further stories about the families who lived in the Shenandoah Park could be told without a continued misrepresentation of who the people were then and who their families are now. In deciding to take on this archival and historical research, I wanted to approach this project as a historical ethnographer, bringing to light a written discourse to complement the oral histories that surrounded my youth. Using the residents' own words, from letters written during a turbulent time, I examine what this writing meant in the past and what it means now as a form of social action.

Writing about and researching the letters written in the 1930s has prompted a new set of correspondence between me and some of the mountain families' descendants. As I shared my research with the families of the displaced, they shared with me stories about their families' experiences as the park was formed. Many families were willing to share their histories and to grant me permission to use their ancestors' letters. Some families were legitimately concerned about a continued misappropriation of their ancestors' lives. The tension among families remains, as many see the research and writing about their ancestors as further mistreatment and disrespect.

Despite my efforts to assure them of my intentions, several descendants stood their ground, and I must honor their concern for the representations of their families. My correspondence with these family members echoes the concern of many researchers, particularly ethnographers and oral historians, about the ethics of interviews and asking participants for permission to use their lives and words in our published research. As I continue to collect oral histories from descendants about their families' lives in the park, I must be aware of the ways that my own relationship to the history of the park, my position as a researcher, and who I am influence the interpretation of the information gathered.

During the summers of 2002 and 2003, while conducting research in the archives for this project, I lived with my parents in their home in Madison County. During the week I went to the archives and studied the letters, and on the weekends my parents and I hiked many of the trails in Shenandoah National Park. My experience of the land only enhanced my desire to understand further the stories of the park. However, my experience of the park, its trails, and its archives is very different from that of many of the families who have granted me permission to quote from their ancestors' letters. I have deep respect for those who have allowed this kind of intimate access into their families' lives so that others might have some knowledge of their stories.

The oral histories and letters of mountain families and their descendants, together with the research of the Park Service's cultural specialists, family historians, archaeologists, folklorists, and regional historians, tell important stories about the ways in which human beings survive displacement. The park's recent visitor center displays, videos, and publications reflect a new commitment to recognize the "sacrifice" made by mountain families. As the past continues to influence the activities of all these groups' professional and personal lives, the mountain residents' stories continue to be told, ensuring a fuller story about the people who once inhabited what is now Shenandoah National Park.

Acknowledgments

This book would not have been possible without the help of many people. I am indebted to the faculty and staff of the Department of English at Louisiana State University. As a junior faculty member there, I received much support and encouragement as I pursued this project and others at LSU.

Thanks to Robin Roberts, Angeletta Gourdine, and Susannah Monta, who read early drafts in a reading group. Thank you to Peggy Prenshaw for her guidance and encouragement. Thanks to Melissa Trosclair for her research assistance. Sarah Liggett mentored me in so many ways, including reading several drafts and talking with me many times about the ideas in this book. Thank you to James Olney for his encouragement and support, and for the valuable collection of autobiography scholarship.

Thanks especially to Malcolm Richardson, who was Department Chair during most of my time at LSU. Thanks as well to Anna Nardo for her support. Thanks also go to my valued colleagues Lillian Bridwell-Bowles, MaryBeth Lima, Petra Munro Hendry, and Becky Ropers-Huilman.

In particular, I'd like to thank Anne Coldiron, who taught me how to be a researcher and to work diligently. And finally, thanks to Katherine Henninger, who read several drafts of this project. Both women are tireless friends and colleagues.

I would also like to share my appreciation for my mentors Debra Journet, Chuck Bazerman, Brian Huot, and Pam Takayoshi, who have provided me guidance for many years. Also, I thank Cassandra Phillips for her friendship and encouragement.

This research was made possible by grants from the LSU Office of Research and Graduate Studies, and in particular thanks to Todd Pourciau; the College of Arts and Sciences Manship Grants, in particular thanks to Dean of the College Guillermo Ferreyra; and the Louisiana Board of Regents Summer Research Grants. I am particularly thankful to Ann Whitmer for her expertise in grant writing and management. This research was also made possible by a Fellowship from the National Endowment for the Humanities, during which time I completed many interviews and located the descendants of the writers discussed in this book. Any views, conclusions, or recommendations expressed in this book do not necessarily reflect those of the National Endowment for the Humanities.

I could not have completed the research or understood the history of the park without the work of SNP's Cultural Resource Specialist, Reed Engle. He read the manuscript twice, and took much time to assist me with historical facts and interpretation of the letters. His work has been invaluable, and I appreciate his kindness in spending so much time with this manuscript. While we did not always agree, his commitment to an accurate history of the park is unquestionable. Reed and the staff at the SNP Archives provided me with invaluable assistance and perspective as I spent many hours in their reading room in Luray, Virginia.

I met Caroline E. Janney while she worked at the SNP Archives and completed her graduate work in history at the University of Virginia. Her tireless efforts to find information for me and to discuss the manuscript are much appreciated. She has been a good friend and colleague. I could not have completed this book without her.

Several people were crucial in helping me find information about families. I would like to thank Julie Dickey, Theresa Cook Angus, Ellen Meadows Early, Debbie Nicholson, Linda Morris, and Anita Shifflett, who helped me with research. Thank you to Ora Meadows, Betty and Jake Hahn, and Alvin and Thelma Meadows for their time. Thank you to genealogists Shirley Breeden and Diane Nicholson Smith for their extensive family research. Thanks also to Charles Perdue, Nancy Martin-Perdue, and Audrey Horning for their crucial research on the folklife, history, and archaeology of Shenandoah National Park. Thanks also to Miriam Fuchs, Peter Mortensen, and Beth Daniell for editing earlier versions of this research. Thanks also to Robert Brooke for reading an earlier draft of the manuscript and encouraging this project.

Thank you to the librarians and staff at the University of Virginia's Alderman Library and the Special Collections and Rare Book Room. Thanks to the Albemarle County Clerk's Office, Albemarle Historical Society, Eugene Powell and Jackie Palmenter of the Greene County Historical Society, Greene County Clerk's Office, Madison County Clerk's Office, Augusta County Clerk's Office, Rappahannock County Clerk's Office, Rockingham County Clerk's Office, Warren County Clerk's Office, and Page County Clerk's Office for research assistance. Thanks to Harold Woodward and Ned Ellerbe, local family historians who provided valuable perspective and resources.

My thanks to the many families of people who were removed from their homes who encouraged this project. The following list includes family members who granted me permission to quote from their ancestors' letters: Larry Baugher, Goldie Helsley, Ruth Janney, Gladys Broyles Jenkins, Lois Cave Hurt, William Dodson, Ila Dyer Weaver, Hubert Cecil Gray, Vivian Taylor Shackelford, Wilsene Scott, Jeanette Pryor, Margaret Jones, Ronald L. Lam, Tammy Randel, Eva Kyger, Virginia Lillard, Charles Nicholson, Dorothy Seal, Susan Trobough, Mr. and Mrs. Carroll R. Shifflett, Florence Nicholson Morgan, George Nicholson, Samuel Richard Nicholson, Wendy Hoge, Ora Meadows, Nellie Haney Sims, Grace Rothstein, James D. Blackwell, Janice Lam Whitlock, Patricia Lam Jenkins, Doris Breeden, Cathaline Hensley, Goldie Seal, Mrs. Owen Baugher, and Harold Breeden.

My family has for many years supported my endeavors and encouraged this research. Thanks to my sister and her husband, Amy and Ray Acors, and their children, Hayden and Cassidee, for showing me what is important in life. My father and mother, Mike and Randee Powell, who have worked for their community for over twenty years, have taught me the value of knowing a community's history. My in-laws, Joe and Fran Scallorns, have also encouraged me along the way. And finally, Joseph Reid Scallorns, my husband, who knows how to be there when it counts.

I am grateful to the people of the park and their families for allowing me to tell their partial stories. There is so much more to their lives than what is here. I want them to know that their stories are worth telling.

A portion of this book was previously published as "Writing the Geography of the Blue Ridge Mountains: How Displacement Recorded the Land" in *Biography: An Interdisciplinary Quarterly* 25.1 (Winter 2002): 73–94, © by the Biographical Research Center, and appears by permission.

THE ANGUISH OF DISPLACEMENT

INTRODUCTION

understanding history through literacy

... nor shall private property be taken for public use without just
compensation.
—Fifth Amendment, United States Constitution

The past is never dead. It's not even past.
—William Faulkner, *Requiem for a Nun*

What defines a relationship of power is that it is a mode of action
that does not act directly and immediately on others. Instead, it acts
upon their actions: an action upon an action, on possible or actual
future or present actions.
—Michel Foucault, "The Subject and Power"

In the early 1930s, the Commonwealth of Virginia condemned the homes
of and displaced some five hundred families from eight counties (Albemarle, Augusta, Greene, Madison, Page, Rappahannock, Rockingham, and
Warren) so that the federal government might form a national park in the
eastern United States and near the nation's capital (see figure 1). The families living in the mountains varied in their socioeconomic standing: some
were wealthy orchard owners, while others were small farm owners, tenant farmers, or sharecroppers. As a result of Virginia's Public Park Condemnation Act in 1928, many landowners quickly sold their homes to the
state at "fair market" price and left to find housing elsewhere. Other families, primarily those who did not own land or who had little means to move,
remained within the park's proposed boundaries under a "special use per-

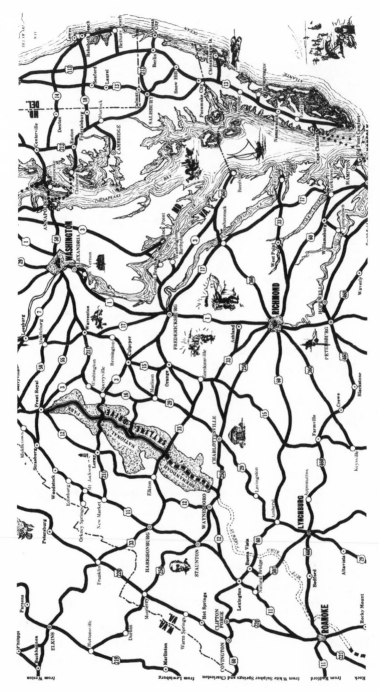

Fig. 1. A map of eastern Virginia and Washington DC. Shenandoah National Park comprises 176,429.8 acres in the Blue Ridge Mountains and extends over eight counties (Albemarle, Augusta, Greene, Madison, Page, Rappahannock, Rockingham, and Warren). The Skyline Drive, which connects to the Blue Ridge Parkway, runs nearly 100 miles from the northern to the southern end of the park.

mit," waiting for government assistance through the Resettlement Administration, the Department of Public Welfare, or the Federal Emergency Relief Administration (FERA). Most stayed in the park for one or two years; others remained four or five years, extending their permits and continuing to live in their homes as Skyline Drive was built and the park developed around them. During this interim period, before all families were vacated and most homes razed, families living in the park wrote letters to park and other government officials. State and National Park Service (NPS) officials and administrators kept meticulous records, saving the letters written to them and copies of their responses to the residents. Located in Luray, Virginia, the park's archives contain the three-hundred-letter collection that is the subject of this book.

Most of the letters collected in the park's archives contain the general business of residents as they were required to write for various permissions. These permissions included those for harvesting crops such as apples or potatoes from their mountain orchards and gardens, grazing cattle, or collecting wood for heating their homes. These activities became regulated once the federal government owned that land, requiring the remaining residents to write for permission to continue their routine living. For the most part, these requests were granted, though park officials reminded the residents of their responsibilities under the permits. When the park became federal property, a few people remaining there were small landowners. Some were tenants who had little means to move from their rental properties. As more and more families vacated their homes, others moved into them, making for a difficult administrative situation for government officials. The process of removing residents involved complex family circumstances and negotiations. Nearly two thousand tracts of land were bought by the state from logging and mining companies, banks, and nearly five hundred families. Of those families, approximately 25 percent remained in the park once it became federal land. The people who wrote letters to either state or park officials included landowners who remained landowners, landowners who had left, tenants who remained, tenants who had left, regional and local community members who were interested and concerned, and others whose lives were affected as they lived near but not within the park's boundaries. Both men and women wrote letters (at a ratio of approximately 3 to 1), and several maintained correspondence over several months or even years. For simplicity, I refer to the people who wrote letters as residents or mountain residents, often conflating the diversity among the people and their individual situations. Where information is known about land ownership, I include information about the individuals as I discuss their letters. It is important to understand, though, that each resident's situation was unique, and the responses of government officials depended on those situations.

In addition to the requests that were granted, several kinds of requests by residents were denied. These often included requests for removing building or fencing materials; moving to other, already vacated homes; and harvesting crops.[1] Some of the letters asked for assistance in settling disputes with neighbors as boundaries and homes changed hands. When one examines the written responses to residents, on the surface it appears that the denials of their requests were arbitrary or at least inconsistent. State and park officials attempted to be fair in distributing various goods and granting requests. But they faced a challenging and complex situation in managing the remaining people living within park boundaries. The letters, then, reveal this challenge and complexity as residents and government officials negotiated the situations. The letters discussed here disclose untold aspects of the story of Shenandoah National Park, stories about who the people were, what they thought about their impending relocation, and what they expected from the government agencies infringing on their livelihoods.

As I will argue in the chapters that follow, the complicated processes of land transfer, relocation, and park administration led residents to write letters that protested not the park itself (it was too late for that) but the way the residents themselves were "seen." The contents of the letters tell the stories of complex people, men and women working to sustain their lives in some way, even as their various ways of life were drastically changing as a result of land condemnation and ultimate displacement (see figure 2). Taken together, the letters exchanged between officials and residents reveal a multidirectional rhetorics of displacement:[2] that is, a system of rhetorical exchange that included assertion, participation, and resistance.

The impetus for these letters is a complicated story, with the makings of a southern gothic novel: people were arrested and forcibly removed from their land, the state was sued, homes were razed, and lives were forever changed (see figure 3). What political, social, and economic conditions must have been present for such a large-scale removal of people from their homes? What simultaneous forces must have been at work for a displace-

Fig. 2. One of the homes razed after the National Park Service took over title of the land from the state of Virginia. The homes in the park ranged from two-story farmhouses to one-room mud and plastered wood buildings. Some structures were used by the Park Service for administrative buildings while others were dismantled and used to build resettlement homes. (Courtesy of Shenandoah National Park Archives)

ment such as this to occur, especially when the displacement was in service of a tourist attraction rather than in fulfillment of a basic need such as a public-use water reservoir?[3] What might make a person living in the Blue Ridge Mountains—a person whose primary source of income would typically be from selling the potatoes grown on a small farm, a person whose living was made from the land, a person who attended school only for a short time—write a letter to a government official? What social practices and values were at work in orchestrating the correspondence between powerful government agencies and people with little more than "plain lumber" houses and barns?

The complexity of events leading a mountain resident to this act of social participation is the focus of this book. I consider literacy as social and symbolic action and explore what individual literate acts make known about public practices.[4] Among the questions that guide my work are the following: How do disempowered individuals represent themselves in written form to those in positions of power? How do their letters counter what was assumed about them? In what ways did women's and men's letters re-

Fig. 3. Walter Lee and Gertie Cave with several of their ten children in front of Panorama Hotel. According to their daughter, Lois Cave Hurt, when they moved, Gertie had "a very hard time" being separated from her extended family. When they received a "notice to vacate," Walter found work in Herndon, Virginia, about an hour's drive from Madison County. (Courtesy of Lois Cave Hurt; used by permission)

flect, or not, expected social roles and values? Finally, how do those in power render others displaceable, and how are rhetorics of displacement discernible across these events?

The mountain families discussed here participated in a public discourse through their letters. However, they were most often private people preoccupied with day-to-day living and with feeding their families and were not necessarily involved in national or regional policy. Few would have anticipated that their letters would have national significance. The archive of their letters, however, sheds light on a significant moment in regional and national history. The establishment of Shenandoah National Park (SNP) prompted these writers to participate in a distinctly public discourse. They wrote letters in order to communicate to government officials their positions, needs, and desires: a significant act of social participation given their circumstances and "available means."[5]

In examining the many facets of the rhetoric about the formation of SNP and the displacement of the mountain families living there, this book places competing accounts of the region and its history alongside one another. While family life and the history of this region have been explored academically in the separate fields of folklore and archaeology, here I examine these events through theories of literacy in order to unveil the complex layers of gender, material condition (that is, health, housing, wealth), and education in determining—and resisting—social position. The tensions and contradictions present in the various ways in which this story has been represented uncover a complex negotiation of power and social determination. The rhetorics employed in these letters by the mountain families counter monolithic discourse written *about* them. As such, these writers resisted the rhetorics of isolation inscribed for them and instead created unique identities that extend the collective memory of this time and place.

The primary objective in contemporary studies of literacy is to understand how language functions in society. Recent work has emphasized the political, social, and historical factors shaping certain literacy events and the ways in which individuals use literacy to operate within certain parameters.[6] The term "literacy" itself has been challenged and now is considered to range in definition from the ability to read and write to a more all-encompassing concept that includes the multiple ways in which people use and have access to literacy depending on context. Where, when, and how a person functions within a particular discourse community matters in terms of how literacy is perceived, determined, and assessed. As a result, literacies in context have become central to our understanding of culture and history. Indeed, as some recent work suggests, literacy, especially "ordinary acts of writing," is crucial to our understanding of historiography.[7] By understanding the ways in which literacy is represented, narrated, and understood, we glean further insights into the culturally constructed ways of knowing about certain events and historical moments.

Out of this understanding of context, or the way in which literacy is "situated," has arisen a new field of "socioliteracy" studies, or New Literacy Studies, that takes into account the various and complex factors surrounding the development and acquisition of literacy.[8] In developing this new social theory of literacy, scholars have argued that "literacy is best understood as a set of social practices; these are observable in events which are mediated by written texts."[9] In their explanation of situated literacy, they suggest that by examining written texts, we must also discern the social practices surrounding those texts if we are to understand the complexities of the "literacy event" itself.[10]

This book focuses, then, on the specific, situated literacy event of letters written by mountain families to government officials in the 1930s. These handwritten, penciled letters were prompted by the families' removal from their land and homes. Their land was acquired under Virginia's Public Park Condemnation Act (and upheld by the constitutional concept of eminent domain) to be used as a public park. Approximately 30 percent of the families who lived there did not own their land but were tenants. In any case, their displacement was imminent and they had no choice but to leave. On a local level, their letters depict a complex dynamic between the people and the government. On a broader level, their letters bring to light a moment in American history when the social, historical, and political climate was ripe for the displacement that occurred. Similarly, the letters expose multifaceted issues surrounding literacy, its use and disuse, and its power in documenting individual stories within broader hegemonic narratives about the Virginia landscape and the mountaineer.

This book examines a local and particular literacy event in order to understand literacy in general.[11] What has been known and generally accepted about literacy and education in central and southern Appalachia, in Virginia, and among Shenandoah National Park residents is subverted by the contents of these letters. However, there is no hidden or true story contained within the letters. Rather, these previously unexamined texts narrate untold aspects of the story. In light of this, I am conscious of constructing a counternarrative about the history of the park and the people who lived there. This re-visioning of the past specifically pays attention to the role of language and literacy in constructing historical narratives about the past. That is, my book is meant to contribute to current conversations about historiography and to argue for the centrality of literacy in understanding narratives and representations of the past.[12]

The Anguish of Displacement examines the letters in the SNP archives as artifacts, comparing the roles they played in the 1930s to the roles they play today. This project views letter writing as a "social practice," where I explore the "texts, the participants, the activities and the artefacts in their social contexts."[13] When the letters studied in this project were first written, they served as documentation of people's thoughts about their situation; but they largely did not function as catalysts for changing governmental policy. Today, however, the role of the letters has evolved. Family historians can read them to find out what kind of writing their ancestors did, or whether they participated in a written dialogue with officials about their land. Literacy scholars can examine them in terms of the complex rhetorical negotiations contained in them, and education scholars can compare the history of educational practice and the literacy skills contained in the letters. These letters are essential to understanding the history of the park and its people. They are also valuable for understanding a larger history of competing literacies, situated in complex contexts of class, region, gender, and race. The very existence of these letters and my analysis of them raise important issues of methodology and reciprocity.[14] And yet, in spite of the work of several scholars to re-narrate Appalachia's story, the region still calls up the image of illiteracy, poor education, and poverty.[15] Examining this literacy event in context highlights the ways in which those in power used the accepted narratives to achieve their own ends.

In retelling and re-remembering the past of the mountains, we recognize the centrality of individual stories to a collective narrative about a place or an event. Understanding the social context of a literacy event is crucial in recognizing how literacy shapes these narratives.[16] That is, the social contexts of individuals' lives make a difference in the kinds of literacy they practice. Issues of power are clearly reflected in the literate practices of the mountain communities. The opinions of the people tended not to matter unless they agreed with those in power. Those who opposed the dominant forces were squashed. The dominant discourses about the region avowed that the mountain families were all poor, illiterate, and ill suited to make decisions for themselves. Early promotional brochures, newspaper articles, and letters between government officials explicitly and implicitly asserted that the mountain people be excluded from the ongoing dialogue of establishing the park.

Unequal power relations, and the stereotypes that supported them, are clear both in the letters written by park officials and social workers and in the letters written by mountain families in resistance to this power. For instance, when two residents could not resolve a dispute, the park superintendent, James R. Lassiter, instructed them not to "be bothering us with all of your petty quarrels and scraps."[17] The circumstances the residents faced were seen to have little consequence compared to the development of the park itself. Indeed, NPS officials were not trained to manage people in this way: because of the interim period, NPS employees faced domestic situations they were not equipped to handle.[18] Letters written by soon-to-be or recently displaced property owners revealed an acute consciousness of the power differential and offered various (strategic) suggestions for how park officials should respond to their concerns. For instance, anticipating that her request to remove materials from her own home would be interpreted under a rubric of "stealing," Rebecca Baugher wrote the following letter, dated February 19, 1936, asserting her (what she hoped were shared) moral values and systems of right and wrong: "Some people will go ahead and take the building and not ask you. But I wouldn't take nothing like that and I am ask you for this building and I hope you will give it to me when we people move out of a park house they allway tear them down and burn them up outside of what people slip around and get. I believe you ought to give it to a poor person that I know I would if I was own it and I surely would be glad and appreciate it very much if you will give it to me." Here Baugher clearly constructs herself as one of the people who would not take something without asking permission. Like many residents' letters, hers reflects a desire to be seen as the right kind of person who would make good use of the materials.

Many residents were concerned that their integrity remain intact and that those in charge see them as good citizens. In another instance, John T. Nicholson (the poet and mountain resident quoted at the beginning of this book) removed windows from his father's vacant home, and Park Superintendent Lassiter wrote him a scathing letter accusing him of theft. Nicholson responded by saying, "It hurts me to know I have offended you," and he spent most of his letter apologizing for the theft and assuring Lassiter he would return the windows immediately. He was adamant about not realizing that taking the windows was wrong and promised Lassiter he would not do so again.

While Baugher and Nicholson construct accommodating tones, Lillie Herring seemed quite annoyed that she was accused of lying. She wrote, "I'm not lieing on no one and I'm not telling you one ward mare that can prave and I am living up to what I say." Her two-page letter was angry. She said that she could prove everything she claimed and she castigated officials for not realizing that she was honorable. Like many residents, she felt slighted that officials would presume these horrible things about her.

The respective writers' tone and sense of identity in relation to park officials are quite different from each other. Their letters are examples of the mountain families' knowledge of the kind of values privileged by those in power. In different ways, the writers examined here construct identities that they believe will be persuasive to those in power so that they might obtain materials or gain access to certain privileges.

Because these letters have never been published in their entirety, this book highlights voices not yet included in current studies of literacy.[19] While it provides new access to an important collection of letters, it also examines the relationship between self-representation versus published representations and thus alters both the story of Shenandoah National Park, Appalachia, and the myth of the mountaineer. In this way, this book responds to works such as *Confronting Appalachian Stereotypes: Back Talk from an American Region*, edited by Dwight Billings, Gurney Norman, and Katherine Ledford, and *Appalachia in the Making: The Mountain South in the Nineteenth Century*, edited by Mary Beth Pudup, Dwight Billings, and Altina Waller. The essays in these collections discuss individual and communal resistance to outside constructs of Appalachia, both historical and contemporary.

However, rewriting the myth of the mountaineer is not the only aim of this book. I also contrast past representations of mountaineer literacy with their own self-representation and ultimately argue for the inextricable link between literacy and identity.[20] The analyses here contribute to evolving theories of identity and autobiography, ultimately suggesting that the rhetorical or autobiographical act of letter writing constitutes a "fundamental challenge to identity."[21] That is, by asserting an identity counter to the one constructed for them, mountain families not only resisted a large government agency but also radically shifted their sense of who they were. This project complicates the notion of a unified identity for the mountaineer and closely examines the ways in which literacy learning is tied to identity. As an autobiographical act of asserting agency and identity, letter writing is, then, a form of both resistance and participation.

What these letters—both those written to mountain inhabitants and those written by them—make clear is that issues of identity are, at their core, issues of power. Identities constructed, enforced, and resisted through literacy go hand-in-hand with larger power dynamics, reinforced by symbolic and sometimes literal violence. When lawmakers, business owners, and state officials discussed the possibility of a park, their discourses easily came in contact with each other. What they never considered in all their negotiations were the implications for the people living on the land. Indeed, they rarely considered who the people *were*. The discourses of the residents were not part of the overall conversation about planning the park. In part, the perceived illiteracy of some of the mountain residents rendered their exclusion possible; in addition, the federal government was not even aware, until very late in the process, of just how large the numbers of residents were. This book places these competing literacies together, examining the tensions and contradictions that affected the removal of people from their homes. It also offers a way to understand how multiple discourses encountered each other, creating a contact zone where they collided with and influenced each other. Those in power used their literate skills to propose and acquire lands for a national park without consulting mountain families who did not have the same literacy. Because they did not have the same skills, they were assumed to be incompetent to participate in the decision-making process. In this way, literacy was imposed in a manner that can be considered violent.

While the acquisition of literacy is most often viewed as a liberating occurrence, the imposition of literacy suggests "a system of oppression that works against entire societies as well as against certain groups within given populations and against individual people."[22] In this interpretation of language acquisition, literacy learning reifies the status quo. Therefore, those in power remain in power, even when literacy is acquired by the underclasses. The chapters in this book therefore examine mountain families' literate acts within the contexts of systemic oppression, elitism, and class prejudice.

In the first chapter, "Literacy, Status, and Narrative Representation," I analyze the "official" rhetorics surrounding the formation of Shenandoah National Park and examine the ways in which mountain residents were constructed, particularly in rendering them displaceable. This chapter situates the rhetorics of the Shenandoah residents within broader conversations in Appalachian and literacy studies concerned with how mountaineers were represented in order to serve political and economic goals. Ultimately, I suggest that the existing stereotypes of Appalachians subsequently affected the ways in which some park officials worked with mountain residents.

In chapter 2, "Representation, Advocacy, and Identification," I discuss how mountain residents represented themselves in relation to and counter to what some government officials assumed about them. As residents wrote requests for tangible items such as keeping their homes, harvesting their crops, or removing building materials, they revealed their identities as citizens concerned with social fairness and responsibility. Their interaction with officials suggests that many community members were interested in the mountain families' situations and sought to help them through established or perceived connections and status. When mountain residents wrote for each other, they mirrored the advocacy and social action expected of those with certain value systems. Their sense of civic engagement, a shared value among community members, identified mountain residents as participating citizens in their neighborhoods as they attempted to maintain their livelihoods while the park developed around them.

Chapter 3, "Genre Knowledge and Assumptions about Class and Education," continues to highlight the kinds of requests made by residents as they became more and more aware of the expectations of park officials. But these letters in turn responded to the assumptions made about them in terms of their value systems and educational background. They carefully adopted cooperative poses while simultaneously working toward advancing individual rights and interests. Their representations of accepted values indicate not only their discursive knowledge but also their ability to convey that knowledge within a written medium.

The adoption of middle- and upper-class values is evident in the letters examined here, yet my research unearthed something more complex than a mere unidirectional flow of power. In chapter 4, "Resistance, Negotiation, and Social Action," I suggest that literacy functions not merely as violence against a group of individuals but also as an assertion of agency and resistance by them. Since the residents had no choice but to leave their homes, writing letters was one means of recourse.[23] They negotiated the system as it existed, rhetorically asserting themselves even if they could not literally change the situation at hand. As written literacy, their letters stand as historical artifacts of the residents' social action, testaments to their resistance of misrepresentation and exploitation.

Chapter 5, "Social Participation and Resisting Cultural Codes," examines mountain families' literate practices in a particular community and what they suggest about larger social, political, and historical issues. This chapter considers the history of letter writing and letter-writing instruction in the late nineteenth century, examining the ways in which contemporary values were reflected in this genre while simultaneously resisting imposed identities. In addition, I explore the significance of mountain residents' use of such epistolary conventions as "I hate to trouble you" and "Just a few lines." The juxtaposition of the mountaineers' letters with other historical documents brings untold stories to the forefront, recasting the history of the region and arguing for the centrality of individual narratives in the telling of communal narratives.

Finally, chapter 6, "Rhetorics of Displacement and the Politics of Eminent Domain," historicizes the rhetorical processes that occur when certain people are deemed dispensable in order to further the "public good." Tracing the history of eminent domain as implied in the Fifth Amendment of the U.S. Constitution, this chapter examines the ways in which large power structures such as government agencies, highway departments, and commercial developers have tended to prevail in disputes over individual property and landowners' rights. In addition, this chapter places rhetorics of displacement in a global context, addressing the differences and the similarities of displacement across types of relocation, including those caused by natural disaster. In the wake of mass relocations caused by catastrophic events such as the tsunami in Southeast Asia and Hurricane Katrina in the Gulf of Mexico, the politics of relocation and human response to involuntary displacement have become global concerns as local and national governments, relief agencies, and volunteers provide assistance to people forced to leave their homes.

Building on the previous chapter's conclusion that individual narratives are crucial to communal narratives, this sixth chapter argues for the early inclusion of individuals' needs and concerns as part of the relocation process. While relocations are inevitable, the inclusion and participation of the residents grants some agency to these individuals. A study of the issues of displacement in this one corner of Appalachian history, this book is meant to offer insight into the issues that have confronted and continue to confront policymakers anywhere who are involved in involuntary displacement and forced migration.

While this book is grounded in the contemporary theories of literacy that other studies have established, it departs from them methodologically by examining the collective literate practices of a particular group writing in a particular genre.[24] It focuses on a common text, the letter, written by several kinds of people, and on how this text fits into the multitude of other written texts concerning this displacement. Knowing this history informs other studies in literacy by showing the necessity of examining multiple genres, including individual examples of literacy, within a particular system to gain a fuller perspective on the event itself. This project advocates an elevated status for genres such as letters, diaries, and oral history because of the profound impact they can have on re-envisioning our historical narratives. By examining texts in this way, I ultimately suggest the simultaneity that characterizes literacy, namely, that it can be both violent and splendid. Literacy is not inherently good or bad: it is literacy's uses within systems of power that make for its results.[25]

As the field of literacy studies has expanded over the last twenty years, several images have been used to describe literacy, emphasizing the ways in which human beings come to and interact with it: as metaphors of adaptation, power, and a state of grace in acknowledgment of the ways in which the uses of literacy depend on situation, hierarchies, and value; as relational, in the way literacy crosses public and private boundaries and deeply affects one's relationship to others and to one's self; as social action, whereby the writing serves to "instruct" others; as violent, often having devastating effects on the users of language; and as an encounter, when local literacies come into contact with global literacies, forming "hybrid literacy practices."[26] My analyses of the letters written by mountain families lead me to argue for a less didactic view of literacy. Rather, I see literacy as on the move—as not only an identity marker but also an act of resistance to and participation in cultural norms.

Whether the mountain residents outwardly protested or not, their letter writing was an act of agency and resistance. Whether the content or tone was acquiescent or defiant, the letters both written and sent denote significant social actions that challenged cultural stereotypes and assumptions. For all their literacy "skills," many of those in power misread those who lived in the mountains. In this book I hope to read the mountain residents differently and to place their own stories in equal standing with the ones previously written about them.

LITERACY, STATUS, AND
NARRATIVE REPRESENTATION

Every image of the past that is not recognized by the present as one
of its own concerns threatens to disappear irretrievably.
—Walter Benjamin, *Illuminations*

As history constantly teaches us, discourse is not simply that which
translates struggles or systems of domination, but is the thing for
which and by which there is struggle, discourse is the power which is
to be seized.
—Michel Foucault, *The Order of Discourse*

The authoritative word demands that we acknowledge it, that we
make it our own; it binds us, quite independent of any power it might
have to persuade us internally; we encounter it with its authority
already fused to it
—Mikhail Bakhtin, *The Dialogic Imagination*

The land that comprises the Appalachian Mountains has had a turbulent
and contested past. According to historian Richard Drake, "Many are those
who consider Appalachia a mysterious region" (vii). What constitutes the
boundaries of Appalachia is continually debated by geologists, historians,
and mountain residents themselves. The landscape and its people have
been written about in literature, and the "myth of the mountaineer" continues to be a point of contention in literary and cultural studies.[1] Scholars
across disciplines have long been interested in the ways that Appalachians
have been misrepresented in the past and in the multiple identities that

comprise the mountaineer. Southerners in general have faced written and visual misrepresentation. According to Katherine Henninger, "The U.S. South has been so visualized—so often represented in photography, film television, and other visual media—that Americans and indeed readers from all over the Western world recognize 'the South' in and as image."[2]

In this chapter, then, I analyze various representations of the mountaineer, highlighting the politically charged notion of Appalachian identity and the role of literacy in constructing it. Doing so enables me to move to the specificity of Shenandoah National Park, and the prevailing attitudes and assumptions of those in charge of developing and administering the park toward those living in the mountains. Through officials' letters to each other and to the mountain residents, several kinds of identities were constructed about and for them, creating a presumed interaction not always fair or accurate.

The use of literacy reinforced stereotypes and myths of the mountaineer, and therefore became a tool for defining their identities. As a consequence, literacy was used to construct identities that made it easier for the state and federal governments to take over the land and displace its people.[3] The remaining chapters in this book present letters that counter those representations, as mountain residents represented themselves through their own literacy and in their own words as strikingly different from the accepted stereotypes.

A Brief History of Appalachia

Appalachia has a long history of ambiguous land ownership. The families who were displaced from Shenandoah National Park (SNP) were not the first to lose their homes in this region. Native American societies lived in Appalachia as early as 6000 BC.[4] The Monacans and the Manahoacs, who were known primarily as hunters and gatherers, lived seasonally in the Blue Ridge Mountains and the Shenandoah Valley.[5] When European fur traders first started hunting the lands in the late seventeenth and early eighteenth centuries, they negotiated a peaceful coexistence with the Native Americans. However, as fur trading became a lucrative business, Native Americans joined the competition and conflict ensued.[6] Hunting became a source of profit only after the white fur traders invaded the land.[7] As white Europeans infiltrated the area, Native Americans became susceptible to their diseases, and many tribes began migrating.

During the eighteenth century, Appalachia evolved from an Indian-dominated forest and fur economy to a yeoman farm economy.[8] At the beginning of the eighteenth century, Virginia's governor Alexander Spotswood recruited wealthy men to develop the Shenandoah Valley to generate capital. Speculators in the valley recruited yeoman from Pennsylvania to work the land, including many Scotch-Irish and Quakers. At the same time, however, Lord Fairfax, the British "feudal proprietor of the Northern Neck domain," thought he laid claim to the land and passed a law forbidding Virginia to make "further grants within his claim."[9] In addition, the "ever-present political tension between English Propriety and the colonial Virginia government heightened as a disagreement flared over the southern boundary."[10] The disputes over who owned the land and the specifics of boundaries made for an extensive history of squatting and disagreement about records and ownership.

Darwin Lambert's *The Undying Past of Shenandoah National Park* describes in detail the complicated disputes over land by Lord Fairfax and Governor Spotswood in the eighteenth century. After the Revolutionary War, a large-scale effort to survey the land and to determine ownership took place. Colonial settlers were encouraged to see the land as common. As Lambert says,

> The Big Surveys encouraged the contrary independence of Americans—thus: Much of the land wasn't noticeably used by owners, so to the public it was pie-in-the-sky, a vast "common." If people needed logs, they simply went up there and got them. They turned cattle loose to browse and hogs to root. They might settle up there, blazing trees around the land, building a cabin, raising a family. It had become an unwritten rule in limitless America that every family deserved enough land to support itself. If your big acreage was idle, and you failed for years to protect it, the county courts just might decide ownership disputes in favor of squatters actually in possession.[11]

During the eighteenth and nineteenth centuries, many Scotch-Irish, English, and Germans settled the land, and most in the mountains farmed small tracts of land. Some owned large apple orchards, which supplied the local communities and the state. By the time SNP was formed, a history of disagreement and lack of true boundaries had been established. That is, people who thought their families had owned land for generations had actually been squatting without ever knowing it.[12] Furthermore, many were the tenant farmers for landowners who lived in the valley and the Virginia Piedmont.[13]

The racial makeup of the Blue Ridge in Virginia is important in understanding constructions of whites living in the mountains. During the time of the park's founding, the mountains were primarily inhabited by whites, while few African Americans lived in the area. While many of the whites living there did not own slaves before the Civil War, there is evidence of slavery in the mountainous region.[14] Drake concludes that "the Appalachian South in the pre–Civil War decades was a quite different 'South' from the plantation South that so dominated the region from 1820 to 1860 and that led eleven of its states to secede and create a new nation."[15] Similarly, John Inscoe points to the variations in the ways mountaineers viewed blacks at the turn of the century. He cites evidence for mountaineers having a spectrum of attitudes toward blacks, ranging from hatred to ambivalence to participation in the abolitionist movement.[16] He concludes, "On either side of the Mason-Dixon line, nineteenth century white America was racist, varying only in degree and in form of expression. The same was true of Appalachia."[17] Contrary to pervading assumptions, Appalachians' racism or lack thereof was not any more or less prevalent than in the rest of the South.

While Appalachia represented the kinds of racial complexities present in the rest of the South, it is important to note that of the nearly 350 landowners displaced from their homes, none of them were African Americans. In the original survey for the park, several of the landowners were African American, but their land did not end up being purchased for the park. There are no records of African Americans writing letters to the Park Service during this time, but their story is yet another layer of the untold narrative about the history of the region.[18]

This story includes the demographic makeup of the region after the Civil War. According to 1930 census data, more blacks tended to live in urban areas after the Civil War and during Reconstruction. In 1930, 2,421,851 people lived in the state of Virginia: 26.8 percent were black and 73.1 percent were white.[19] Between the 1920 and 1930 censuses, there was a steady migration of blacks from Virginia's rural communities and a steady influx of whites. For instance, in Page County 6.1 percent of the population in 1920 was black, whereas in 1930 only 4.9 percent of the population was black.[20] While these trends suggest that many blacks left rural areas for the opportunities in urban areas, several African Americans owned property in rural areas during this time. In Augusta County, for instance, 9.2 percent of the population was classified as "Negro," yet 514 owned property.[21] Five African Americans in Augusta County and one in Madison County, listed as "colored" in the park's land records, owned property within the park's authorized boundaries; however, while these properties were within the original 321,000 proposed acres of the park, they were not part of the 176,429.8 that became the park and were therefore not displaced.[22]

African American history in this region is important to understanding white identity in this region.[23] Many of the people living in the mountains were not slave owners, as many did not have the money to buy slaves.[24] As identities for mountain residents were constructed by those living outside the area, their whiteness was called into question. While some from the middle and upper classes understood African Americans' preclusion from literacy, those same people often did not understand why poor whites could not read or write. That is, though mountain residents were white, they were not the "right kind" of white, and therefore were viewed as needing "help" from those who thought they knew how to provide it for them.

It is important to understand this inhabited past of Appalachia and the Blue Ridge in particular. The complexity of who lived there, who owned the land, and who had rights to it has been a standing debate throughout the region's history. Resistance and strife epitomized the dominant narratives about the people living in the wilderness, and as these narratives became commonly understood and accepted, it became increasingly difficult to believe that anyone with any education or "class" could live in the untamed terrain of the mountains that was not suitable for agriculture or industry.

Representations of mountain residents as illiterate and uneducated were closely linked to the general sentiment in the country about the South during and after Reconstruction, to standardized education, and to the Progressive Era in social and educational reforms. According to William Link, a prominent historian of Virginia's progressive education movement, "Local power over education was more apparent in rural schools, which, between the mid-nineteenth century and World War I, flourished in isolation from their urban counterparts."[25] Standardized curricula were a rarity in rural schools, although there are some records of various texts that individual schools used. Schools located in the mountain region of Virginia used primers such as *The McGuffey Reader*.[26] Public education was instituted in the United States in 1870, and the Commonwealth of Virginia enacted compulsory education for children ages 5–18 in 1908, which included attendance for only several months of the year. However, several schools existed in the mountains before this legislation, schools that were funded primarily by parents and local communities. Changes in public education at the turn of the century paralleled the general changes in attitudes about social programs and reform. Link suggests that "in a region that more than any other valued individualism, familial identity, and personal honor among white males, hostility toward public control of youth socialization was a virtual certainty. In the antebellum southern belief system, education remained a matter of private choice and an area in which central, outside government had no place."[27]

When reformers suggested making changes in rural education at the turn of the century, they thought that the "regional uplift" depended on educating white southerners. As was typical, poor whites were described as "semi-civilized" and "poor and ignorant."[28] The reformers' elitist attitudes about poor whites influenced politicians and businessmen, such as those interested in establishing the national park in Virginia. As a result, rhetorics of paternalistic reform were used to persuade local communities that moving people out of their isolated locations and close to education was not only "good" for them as individuals but also good for the general rebuilding of the South.

Little research exists about educating the poor, particularly women, in the South, and most historical studies of education in the South focus on those in the middle and upper classes.[29] What is known, however, is that when SNP was formed, several mountain schools—including Old Rag, Hazel Mountain, Sims Gap, Hull, Sunny Side, and President Hoover's— were closed.[30] The children attending those schools were then required to attend the larger schools in the lowlands, shifting children's access to and attitude toward education.[31] According to Nellie Haney Sims, whose parents boarded the schoolteachers for Sunny Side School at Fern Hill, and who were displaced from park land in Greene County, everyone was sad about having to move, "and the children they didn't know what to do because they take them out of school there where they'd been all their lives."[32] Many in the mountains valued education and went to great lengths to send their children to school. Therefore, when so many people, like the Haneys, were forced to move from their homes and were then educated in different places, their sense of literacy and education inevitably shifted.[33] The broader political and economic climates directly impacted individuals' education and literacy.[34] Indeed, it was the lure of moving closer to schools that prompted some mountain residents to abandon their resistance: they were told by some park promoters that moving to the lowlands would provide their children with greater educational opportunities. Businessmen and other community members supporting the park's founding assumed that more regulated education would benefit the mountain families.

For instance, Superintendent Lassiter's letter to Senator Harry F. Byrd in 1937 reiterated the perceived educational benefit to mountain residents.[35] In his response to Byrd's concern for a particular resident, Lassiter said, "Explain to him [the resident] that he will be better off if located in a small place in the valley where he can obtain some work" and where "he will also be nearer to schools, churches, medical care, and welfare." Not only was the general sentiment that mountain families "needed" better access to education, it was also assumed that mountaineers could not make decisions about education on their own. The perceptions and biases of social workers, government officials, and the surrounding communities were similar to the country's general sentiments about the mountaineer.

A large body of knowledge exists within Appalachian studies that addresses the "myth of the mountaineer," a phrase coined by Henry Shapiro in his study *Appalachia on Our Mind*. Several Appalachian studies scholars have examined the social and cultural factors that have contributed to the ways in which Appalachians have been misrepresented and stereotyped. According to Dwight Billings, "While the peoples and cultures in the Appalachian Mountains are decidedly plural, outside the region in the arts, the academy, and popular culture, many representations of them now, as for the past one hundred years, are often monolithic, pejorative, and unquestioned. But they are challenged in the region. Appalachian scholars have been engaged in the sustained critique of these stereotypes for many years, and the people of the region 'talk back' to stereotypes of themselves by who they are and how they live their lives."[36]

Appalachians are often characterized as individualistic, self-reliant, traditional, fatalistic, religiously fundamental, illiterate, hostile, and peculiar.[37] According to recent scholarship in Appalachian studies, these characterizations, including those in literature, have contributed to various economic, political, and social decisions made about the region.[38] Scholars have theorized about how these assumptions could have been made in the first place, and furthermore how these limited representations and assumptions could work against the people of Appalachia. Theories about the region have shifted from a culture of poverty, to internal colonialism, and finally to social class relations.[39] Contemporary scholarship is interested in the external ownership of the region and who has control of natural resources.[40] Both of these issues are tied to the issue of class and the relative power certain groups have in the region. As Foucault's quote at the beginning of the chapter suggests, the language itself and its use in describing a group of people has been a constant source of struggle for Appalachians.

Of all the representations, however, the most damaging has been that all Appalachians are the same. Contemporary scholars in Appalachian studies seek to subvert the notion of a homogeneous population and to document the rich and diverse cultures of the region. In an effort to understand the sources of poverty and lack of education that did and does exist in the region, scholars have shifted their attention to the political, cultural, and economic factors responsible for the various conditions present in Appalachia. In literacy studies, there has been a similar shift. Scholars in both Appalachian studies and literacy studies are interested in similar issues of economics, class, politics, and social reforms. The parallel directions that each field has taken are indicative of contemporary attention to the cultural and political factors that can shape a region's and an individual's identity. While many studies exist about current literacy programs in Appalachia, few have focused on the historical issues of literacy and education, specifically in Virginia. While some of the current research has briefly mentioned the literacy of mountain families, few focus on the history of literate practices of the region and the influence of contemporary culture on those practices.[41]

This study is situated within contemporary thought in Appalachian studies in terms of class conflicts; however, it departs from many studies in this field by having literacy and rhetorical construction as its central foci. Like many projects concerned with the Appalachian region, this study focuses on the "economic exploitation and political domination" and "operations of cultural power" that occurred in the Shenandoah region to precipitate a large displacement of people.[42] However, with literacy and rhetorical strategy as central issues, the significance of letter writing as an act of resistance can be discussed. In terms of literacy and language learning, therefore, we see how mountain residents saw themselves through their own words.[43]

Mountain residents' letters to government officials were not necessarily "ordinary"; rather, residents were prompted to write these letters by their very displacement. Whether engaging in written literacy was routine in their lives or not, they were asked to engage with power structures that had drastic effects on their lives.[44] While the establishment of SNP through its land conservation was on the surface a resistance to industrial change and development, it was also part of a government agency, the Department of the Interior, steeped in its own sets of values and goals.[45] Thus, its intrusion on the community had inevitable effects on the literate and social makeup of the people living there, both in and outside its boundaries.

Throughout the history of Appalachia, including the Blue Ridge Mountains of Virginia, people have been made to feel that they must defend their positions, either physically or metaphorically. Resistance and strife continue in contemporary Appalachia as people are placed in positions where they must defend their identities and their ways of life, taking activist stances against various power structures.[46] The letters discussed here, as acts of resistance, fall into the notion of anonymous action, insofar as they were not known to a larger public and ultimately had little result in terms of resisting relocation. That is, the letters appear to have had little effect. Whether or not the letters are deemed "successful" depends on how "success" and "action" are defined. If by successful we mean that the letters moved the park officials to grant most requests, then no, they were not successful. But to characterize the letters as unsuccessful would be misleading. While they did not necessarily incite the desired action from government officials, as the analyses in this book show, the rhetorical power of the letters in terms of individual and collective agency establishes the letters' rhetorical and symbolic achievement. The letters' legacy, longevity, and ability to prompt response both in the past and in the present sanction their worth in the historical record. Collectively, these letters suggest that enough people saw it necessary to resist what was thought of them by those in power, and to request, advocate, and sometimes demand what was left of their rights.

The park's founding and establishment are inextricably tied to the historical notion of Appalachia and in particular to the southern mountaineer. These dominant discourses, together with the turn of the century's move toward business and tourism, made for a moment where displacement could occur. Though collective efforts to resist the park's founding were minimal, it was the anonymous actions such as writing letters that indirectly resisted assumptions about mountain residents. As literacy became a commodity more and more valued in contemporary society, the letter writers examined here can be seen as attempting to participate in the emerging value system of the country.[47] Understanding the historical and economic factors contributing to the founding of the park is essential in realizing the impetus and the analysis of these letters.

As this brief history of Appalachia suggests, displacement and politics are integral parts of the region's history, and the people here were not entirely naive. Indeed, as the remaining chapters of this book demonstrate, the people living in the mountains in the 1920s and 1930s were savvy rhetoricians, capable of making their own decisions and participating in the discourse of the park. That they were at once innocent and shrewd makes for the complicated moment in the history of the park: all the conditions were set for this large-scale development and ultimate removal of nearly five hundred families.

The History of Shenandoah National Park: A Story of Business, Tourism, and Displacement

As Congress and Virginia businesspeople first conceived of a national park in the Appalachians in the 1920s, major social and political events were unfolding and therefore changing the United States. Prohibition had been ratified by the Eighteenth Amendment in 1918 and women had just gained the right to vote in 1920. Flappers, speakeasies, and jazz clubs were prevalent in the major cities, yet the economic depression had already begun to hit the rural areas of the country. In Virginia, for instance, a major blight had killed the chestnut trees that many mountaineers sold for firewood and lumber. The rural economy was depressed before the stock market crash of

Fig. 4. Local moonshiners pictured with a federal agent. This photograph and others like it were used to represent a monolithic portrait of the mountaineer as lawless. Contemporary examinations of visual representations of the mountaineer take into account the social and economic factors of manufacturing alcohol during Prohibition and the representations of those who did so. (Courtesy of Shenandoah National Park Archives)

1929. Prohibition, together with the blight, prompted some living in the Virginia mountains to sell moonshine illegally, even though the production and selling of liquor had previously been legal and a major source of cash for some. Consequently thought of as lawbreakers and a general menace, those "running shine" through the mountains created conflicts with local authorities (see figure 4).

Virginia's mountainous communities reflected some of the general tensions across the country. For instance, a group of World War I veterans camped out on Capitol Hill to ask Congress for their pensions early, because of their financial hardships after returning home from the war. The "Bonus March" requests were denied by Congress, and army forces were sent to remove the veterans from the lawn in front of the Capitol. While on the one hand the country's identity consisted of isolationism and individualism (Woodrow Wilson's League of Nations had been voted down), various writers and artists such as Ernest Hemingway and Gertrude Stein were fleeing the country seeking broader-minded thinking in Europe. The Harlem Renaissance was in full swing, Charles Lindbergh had crossed the ocean in a single-engine aircraft in 1927, and the Scopes trial debating the legality of teaching evolution divided the nation. While Adolph Hitler rose to power in Germany, U.S. president Franklin D. Roosevelt's Works Progress Administration (WPA) and Civilian Conservation Corps (CCC) programs were well under way as the country tried to rebuild after the Great Depression.

In Virginia, as in much of the South, the rebuilding after the Civil War exacerbated some of the problems between the North and the South. The rebuilding of the South continued through the beginning part of the twentieth century, culminating in social and educational reforms.[48] The Progressive Era of social and educational reforms, while making great strides in public education and relief, was steeped in paternalistic attitudes toward the lower classes. Many involved in the reforms, however, were sincere in their efforts to provide mass education, health care, and financial assistance.

While the National Park Service (NPS) was created in 1916 by President Woodrow Wilson, it was in 1907, during Theodore Roosevelt's presidency, that Congress voted in favor of a proposal for an eastern national park. When President Wilson created the NPS, fourteen parks and twenty-one monuments were already in existence. The NPS then surveyed the entire country to determine the best sites for wilderness preservation. Many of the national parks founded during this time (such as Yellowstone and Grand Canyon) consisted of land already considered wilderness. The East Coast, however, was largely developed. In 1924 Secretary of the Interior Hubert Work established the Southern Appalachian National Park Committee (SANPC) with congressional approval. The SANPC distributed questionnaires to solicit public opinion about locations for a park. Several states lobbied for the park, including Virginia, whose prominent business owners saw a national park as a way for the state of Virginia to progress, and also as a way to generate funds for road development. Several states in the country were moving toward industrialization, and Virginians interested in business and politics were concerned about preserving a state they felt was too beautiful to mar with factories.[49] Certainly Virginia did have industry (coal, tobacco, and timber), but when a group of wealthy businessmen suggested preserving a small portion of the Virginia landscape for tourism,[50] most Virginians approved of the idea based on a tradition of respect for the land and state.[51] However, many of the people involved in the park's development saw it as a lucrative business opportunity, and though preservation was the outcome, their motivation also involved profit.[52] In order to promote the park to other Virginians and to Congress, early pro-moters constructed the region as picturesque and unspoiled, and they played off a sense of returning to nature and the beauty of the mountains.

For instance, Shenandoah Valley, Inc., was formed to persuade Virginia's public and the federal government to locate its next national park in Vir-ginia.[53] George Pollock, a prominent businessman and owner of the moun-tain resort Skyland (located in the middle of the park) and a member of this newly formed group, responded to SANPC's questionnaire about possible locations for an eastern park. In his response, he described the area by say-ing, "There are within this area, of course, a few small mountain farms, of no great value."[54] The Shenandoah National Park Association (SNPA) used similar language in a promotional brochure, stating that the population from "the new national park [is] to be located in Virginia's scenic wonder-land." The brochure described the area as having "magnificent waterfalls, rugged cliffs, fine trout streams, stands of original timber."[55] Meant to per-suade local communities to support the park, the brochure included only minor mention of the people who inhabited the area or what might become of them should a park be approved, and it misrepresented the diversity of housing and socioeconomic status of the residents living there. It also cre-ated a sense that "small mountain farms" were of no value, that the homes themselves and the people living there could easily be moved, dismissed. Later, when the issue of families living within proposed boundaries could no longer be ignored, they were represented in a way that reinforced as-sumptions made about them: that they could not appreciate the beauty of where they lived and that they "needed" the middle and upper classes to help educate and conform them. For instance, in a December 25, 1924, issue of the *National Parks Bulletin*, published by the National Parks Association, mountain residents were only briefly mentioned, and that was in context of the "thrilling" landscape: "For here was fought the finish of a celebrated feud in which three men were shot to death. The neighborhood has been famous for its moonshine for many years. Many years ago the Blue Ridge was a haven of refuge for bandits and desperados who preyed upon the neighborhood settlements."[56] In the same bulletin, SANPC's full report to Congress was reprinted. Included in the report are the rules that guided the committee in its recommendation for a park in the eastern part of the country. One of these rules stated that the area have "a substantial part to contain forests, shrubs and flowers, and mountain streams, with picturesque cascades and waterfalls overhung with foliage, all untouched by the hand of man."[57] While the mountains were beautiful as described, there were a significant number of people living in the forests and using the water sources. In these early documents, if the people were not ignored completely, there were represented as unlawful and violent.

Once the decision was made by influential and wealthy political and business figures to establish SNP, then the contested processes of displacement began. The remaining sections in this chapter delineate the competing discourses examined in the book: (1) the rhetoric of the park promoters and the outside community in favor of establishing a park, and (2) the counterdiscourses by mountain residents begun only after a governmental decision was made to remove them from their homes. The interactions of these competing discourses resulted from a complicated set of circumstances surrounding the approval, planning, and development of the park.

Most of the histories written about the park emphasize the complicated turn of events and specific details necessary for such a large-scale effort to be successful.[58] SNP, unlike the other national parks in the west, was created by reclaiming land inhabited and owned by families, some for generations. In addition, the lands in the West were mostly already federally owned lands converted to "park" land with specific regulation for conservation. However, when SNP was first discussed, marketed, and established, the families living in the mountains were not considered; indeed, the NPS was largely unaware of the significant numbers of families living there. According to SNP cultural resource specialist Reed Engle, the NPS "had been told in the questionnaires that there were a 'few small farmers' in the mountains when in fact there were many, many residents. Congress was lobbied by Byrd, et al., and accepted the recommendations of the Southern Appalachian National Park Committee (which had been intensively lobbied and been wined and dined by Shen. Valley Inc.,) that SNP would be purchased and donated by the Commonwealth with no problems."[59] Since the land was to be donated by the state to the federal government, the process of surveying the land was the responsibility of the state (see figure 5). In 1925, the SNPA, a group of interested parties that overlapped with Shenandoah Val-

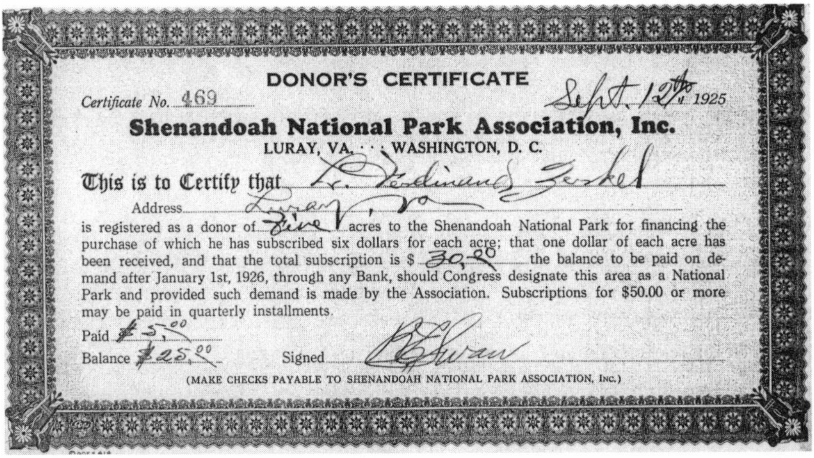

DONOR'S CERTIFICATE

Certificate No. 469 Sept. 12th 1925

Shenandoah National Park Association, Inc.

LURAY, VA. · · · WASHINGTON, D. C.

This is to Certify that L. Ferdinand Zerkel

Address Luray, Va

is registered as a donor of Five acres to the Shenandoah National Park for financing the purchase of which he has subscribed six dollars for each acre; that one dollar of each acre has been received, and that the total subscription is $ 30.00 the balance to be paid on demand after January 1st, 1926, through any Bank, should Congress designate this area as a National Park and provided such demand is made by the Association. Subscriptions for $50.00 or more may be paid in quarterly installments.

Paid $5.00

Balance $25.00 Signed

(MAKE CHECKS PAYABLE TO SHENANDOAH NATIONAL PARK ASSOCIATION, INC.)

Fig. 5. This "donor's certificate" was used by the Shenandoah National Park Association to promote a national park in Virginia. Through these donations, the association could prove to Congress that citizens of Virginia supported the establishment of a park in the region. (Courtesy of Shenandoah National Park Archives)

ley, Inc., was formed in order to raise funds to purchase the land within the proposed site.

A complicated series of events occurred in order to establish SNP, and it was not until late in its development that the people living there became an "issue" that the state had to address. In 1926, then governor Harry F. Byrd established the State Commission on Conservation and Development (SCCD) in order to control the collection of funds for purchasing land.[60] The first chairman of the commission, William Carson, was charged with surveying and appraising the land within the proposed site. This tract-by-tract inspection and survey of properties, conducted in 1932 and 1933, included a census of landowners and residents in the proposed park area.[61] During this time, Virginia officials interviewed mountain families, informing them of the state's intentions to form a national park and trying to persuade residents to sell their land willingly.

During this survey period, rumblings of resistance circulated among the people in the eight counties affected by the park's proposed boundaries. As might be expected, many people did not want to give up their mountain homes, even for a "fair market price." However, organized resistance did not occur or was not successful for several reasons. First, many people living in the mountains were not informed of the park's proposal until much of the decision making had already occurred. Second, some may not have known their options in resisting government decisions and laws. Third, the park's development, whether purposefully or not, was misrepresented to the people living there. This was in part due to a change in presidential administration. According to Engle, "[President Herbert] Hoover's Secretary of the Interior, Ray Lyman Wilbur, stated that residents would not be forced to move unless in the direct path of development."[62] However, in 1934 and under the Roosevelt administration, new NPS director Arno Cammerer said that all residents *would* have to leave in order for the federal government to accept title to the land.[63]

Changes in administrations and policies were emphasized in several oral histories and newspaper accounts, where residents recounted how they were told that they could continue living in the park but their land would be considered park property. Estelle Nicholson Dodson, for instance, whose father Eddie Nicholson's property was condemned by Virginia's Public Park Condemnation Act, suggests that residents felt tricked. In the following excerpt from her oral history, Dodson describes how several residents felt when state officials first told them about the park project:

> We were glad when the Park taken over it. Cause they made such a promise to us. We thought it was the finest thing ever happened. What they didn't hold out. . . . Well, taken homes away from you after they moved you outa here. Make ya . . . when they first come around they said that uh, well when they first started it up, they come around and tell you sweetest mouth you ever heard in your life to get your home. What they first wanted uh take the Park over and they want everybody that was able to . . . to donate as much as $10 to help out on it. Or then to give them an acre of land. Course we didn't have no land. And I don't know anybody that did, but that was what they wanted you know. But then they said you won't never be bothered again. We thought it was the finest thing in the world. But that wasn't true.[64]

Dodson felt misled, though changing administrations and subsequent changes in policy contributed to the confusion experienced by residents. Virginia state officials who talked to Dodson's family first most likely believed in what they were saying about residents' ability to live in government-provided homesteads. However, the federal government's Resettlement Administration (RA) had certain eligibility parameters for homesteads. Some residents were excited about the prospect of living in a "new" home, one made available to them through the RA. However, homesteads were available only through government-assisted loans. That is, if they qualified (residents withstood more interviews by home economists to determine their eligibility), they were able to incur debt on their resettlement home. Many residents had never paid a mortgage; they made their living off their land in the mountains. Consequently, many could often not make their loan payments on their resettlement homes. Dodson addressed this dilemma in her interview: "After they moved us down in here, they said these homes . . . before they moved us here . . . they said these homes would be our homes for life . . . by paying $20 a month and then for twenty years they would give us the deed to it, but they wouldn't let us stay no twenty years. They'd come up and 'save' it. That's why we have to move . . . our home was taken away again." Dodson's narrative tells an untold story about the park. When families were promised resettlement, it was only if they "qualified" for a loan on the home. Often people could not pay the loans (and were consequently turned over to the Department of Public Welfare) and therefore they lost their resettlement homes, a second loss to them after their original displacement from the park. More important in her narrative, though, is the feeling of betrayal that Dodson reflects toward those in authority. This feeling of betrayal has remained with some people who live in the area today.[65]

Once President Calvin Coolidge signed the bill in 1926 that authorized the creation of the park in the Blue Ridge Mountains to consist of 521,000 acres, SCCD chairman Carson conducted land assessments. While some, like Dodson's father, willingly left their property, opposition came from some landowners in the form of inflated land prices, and it became clear that the park faced some resistance. In order to avoid a lengthy delay because of resistance, Chairman Carson persuaded the Commonwealth's legislature to pass Virginia's holistic condemnation law so that appraisers could establish fair market value.

The Public Park Condemnation Act was passed in the Virginia legislature in the early part of 1928. As opposition to the park continued, several people were able to persuade officials not to include their land within park boundaries, in part because of their influence and in part because their appraised values were much higher than anticipated. In 1932, the SCCD proposed another reduction in the acreage to be condemned for the park. The land was resurveyed by the director of the National Park Service, Arno Cammerer. All of the land approved by the NPS, some 321,000 acres, was condemned by Virginia through the Condemnation Act. Land was bought from landowners at a "fair market price" and then "donated" to the federal government. The process of removal began, and construction of the Skyline Drive (on a 100-foot right-of-way given or sold by landowners who were glad to have an improved road) began while the formal handing over from state to federal government took several years of legal review and paperwork.[66] A layered process of people vacating their homes and building roads began under the SCCD's direction. The Skyline Drive, for instance, began with federal drought-relief funds in 1931, under the Emergency Construction Act (see figure 7), long before the SCCD owned deeds for the land proposed for the park. President Hoover, who had purchased his fishing camp within the boundaries of the park, approved spending the drought-relief funds to build the drive and to send relief to the families who lived in the area. Local residents were employed during this time to begin construction of the Skyline Drive, which at this point consisted of removing trees and rocks in order to build a roadbed. In 1933, Roosevelt's CCC workers began work on the Skyline Drive and on other park projects after its official transfer in 1935, and the CCC hired "upwards of 300 local men."[67] As the transfer of ownership from state to federal government became inevitable, it became evident that the people living within the park's boundaries posed several kinds of problems for state and federal officials.

It was during this time that park promoters began a campaign to assuage local opposition by representing mountain residents as in need of the services to be provided them once they were removed from the park. The rhetoric used by those in power to describe the mountaineers drastically affected residents' lives. Various published narratives composed by competing parties created contradictory representations of the region and its people that were steeped in political and cultural assumptions. One of the earliest representations of the region's inhabitants was contained in *Hollow Folk*, written by Dr. Mandel Sherman and Thomas Henry and published in 1933. Sherman, the director of the Washington Child Research Centre, hired several psychologists and sociologists to conduct surveys about the living conditions, mental states, and nutrition of families living in hollows within the park's proposed boundaries. Miriam Sizer, a local teacher and a

Fig. 7. Construction of Skyline Drive. Contractors, who hired some local residents, began work on the drive in 1931 with funds made available through Hoover's Emergency Construction and Relief Act. When Roosevelt's WPA programs began in 1933, the "CCC boys" continued the development of Skyline Drive, and more local residents were hired. (Courtesy of Shenandoah National Park Archives)

graduate student at the University of Virginia, assisted with the survey. According to archaeologist Audrey Horning, Sizer's generalizations fueled negative assumptions about park residents.[68] In addition to her work with the Centre, Sizer compiled a report titled "Tabulations," which made written recommendations to the RA and the state's welfare officials about the relocation issues of mountain families (she had already made these recommendations at a meeting with state officials in 1932). Sizer was later employed by the federal government's RA (which became involved in 1934) and proposed that mountain residents living in the park and unable to move of their own financial accord be relocated to homesteads subsidized by the government. This proposal was accepted by the RA, and a relationship between the Virginia Department of Public Welfare, the Park Service, and the RA (part of the Department of Agriculture's Farm Security Administration) was subsequently established. Ferdinand Zerkel, a local valley resident and member of Shenandoah Valley, Inc., later was employed by the Division of Subsistence Homesteads and conducted surveys of mountain residents to determine their eligibility for homesteads.

It is evident in Sizer's reports that she was genuinely concerned with the mountain folk and their well-being. Based on her interviews with families in several mountain hollows, she believed that people largely did not understand what would happen to their families, and that "to send such individuals into the competition of modern life would be, in all probability, to thrust them into either the pauper or the criminal classes."[69] Despite her concerns, her tone was patronizing and patriarchal, and focused primarily on the poverty-stricken. Based on her survey results, several months of teaching at a school near Old Rag Mountain, and interviews with families in several hollows, Sizer concluded the mountain people to be "irresponsible, untaught, untrained, often non law-abiding."[70] Families presumably trusted the schoolteacher initially as she asked them questions about their education, work, and social habits. She was sympathetic to their plight, and suggested to those in power that they provide financial assistance.[71] However, Sizer's generalities failed to recognize the complexities of the area. Many residents later despised Sizer and felt she was conveying an inaccurate description of their lives, descriptions eventually used against them.[72]

As the park's establishment was reported in local newspapers, the *Washington Herald*, and the *Baltimore Sun*, mountaineers were described as poverty-stricken, sexual deviants, and "'a community of perennial starvation and penniless squalor . . . [where] sisters and brothers have intermarried." They were described as illiterate and unable to communicate with the outside world: "They speak a queer, Chaucerian English, almost un-understandable. They say 'holpen' for 'to help,' and 'withouten' for 'without.'"[73] A *New York Times* article also described dire living conditions, suggesting that mountain residents were living in "bleak simplicity" and that "there are no social activities, no toys, no group diversions."[74] These and Sizer's generalities grossly misrepresented the more complex social, economic, and political systems that existed in the mountains.[75] Sizer's documents and letters to government officials implore them to establish programs for the mountain people: it is clear she thought she was helping them. However, her paternal attitudes about the residents influenced the decisions and policies made by state and federal officials.

Skyland owner George Pollock supported Sizer and her patronizing views of his mountain neighbors. In his reminiscences of his time operating Skyland, he described mountain families as "quarrelsome." In his chapter called "*Our* Mountaineers" (emphasis mine) he said, "For the forty years all of the mountain people seemed to consider the Skyland kitchen as their headquarters and there would usually be four or five of them lurking around like a pack of hungry wolves. I never had a cook who could keep a drunk mountaineer out of my kitchen, and whenever I had to intervene, a row usually resulted."[76]

The emphasis on the poverty-stricken or the violent in the mountains ignored the multiple levels of self-sufficiency, wealth, and education of the population as a whole. While there were some who lived in dire conditions, recent research has revealed a more complex history of the residents living the park's boundaries. Scholars such as archaeologist Audrey Horning and historian Darwin Lambert have recognized the limited representations of the residents removed from the area that is now the park and have theorized about how those limited representations have affected our cultural and collective memories about a specific place.[77] When *Hollow Folk* was published in 1933, readers were presented only with images of "unlettered folk . . . sheltered in tiny, mud-plastered log cabins and supported by a primitive agriculture."[78] The written images of poverty in *Hollow Folk*, together with Farm Security Administration photographs taken in the 1930s, had a lasting effect on the country's assumptions about the mountaineer, assumptions that included poverty, illiteracy, and isolation.[79] Because local community members and politicians were persuaded by the dominant rhetoric about mountaineers' lack of education and self-sufficiency, local resistance to the park was seemingly minor and lacked collective organization.

By the time Franklin D. Roosevelt became president and established federal work programs such as the CCC in 1933, development of Skyline Drive was under way and could be used as a selling point for the kind of work that could be accomplished through Roosevelt's WPA programs. According to Engle, "After FDR's inauguration in 1933 and the establishment of the six Civilian Conservation Corps (CCC) camps in Shenandoah by year's end, construction and development exploded—primarily as highly visible public relations efforts to bolster Roosevelt's campaign to fight the negative psychological impacts of the Great Depression."[80] After the land transfer in 1935, young men from Pittsburgh, western Pennsylvania, western Maryland, and Washington DC came to the area to build the Skyline Drive and to raze the various buildings (as instructed) within the park that were slowly being vacated as people willingly and forcibly left their homes.

At the same time the first CCC camps were established within the park in mid-1933, James R. Lassiter was named as the NPS engineer-in-charge of the Shenandoah Project. As engineer-in-charge, Lassiter supervised all the operations concerning the building of Skyline Drive, the razing of various buildings, and the general "improvements" of the area consistent with a natural landscape. During the first year of Lassiter's position, the state of Virginia still officially owned the land—the NPS did not have full authority over the land until late in 1935. So while the park was being developed and residents were slowly moving out of their homes and asking Lassiter for various permissions, Lassiter had to refer residents' requests to the new SCCD chairman, Wilbur Hall. This administrative changeover and delay is crucial to understanding the complexity of the park rules and regulations. The changeover caused much confusion and frustration as Lassiter and the SCCD apparently administered the lands differently. Ultimately, Lassiter would have jurisdiction over the land and residents' actions within the park, but this initial stage rendered him powerless in making decisions for residents. The SCCD had jurisdiction, but had no intention of long-term administration of the various requests and needs of the residents remaining in the park. No consistent set policies and procedures had been established, and there was much confusion over what was allowed. Because the federal government would not accept any deeds from the state of Virginia until all residents were accounted for, more than two years of passing decisions back and forth left residents, and administrators, confused and frustrated.

Part of the reason for the delay in transferring land from state to federal government was a pending civil suit against the state of Virginia by mountain resident and wealthy landowner Robert Via. The federal government could not accept title to the deeds until all lawsuits were settled. Via owned a 100-acre apple orchard in Rockingham County, which was included within the park boundary and therefore condemned by the state of Virginia. Via filed a suit with the U.S. Supreme Court on the grounds that condemning a person's land was a violation of that person's constitutional rights. While waiting for resolution in Via's case, the federal government would not accept the deeds from Virginia, and the administration of the park remained in a state of confusion and standstill. The building of Skyline Drive continued and willing landowners left while SNP and state officials were hard-pressed to provide remaining residents definitive answers to their questions. Some residents, not aware of administrative delays, only knew that their individual requests were often denied for reasons that seemed arbitrary. Via's court case, along with other examples of prominent business owners who lost property (such as J. Allen Williams, who owned the Panorama Hotel, and Addie Pollock, George Pollock's wife, who owned property at Skyland), illustrate that there were varying degrees of socioeconomic status among residents in the park's boundaries. In addition, residents who were not landowners were not necessarily accounted for at this time.

In 1935 the U.S. Supreme Court refused to hear Via's case, essentially upholding Virginia's condemnation laws. At this time the federal government accepted deeds from Virginia. The deeds totaled 176,429.8 acres and included land from eight counties in the state. Of the 500 families displaced from their land to form the park, approximately 350 remained during the interim before the land was transferred and their homesteads were made available. During this entire interim period, from approximately 1931 to 1938, mountain residents wrote letters to government officials, requesting various permissions. In addition to writing responses to residents, officials also wrote to each other about residents as they worked to address their needs. In the remainder of this chapter, we see the ways that government officials represented mountain residents, and how assumptions of some officials affected their interactions with residents and the decisions they made about them.

The Process of Removing Residents from Their Land: Written Representations of Mountaineers

As the work of removing residents from within the boundaries of the park began, SNP, the Virginia Department of Public Welfare, the RA, community missionaries, and local attorneys corresponded as they coordinated moves, assessed homestead eligibility, and delineated removal procedures. The confusing procedures for approval and the multiple parties involved in making these decisions added to the overall tension between the residents and the overarching government entities who had control over them. In the remainder of this chapter, I discuss the ways those working for these agencies tended to represent some mountain residents. After this discussion, the following chapters then place the letters of the mountain residents themselves alongside the discourses written about them, suggesting the residents' overall resistance not only to the park itself but to the assumptions made about themselves.

Those working with mountain residents often represented them negatively. When they were not negative, they were patronizing. That is, they took on a paternalistic tone of "helping" the residents gain access either to relief funds, to moving assistance, or to permissions from park officials. If mountain residents were not "good citizens," then they were assumed to have character deficiencies, especially when they were poor. Similarly, they were assumed to be ignorant and illiterate, and many of the letters from officials take on a condescending tone. Several letters reflect that some mountain residents were seen to be disagreeable, to have uncooperative attitudes, or to outright resist park procedures and rules. Park officials expected that mountain residents would live in harmony with each other and that they would adhere to the rules of the park. However, the rules of the park changed as the land changed hands from state government to federal government. Many residents, as Dodson's oral history suggested earlier, believed they had been "misinformed" about the services and rights they would have once they turned over their land to the government. Many of the letters written by park officials reflect a frustration with having to "deal with" people at all, as their primary job (and expertise) was to establish a park, not manage people.

When the National Park Service was first formed, it was a small organization and Lassiter "had to follow every Federal regulation with care."[81] According to Engle, part of Lassiter's refusal to grant requests was because his bosses in Washington DC watched his administration carefully. For instance, he was limited in granting requests to allow others to occupy vacated homes because of his responsibility to conduct a "historic survey" of all the buildings in the area. However, as Lassiter worked with residents and attempted to administer the park, his frustrations increased.

Some of the letters discussed below were written by government officials directly to mountain residents, either responding to their requests or alerting them to certain park rules that had been broken. Others include correspondence among various agencies, discussing various residents' actions or eligibilities for certain services (such as relief, or moving by the "CCC boys"). The discourse written by some in power reflects the general sentiment about southern mountaineers at the time, indicating that they were influenced by those stereotypes and, in turn, contributed to those stereotypes, despite their close proximity to and work with mountain residents.

Before the land was officially transferred to the federal government late in 1935, Lassiter and the SCCD were compelled to work together as they figured ways to help residents in the removal process. Of all the government officials, Lassiter responded the most negatively to managing the human aspect of establishing the park. As he and new SCCD chairman Wilbur C. Hall corresponded about residents' questions and requests, Lassiter's resentment toward the mountain families was evident. For instance, in the following letter from June 29, 1935, Lassiter said to Hall:

> In administering this area, which is virtually "No Man's Land", we are
> attempting to handle a large number of people who are not very clear
> on the conception of "mine" and "thine." Most of the residents of the area
> are residing therein on permits, which carry a clause stating that the
> permits are to be cancelled if any of the provisions are violated. Inasmuch
> as most of the remaining residents are without means of moving else-
> where, it is impractical to enforce this provision. Other dwellers remain
> in the area without permits, which reacts unfavorably upon those who
> have permits and try to live up to the provisions of the permits. The lat-
> ter feel that they are being treated unjustly when their neighbors do
> things, without permits, that they are prohibited from doing while hold-
> ing a permit. . . . The actions of these men, in maintaining and establish-
> ing places of business within the Park area, without permits of any kind,
> is an indication to the public, in general, and Park dwellers, in particular,
> that they are free to do as they please, without fear of reprisal.

Lassiter's letter to Hall explains the dilemmas that he faced in administering the special use permits (SUPs), and the resulting frustrations at a difficult situation. But in doing so he reveals his attitude about many of the people. He saw some residents as dismissive of the law and constructed their dwelling as "No Man's Land." Indeed, his invocation of the World War I no-battle zone highlights his inability to make decisions about this land that was going to be a national park but was not yet a national park. Some residents were living on the land without SUPs and therefore were breaking federal regulation. He was highly frustrated at the situation, because he had no official authority until late in 1935. Arguably, his rendering of the land as unlivable deemed some of the people living there as no men, not human, and not capable of adhering to accepted values of respecting others' property. In his letter he admonished Hall for favoritism, explaining federal laws against private filling stations on federal land. Lassiter's advice to Hall was at once concerned with fairness and procedure, while at the same time derogatory toward the people he worked with.

Lassiter was, in fact, very concerned with proper procedure and rule following. However, in expressing this concern, he also revealed what he thought about particular people. In his response to an employee of the RA—"All I can say in reply is, that if I grant this request, what reply am I going to make to . . . others when they ask for a building?"—Lassiter listed several names of people presumed as troublemakers. Lassiter consistently seemed to maintain that rules must be followed; however, during the beginning of his leadership in the park as engineer-in-charge, he did not have jurisdiction to make certain decisions. While he tried to be consistent, the SCCD granted requests that would have otherwise been against the park's policies. Therefore, when Lassiter assumed control over land, people expected him to continue granting similar requests. In his correspondence with the SCCD and the RA, Lassiter discouraged certain requests, but he made his argument based on his assumption that a certain "class" of people were making these requests.

Early on in the process, Lassiter and the SCCD did allow people to cultivate land. However, Lassiter did not anticipate how doing so would cause problems with some of the residents. In a letter written to a local missionary on June 12, 1935, he said, "We did do this [grant cultivation requests] in several instances which resulted in so many disputes among the mountain people that is has become necessary to refuse all requests to cultivate other lands." Lassiter was bound by federal government rules, but also determined that granting requests to some residents and not to others would be unfair. Because of an apparent shift in policymaking from the SCCD to SNP, and within SNP as circumstances changed, some residents assumed that earlier decisions were based on favoritism.

Lassiter's attitude toward some mountain residents was also reflected in his letters to the residents themselves. In his letter dated March 20, 1935, he reminded a resident of their agreement: "I intend to see it that this is carried out for I do not expect to permit him to sit there all summer and live on what someone else produces. Similarly I do not expect your son to sit at home and reap the benefit of what someone produces on this land on a share-basis." Lassiter instructs this resident on the rules he should follow but also on the morality involved in their agreement.

In another example, Lassiter stresses the value he placed upon residents' cooperation with the procedures of the park. He followed rules closely, and his letter illustrates the importance of residents' history of following those rules. In response to a resident's request to farm a garden, Lassiter said on April 16, 1935, "You have not co-operated in any way and have refused to sign any permits at all times, therefore, nothing at all can be done for you at any time." How residents proceeded during their relocation played a large role in whether they were able to obtain certain services.

In addition to his frustration with certain individuals' lack of adherence to the rules, Lassiter also revealed his general frustration with residents as they negotiated their ways of living. For instance, in a July 8, 1935, letter to a resident, Lassiter responded to his complaint about a neighbor not letting him pasture his cow: "Why in the world can't you two men get along together? You are living on a piece of land containing about 100 acres of pasture and you two fight so much you can't even find space to graze one cow. You are urgently requested to try to live neighborly and help one another rather than fight like cats and dogs. If there is any fruit on the whole place I see no reason why the two of you can't divide it so that both of you will have plenty." Lassiter's plea that the two men live as neighbors indicates his narrow view of their problem. Lassiter did not take into account that the residents were losing their homes, their livelihoods, and that securing pasture was a small part of the larger problem they faced. Lassiter could not *see* any reasons that the two could not be agreeable, in part because he saw them as men incapable of doing so. He apparently could not fathom why two men would not want to share or cooperate, even with their neighbors. In a situation where they felt they had been lied to, where they felt their land had been taken from them unwillingly, their resistance to cooperating was not met with sympathy or understanding. Rather, they were held to almost biblical standards, requested to "do unto others" in the way that the government expected them to.

The condescending tone expressed by Lassiter and the park rangers toward mountain residents is also evident in the correspondence from higher-ranking officials. Arno Cammerer, director of the Park Service from 1933 to 1940, wrote to a resident on October 10, 1936: "We regret that we cannot accommodate you in this matter [the removal of building materials and dead chestnut trees], but hope you will experience no great difficulty in getting the necessary building material and firewood from sources outside the Park." Cammerer was clearly ignorant of the situation of many mountain families. They had little means to obtain materials. The park was full of building materials not being used (though many were recycled as resettlement outbuildings), and residents saw some instances where materials were occasionally burned by the CCC boys. Per federal regulation, park officials were not allowed to give materials away, and as Lassiter said in several of his letters, if he gave some to a few, to be fair he would have to give some to all. Government officials attempted to follow procedure, but what residents saw was waste. Yet in their correspondence, officials seemed ignorant or uncaring of the issues mountain residents faced.

While Lassiter's letters revealed frustration and impatience with mountain residents, Ferdinand Zerkel's letters indicated his desire to instruct residents in the actions that government officials valued. Zerkel, a resident of the Shenandoah Valley and executive secretary of the SNPA, earned a position in the RA as the Homesteads Project Manager and therefore worked closely with Lassiter, RA home economists, and Virginia social workers regarding the status of mountain families during the relocation process. He also corresponded with many of the residents themselves, clarifying procedures and informing them of their status. For instance, in his September 2, 1936, letter to a resident, Zerkel reestablished the resident's responsibility over an orchard: "The matter of supervision of the distribution of the apples on the several orchards in the Park Area west of the CCC Camp was placed with you again, with a view to your assisting the worthy mountain families and who are prospective homesteaders in getting all the apples they need for their own family use and preventing a scramble and wasting or misuse of the apples by anyone." Zerkel described families who were allowed apples "for their own family use" as "worthy" of them. In other words, Zerkel asked the resident to distribute the apples fairly to those who *deserved* them. Based on several of his other letters, those who deserved the apples were presumably those who had been cooperative with the government and who were part of the homestead program. Those qualifying for the homestead program participated in extensive surveys and interviews by the state's public welfare organization and were deemed "worthy" as well.

Being worthy also included being capable of making homestead loan payments and being of good "mental condition." In many of the letters written by Lassiter and some of the park rangers, they seemed to expect that the mountain residents should already know how to "act." Zerkel, however, provided much explanation in his letters about the rules and procedures, in what appears to be a sincere attempt to help residents as best he could. For instance, in a letter dated April 3, 1937, Zerkel tells one resident that

> Miss Cowden [home economist, FSA] plans to call to see you in the
> near future and I feel sure that she or Mrs. Humrickhouse will be able to
> work out with you a plan of relocation which you will find satisfactory.
> Your letter of March 26 confirms the feeling which you know I have con-
> sistently held that it is now and has been your desire and intention to
> co-operate with all Governmental agencies—Federal, State and local. I
> feel sure that you and your neighbors received from unofficial and some-
> what antagonistic sources a considerable amount of misinformation in
> the early stages of the Park and Resettlement programs and I sincerely
> hope this situation is or very shortly will be reversed, through the con-
> tacts with the personnel from this office and that of Mr. Lassiter.

Both Zerkel and Lassiter were aware of the ways that the procedures of the park and families' removals had been misrepresented by state and federal officials. When the SCCD was in control of the land, promises were made that could not be kept once the federal government took control. Zerkel, unlike Lassiter, took time in his letters to explain to residents what happened, and to empathize with their frustration and anger over unexpected changes. In addition, he was rhetorically aware of the values held by those in power, and in an effort to assist residents in getting what they needed, he taught them the value of cooperating with the government so that they might obtain all the services they could.

Zerkel, who genuinely seemed to have mountain residents' interests in mind and generally gave residents the benefit of the doubt (albeit in a paternal way), also favored people with standing and who exhibited certain values. Consistently in his lengthy, detailed letters, he explained to residents why decisions were being made in regards to their land or their eligibility for homesteads. In a letter to one resident, Zerkel granted an extension on his SUP, even though the resident had not requested it. He said on January 21, 1935, "I might suggest, further, for your PERSONAL and CONFIDEN-TIAL information only and positively not for your passing this idea to oth-

STATE COMMISSION ON CONSERVATION AND DEVELOPMENT

WILLIAM E. CARSON, CHAIRMAN, RIVERTON
COLEMAN WORTHAM, VICE CHAIRMAN, RICHMOND
JUNIUS P. FISHBURN, ROANOKE
E. GRIFFITH DODSON, NORFOLK
MARSHALL B. BOOKER, HALIFAX
THOMAS L. FARRAR, CHARLOTTESVILLE
LEE LONG, DANTE

R. A. GILLIAM,
EXECUTIVE SECRETARY AND TREASURER

RICHMOND, VA.

SHENANDOAH NATIONAL PARK DIVISION

PHONE 84, FRONT ROYAL

ADDRESS YOUR REPLY TO
FRONT ROYAL, VA.

BUREAUS OF THE COMMISSION
GEOLOGICAL SURVEY
WATER RESOURCES AND POWER
FOREST SERVICE
PARKS AND LANDSCAPE ENGINEERING
ARCHAEOLOGY AND HISTORY
STATE PUBLICITY

ADDRESS REPLY TO UNDERSIGNED

NOTICE TO VACATE

To all persons living within the Shenandoah National Park Area who have signed "Special Use Permits" permitting them to use certain buildings and harvest certain crops within the park area for a period ending not later than November 1, 1934.

Please be advised that the premises occupied or used by you under your "Special Use Permit" must be vacated not later than November 1, 1934. If the premises are under lock and key, we would appreciate the courtesy of your mailing the keys to the Shenandoah National Park Office, Front Royal, Virginia, with a letter or post card advising that you are sending them, and vacating the premises.

Wm. E. Carson, Chairman
STATE COMMISSION ON CONSERVATION AND DEVELOPMENT

SPECIAL NOTICE TO APPLICANTS FOR HOMESTEAD PRIVILEGES

Special notice to persons now holding "Special Use Permits" who have applied or desire to make application for Homesteading Privileges.

A new "Special Use Permit" may be issued to any person now holding a "Special Use Permit", who will make application to Mr. Ferdinand Zerkel, Assistant Manager, Shenandoah National Park Project, Division of Subsistence Homesteads at his office, in Luray, Virginia, if such person purposes or desires to apply for Homesteading Privileges.

Under this new "Special Use Permit" the time allowed for vacating the premises in the "Special Use Permit" may be extended to April, 1935. But such extension will only be made on application to Mr. Zerkel; and unless a new permit is issued the premises must be vacated by November first.

Wm. E. Carson, Chairman
STATE COMMISSION ON CONSERVATION AND DEVELOPMENT

Shenandoah National Park Archives
Shenandoah National Park Resource Management Records, 1880-1996
Box 101 Folder 9

Fig. 8. Notice to vacate. This notice, different from a writ of conviction, was distributed to mountain residents early in 1934, by mail and by publication in local newspapers. In addition to land appraisals and appeal notices by the Resettlement Administration, this was one of the written notices landowners came in contact with as they were faced with leaving their homes. Many tenants, however, did not receive such documents, as the SCCD assumed landowners would notify them. Once the SCCD owned the deeds to the lands, officials then contacted tenants with the more threatening writ of conviction. For some tenants, this would be the first notification of their obligation to leave. (Courtesy of Shenandoah National Park Archives) ers, that you just stay on there until you hear further from me." While he offered the extension, he also discouraged the resident from telling others, assuming his power in distributing favors. Zerkel suggested that just staying there with an extension until he was forced out would allow him to stay longer. He did not, however, want others knowing this, presumably because giving out too many permits had become a problem for the park service. In a letter to another resident on April 21, 1934, Zerkel said, "Therefore, with only the friendliest of feelings and a wish to serve you and at the same time to see the Park Area protected in its best condition for early transfer to the Federal Government, I would urge that you sign and abide by the permit."

On January 19, 1935, Zerkel wrote to SCCD attorney William Armstrong that a resident's request "has had full consideration and his present attitude directly invites eviction or at least the issuance of an eviction writ similar to those which were issued some weeks ago in the various Park Area Counties" (see figure 8). Contained in the letter is also the Family History Enumeration, which lists the names and ages of all the people in a family and their various possessions. It also includes the family's source of income: "I have been told he and son live almost totally from moonshining. He has the name of being the fastest runner in the mtn. when officers are near." Though Zerkel did not say so directly, apparently the resident's "present attitude" included lawlessness and to Zerkel this was cause for eviction. Many of the letters from officials reflected this sentiment— whenever mountain residents expressed their anger or resisted rules they were seen as uncooperative and undeserving of services.

While some residents seemed uncooperative either because they were ignorant of the rules or because of preexisting conflicts with neighbors, some were consciously resistant to the rules. In the following letter from Zerkel to the NPS's legal division, Zerkel informed them of the status of people evicted from the park. He noted on April 20, 1935, that the "old mountain preacher" had been granted "the special privilege of a belated signing of the original and extension permits." Zerkel explained why the preacher had been granted an extension: "[He] tried to secure signatures to permits from all of the neighbors in Dark Hollow but returned the blanks somewhat later with the report that his nephews and other neighbors whom he had contacted on this matter had refused to sign the permits." Therefore, the resident was granted an extension for trying to persuade the others to cooperate. This is an example of "special privilege" granted because a mountain resident cooperated with the government. In addition, Zerkel's letter reflects the resistance that occurred from residents. By signing a federal SUP, residents were recognizing legally what was already true about their property: that they had lost their rights to their land through the Virginia Condemnation Act. Many residents refused to do so. Then later, when the park's establishment was inevitable, some residents tried to sign the permits so they might remain on their land for as long as possible. Many of the letters from the rangers, Lassiter, and Zerkel were responses to these requests, and often they were denied because they "refused to sign" at the outset, again attesting to officials' value of cooperation.

Several families actively resisted leaving their land and were forcibly removed from their homes. This act of resistance has been written about in contemporary studies as an admirable way of asserting one's agency in the face of a kind of oppression. However, park officials (and the Virginia magistrates who carried out removals before 1936) saw forcible removal from one's home as an embarrassment, and they constructed it as such in their letters. For instance, in this letter dated December 19, 1935, Zerkel says to a resident, "There is enclosed herewith permit you signed the other day which has been approved by me and Deputy Sheriff Lucas of Elkton. This permit was issued primarily for the purpose of giving you notice that you must move out of the Park and allowing you until April 1 to find a new location and make your move. You are advised to lose no time in locating a place to which you can move, as we do not want the embarrassment of having to have you evicted from the Park area." Zerkel constructs his letter so as to provide information for the resident, but also to empathize with him, albeit in a patronizing way. He assumes that eviction would be an embarrassment, seen as an instance of social shame rather than an instance of resistance to an unfair situation. Zerkel's attitude toward residents was a paternal one, illustrated by his willingness to help them and his attempts to educate them as they negotiated their struggles. Rather than castigate them for their behavior, he primarily wrote lengthy instructions on how to behave.

In addition to expressing values about work and fairness, park officials also spent time instructing residents on the regulations of the park. In this letter from December 9, 1935, the CCC camp superintendent says to a resident, "Your objection to leaving the gates [of the park] open, is that grazing stock of individuals, get together. Please refer to your 'Special Use Permit' which in paragraph 7 forbids the grazing of stock. Please believe us

willing to cooperate whenever possible, but we also expect your cooperation in abiding by your permit" (see figure 9). While he reminded the resident of the regulations, he also instructed her on the moral values of cooperation and following the rules.

In addition to the CCC camp superintendent, the RA's home economists
were involved in residents' lives as they proceeded to relocate. Mozelle Cowden, who began her work as a family selection specialist, worked as a home
economist in the Blue Ridge Mountains, assessing families' abilities to qualify for government-assisted loans for resettlement housing. She communicated with Zerkel, Lassiter, and several park rangers as she updated them
about various families' statuses. As is evident in the letters from officials,
they communicated with each other about residents' statuses in terms of
location, eligibility, and general behavior. In this letter from November 16,
1937, for instance, Cowden wrote to the park's chief ranger, Taylor Hoskins,
that a resident "wants a place at Flint Hill [homestead] but until his physical appraisals are complete he cannot be assigned a definite place. His wife
and son were not able to be at the physical Appraisal clinic held in Nicholson Hollow November 6 but he promised to have his family doctor make
those examinations sometime soon. . . . I have not been able to do any surveying recently in Rappahannock County but just as soon as I can get over
there I will let you know what their plans are for moving." Cowden's correspondence with Hoskins here exemplifies the many letters between the
resettlement administration and park officials. They often communicated
in writing (though it was clear the telephone was used as well), keeping
track of the various needs of residents and where they were in the process
of resettlement. Both kept organized records and informed each other of
residents' activities in the park. The process of organized relocation and assessment, though, came only after residents' land had been assessed and
approved for the park, making their removal inevitable. In Cowden's reminiscences, she recounts that one mountain resident expressed frustration at
her evaluative interview, telling Cowden, "I've just answered so many questions for so many people. Don't you people that write-down never show each
other what you have wrote down?" The process of surveys, interviews, and
assessments over the years frustrated residents, especially when they were
held to strict standards of following regulation and rules.

Park officials also worked with the men employed in the CCC camps. The
interaction of residents with CCC workers is evident in their letters, as the

STATE COMI 3SION ON CONSERVATION N DEVELOPMENT
RICHMOND. VIRGINIA

SHENANDOAH NATIONAL PARK

NO. _____

SPECIAL USE PERMIT

In consideration of his (her) agreement to promptly vacate the premises at the expiration of the authorization hereby granted, and subject to which this authorization is expressly conditioned, _____

of _____ (P. O) _____ _____County, Virginia, is hereby authorized, from _____, 1934, to and until after the harvesting of crops to mature during the growing season of 1934 and in no event after November 1, 1934, to use the buildings occupied and such part of the land as was cultivated by this permittee last year in the above-named national park area; for the purposes of cultivating and harvesting the crops maturing during the growing season of 1934; justification being the protection of the forests from fires and the cultivation of the land until it is determined what use is to be made of this property; subject to the following conditions:

1. Permittee shall exercise this privilege subject to the supervision of the State Commission on Conservation and Development and shall comply with the regulations of the Secretary of the Interior governing the same upon the acceptance by the United States of the area embracing the land in question for park purposes.

2. Use by the permittee of the land covered hereby is subject to the right of the Director of the National Park Service to established trails, roads and other improvements and betterments over, upon, or through said premises, and further to the use by travelers and others of such roads and trails as well as those already existing.

3. No building or other structure shall be erected under this permit and existing buildings and their premises and all appurtenances thereto shall be kept in a safe, sanitary, and sightly condition.

4. Permittee shall dispose of brush and other refuse as required by the State Commission on Conservation and Development or the National Park Service.

5. Permittee shall pay for damage resulting from his use of this property, usual wear and tear excepted.

6. Land not cultivated last year shall remain not cultivated or disturbed in any manner this year.

7. The milk cow or cows owned by the permittee hereunder may be grazed on the land similarly used last year bu on permittee's sole responsibility for damage by or to or loss of such milk cow or cows. However, grazing of cattle will not be allowed in the section of the Park Area between the Lee Highway and the Spottswood Trail and, in the other sections, special authority must be gotten for any grazing other than a family's own milk cow as above indicated.

8. No living timber of any kind may be cut or destroyed.

9. It is understood, however, that the manufacture and (or) sale of liquor either within the park or outside of same as prohibited by law, by permittee or any member of permittee's household or any persons residing on lands leased hereunder, shall automatically render this permit null and void.

10. This permit may not be transferred or assigned.

11. This permit shall terminate upon the violation of any of the conditions hereof.

12. Permittee, members of his family and his employees shall take all reasonable precautions to prevent forest fires and also shall assist the representatives of the State Commission on Conservation and Development or the National Park Service to extinguish forest fires in the vicinity of any tract which may be used hereunder, and shall assist these representatives in the preservation ot good order within the metes and bounds of the park.

13. In consideration of this permit, permittee agrees to prevent fire from originating on said premises, to fight fire voluntarily and free of charge within one mile of his leased habitation, and in event permittee is unable to immediately put out such fires, to notify the representative of the State Commission on Conservation and Development or the National Park Service in charge. Permittee further agrees to fight fires elsewhere voluntarily and free of charge when called upon by the proper authorities.

14. This permit is issued with the express understanding that the same is issued for a temporary period and the authorization under this permit carries no obligation on the State Commission on Conservation and Development or the National Park Service for its renewal or for the continuance of the operation in any matter whatsoever upon its expiration.

The undersigned hereby accepts the above permit and the right to exercise the privileges granted, subject to the terms, covenants, obligations and reservations, expressed or implied, therein.

TWO witnesses to signatures.

_____   Permittee _____
          Witness
                                 Address _____
Address _____

_____
     ENUMERATOR   Witness _____

Address _____

                    APPROVED:

_____   _____
     William E. Carson   Arno B. Cammerer
CHAIRMAN. State Commission on Conservation and Development   DIRECTOR. National Park Service

Fig. 9. Special use permit. Mountain residents who remained on their property during the interim period were required to sign this permit and were expected to follow its instructions or face eviction. Because of administrative delays, residents could remain beyond the original November 1, 1934, relocation deadline. Those remaining could request extensions for their permits. Some families remained in the park as late as 1939, extending their permits every year and consequently living under federal law. Annie Shenk, a life-tenure resident and the last resident remaining under SUP, died in her home in the park in 1979. (Courtesy of Shenandoah National Park Archives)

CCC did much of the work of building removal and general park maintenance. The frustration of park officials helping those in need was also felt by CCC camp superintendent C. V. Bert. He wrote to Lassiter on November 3, 1938, "I suppose, as the Park has accepted the responsibility of keeping these indigent cases in the Park, no criticism of relief efforts will be advanced." As more and more families were found ineligible for resettlement housing, the Department of Public Welfare was tasked with finding assistance for them. Bert's sarcasm stems from his criticism of the NPS for not moving families out sooner. Bert's frustration, not unlike Lassiter's, came from not being equipped to manage the many problems of mountain residents. In the same letter, Bert told Lassiter, "This old lady, about eighty years old, I realize, is up against it, and I don't suppose will last very long, so, if we slap up a meat house and haul her a couple of loads of wood, that would be the easiest way out of the situation. Personally, I don't see that this is the function of the Park service but, as we have it thrust upon us, we will have to make the best of it for a little while" (November 3, 1938). Bert, like many officials affiliated with the park service, was frustrated by the requests of the mountain families, as they were extraneous to the issues of building Skyline Drive and reestablishing plant life in certain areas. The mandated tasks of managing the work of the CCC boys and of maintaining the land for public access and use often conflicted with management decisions about the people living in the park.[82]

When mountain residents were interviewed by Cowden and then assessed for their eligibility for resettlement housing, their names and family situations were then written about and discussed by Cowden, Lassiter, and welfare agents. In one letter dated October 4, 1937, Lassiter wrote to U.S. Senator (and former Virginia governor) Harry F. Byrd about one of the mountain residents who challenged his pending move: "I think he is scheduled for re-establishment outside of the Park by the Virginia Department of Welfare, as he is too old to be considered a good risk for the Resettlement Administration. . . . [His] family consists of his wife, daughter about ten years old, his fifteen-year-old daughter, and her husband. [He] himself seems to be a pretty good character, but his wife, two daughters, and son-in-law are objectionable, especially the latter who is rather weak mentally and is anxious to fight with any one he meets."[83] Lassiter's information about this family came largely from Cowden and others at the welfare office. Though the resident owned property, he would not be eligible for a homestead because his age made him a "risk." Further, the character of his son-in-law factored into the homestead decision. Therefore, this family was relocated, through the Department of Welfare, to a location that Lassiter assured Senator Byrd would be good for the family, based on proximity to schools.

SNP was not the only project where the NPS and social welfare projects were linked.[84] Like Skyline Drive, the Blue Ridge Parkway "accentuated job creation as their primary motivation, declaring that the construction of a new scenic highway in the Virginia and North Carolina Blue Ridge had the potential to improve conditions for people living in Appalachia, an economically distressed region."[85] However, despite the ways in which the parkways were marketed to benefit locals, "the people who provided the land on which the parkway was built benefited relatively little from the road."[86] Cultures and traditions were forever changed, accelerating the ways that mountain residents' lives would change.[87]

This important link of public works projects, New Deal programs such as the CCC, building roadways such as Skyline Drive, and new social reforms such as public welfare helps explain the confusing ways that residents were presented with incoming programs and their implications for their relocation. Residents were told conflicting information, likely not maliciously, but rather as a consequence of evolving governmental programs and new communication and bureaucratic networks across agencies. However, when residents responded to this confusion with frustration or resistance of any kind, they were met with derision at worst and condescension at best.

Lassiter's letters in particular reflected frustration with residents for being disagreeable or displaying an uncooperative attitude. In addition to instructing residents on the various procedures of the park, Lassiter also instructed them in cooperating with the welfare agents assigned to assist them. In the following letter, written March 5, 1938, Lassiter indicated to a resident that only by cooperating could he receive service: "Mrs. Humrickhouse, Supervisor of the Department of Public Welfare, has informed me that you are not making an effort to co-operate with her in finding you a place to move. As you know, your permit to remain the Park expired on January 1, 1938, and if you do not change your attitude and give her the proper co-operation, we will be forced to secure a writ of eviction and put you out of the Park." By this time in 1938, Lassiter's frustration at handling the relocations of residents had reached a high level. As residents resisted the help of public welfare, Lassiter threatened them with eviction, knowing full well that was precisely what they did not want. The welfare agent referred to in this letter, Mable Humrickhouse, supervised several social workers through state offices in Richmond, Virginia (approximately ninety miles from SNP). Humrickhouse reported to Lassiter about various residents' standing in the removal process and asked for Lassiter's assistance in getting residents to cooperate. In a similar example, Lassiter wrote to a resident and "advised" him to cooperate with the Department of Welfare:

> I have been notified by Mrs. Mable B. Humrickhouse, Supervisor of the Department of Public Welfare that she has been unable to make satisfactory arrangements with you about moving out of the Park. Further, that on numerous occasions as you have told her that you would make your own arrangements and have refused to let her help you find a place outside of the Park area. This is to advise that unless you make an effort to co-operate with her at once or else move out within a reasonable time unassisted, a writ of eviction will be secured from the United States Court and you will be put out of the Park.

Residents hoped to live in their homes as long as possible, and Lassiter's threat of force, not only from SNP but from the federal government, was meant to reiterate the severity of their perceived lack of cooperation.

Humrickhouse's frustration with residents is also indicated in her letters to Lassiter, as she explained that, because residents would not cooperate, they would be the sole responsibility of SNP—the last thing Lassiter wanted. She wrote to Lassiter on February 3, 1938, "Miss Taliaferro [Assistant Director, Department of Public Welfare] went to see [the resident's] son-in-law . . . and he advised her that it would be perfectly agreeable with him for [the resident] and his daughter to come to live with them, but he is refusing to go. We feel that this is all we can do for [him] and I am, therefore, advising you that no more work will be done with him and it will be left to the Park Service to see to it that he is out."

While much of the rhetoric in agents' letters about residents was condescending and paternalistic, they were also genuinely concerned for residents' welfare as they implored park officials to help those who needed assistance. June Taliaferro, referred to in Humrickhouse's letter, was an assistant supervisor located at the Department of Public Welfare's office in Elkton,

Virginia. Her letters, written both to Lassiter and to park rangers, referred to multiple families, updating park officials on where families were in the process of moving or of securing eligibility for homesteads or welfare assistance. In one letter to a ranger on November 18, 1937, she requested that CCC trucks move a family and advocated keeping another citizen out of jail. Since some families did not own trucks, the CCC assisted with several moves. She said, "If there is anything that you can do to enable them to carry out their plan, I believe it will help the whole situation." As residents faced moving from their homes, tensions among residents and with park officials mounted. Taliaferro's letter urged park officials to attend quickly to the situation, so that further conflict could be avoided. Her letter documents the government's assistance, through the CCC, in moving families from their homes. While this assistance was helpful to residents without large trucks, it was also a way to remove families more quickly from the park area in these final phases of relocation.

The following letter from Humrickhouse to Hoskins, written October 27, 1937, is typical of the communication found in the park's archives between social workers and park officials.[88] In it, Humrickhouse wrote to the ranger on behalf of a resident who was having difficulty obtaining firewood, and requested permission for her son to gather dead wood from SNP. Humrickhouse said that the resident's son "agrees to gather nothing but dead wood and I feel that he is a very dependable person and will do as he says."[89] Requests for removing dead wood from the park, or collecting berries from within park boundaries, continued throughout the process of relocating families and, according to Reed Engle, continues today (e-mail correspondence). Humrickhouse's comment on the resident's character echoed the common strategies used by many advocates for determining a resident's worthiness in granting requests.

The determination of a person's "worth" in receiving public assistance was steeped in Virginia's history of social reform. While public programs for widow's pensions, relief for the poor, and working conditions were being developed, who "deserved" access to aid became a prevalent question for state officials. After the Civil War, rhetorics of worth and moral value permeated the controversies over how much state funding was allocated to public relief programs.[90] The New Deal greatly affected Virginia's (and the South's in general) social and welfare policies, but the poor "still had to practice their dramatic skills as they approached new gatekeepers of relief in the 'theater or charity.'"[91] As mountain residents figured ways to obtain the services or assistance they needed, they were forced to participate in a discourse from which they were largely excluded. As residents came in contact with more and more written documents from various government representatives, they shaped their own rhetoric to perhaps remedy their immediate needs, and for certain to remedy how others saw them.

Conclusion

The ways that park officials, home economists, social workers, and resettlement administrators interacted with some mountain families were steeped in stereotypes and assumptions that had already been formulated for the people living in the mountains of Appalachia. Their letters to each other reflect the stereotypes commonly accepted about the mountaineer that contributed to the acceptance of their displacement in the first place. The representations accepted about residents included the perception that they were worthy citizens, only in that they acquiesced to their displacement. But they were also often assumed to be morally degenerate and uncooperative. These assumptions consequently turned mountain residents into "no men." As they were considered subhuman, they were consequently rendered displaceable, and this rendering continued throughout the park officials' interaction with them. Out of the history of the Blue Ridge, where there were contested land claims, racism, insularity, and small farming, arose myths and stereotypes about mountaineers that not only affected how park officials dealt with mountain residents but ultimately made the establishment of the park possible by transforming it into No Man's Land, a place where men, and certainly not women, could live as the kind of citizen that those in power valued.

The materiality of the letters themselves reflect the social status and positioning of the mountain residents and government officials. Officials' letters were typed on formally printed government letterhead and contained a discourse of authority and propriety. Many, though not all, of the mountain residents' letters were mostly handwritten, in pencil and on school notepad paper. Since the wealthier or more educated residents had either the foresight or the means to leave, by the time SNP took over officially late in 1935, the residents left to write letters were those with less means and with less education. That is, the residents writing the letters discussed here are not representative of the entire population displaced from the park. On the surface, the discourse used in these letters reflected a lack of education. However, as the following chapters that highlight rhetorical strategy suggest, the representations contained in mountain families' letters directly counter those constructed for them. Not only can their acts of resistance be seen as acts of resistance to identity, but also this very specific literate act, that of writing letters, illustrates an act of social participation. While the conditions were ripe for displacement and exploitation, there was no one person or group necessarily to blame. The series of events and the prevailing yet erroneous attitudes about the mountaineers made this large-scale displacement possible. The following analyses of letters, and specific literacy events, places literacy as the central factor in understanding this historical moment and its continued significance today.

REPRESENTATION, ADVOCACY, AND IDENTIFICATION

A speaker persuades an audience by the use of stylistic identifica-
tions; his act of persuasion may be for the purpose of causing the
audience to identify itself with the speaker's interests.
—Kenneth Burke, *A Rhetoric of Motives*

Such definitions [of rhetoric] contain a male bias because of their
emphasis on conversion and conquest—on the effort to change
people and things.
—Karen A. Foss and Sonja K. Foss, *Women Speak*

Chapter 1 discussed the ways that people were represented by some of the
local businesspeople who promoted the establishment of a park in Virginia,
and by some of the state and federal officials involved in making Shenandoah National Park (SNP) a reality. The representations of mountain residents by these groups of people consequently resulted in misperceptions of
mountain families as they were forced into the processes of vacating their
homes and relocating. Once the park land was transferred from the State
Commission on Conservation and Development (SCCD), located in Richmond, Virginia, to the federal government (with offices in Luray, Virginia,
and Washington, DC), a series of interactions began with park officials—
interactions between the residents who owned land, the residents who
were concerned advocates, and generally the people living near the park's
boundaries,. Because state officials had simply not fully anticipated the
logistics involved in relocating families, the SCCD did not have formal policies in place when faced with questions of removing building materials and

cultivating crops. To make matters more confusing for residents, the SCCD and the National Park Service (NPS) were cautious in granting permissions, since jurisdiction over the land was to change at any moment.

Once jurisdiction of the land was transferred to the NPS, any requests that came through the SCCD were forwarded to SNP. However, because legal transfer of the lands did not occur until December 1935, many requests forwarded to Lassiter were bounced back to the SCCD because he did not yet have legal authority to make decisions. Lassiter often deferred to the SCCD on these decisions, creating a complex exchange of letters, suggesting that neither agency felt it had the authority to make significant decisions about property and land, primarily because of the tenuous nature of that authority. During this delay, many conflicting messages, both written and unwritten, were sent to residents about the rules for proceeding while living on what was once their land and what would imminently be government property. Many residents continued to take materials or harvest their crops, which the SCCD had originally led them to understand they could do, as indicated in several letters. However, these residents later faced repercussions when they were served with violation notices by SNP. These notices were the impetus for many letters of request, as residents and local community members advocated for the fair treatment of the people living in the park's boundaries.

As residents remaining in the park's boundaries awaited homesteads or other government assistance, they continued to live their lives by growing food, cultivating crops, and grazing animals. At this time, at the beginning of the federal government's jurisdiction and during a time of confusing or contradictory policies, residents wrote letters that requested tangible things, such as removing materials, harvesting crops, or remaining in their homes with an extension of their permits. In this chapter, I focus on the letters written by residents who sought to represent themselves as worthy of the requests they made. In writing these letters, they represented themselves differently than what had previously been published or generally accepted about mountain folks, and in doing so they affected rhetoric they assumed would be persuasive to those granting the requests.

As discussed in chapter 1, early published representations by park promoters of the park's benefits to the state of Virginia reflected a universal support of the park's establishment with very little attention to the fact that people would have to be relocated. Indeed, some park promoters assumed that people living on the land could continue to do so even after the NPS assumed authority over the land. Some community members were supportive of a national park in Virginia's mountains for its anticipated economic and tourist benefits. In one promotional booklet, published in 1929 by the Shenandoah National Park Tourist Bureau, Shenandoah National Park Association (SNPA) secretary Daniel P. Wine said, "Of the native people [the photographer] visited, the fact that they speak a language and follow customs that resemble the Eighteenth century more than the present, indicates that they have long been living to themselves away from the influence of other people."[1] In another essay in the same publication, Harold E. Phillips said, "Here, [God] decided, should forever be preserved a sanctuary, where man might come eons later to rediscover himself among nature's birds and trees and among her eternal hills. Thus, the history of the Shenandoah National Park must have begun." His rhetoric implies that it is the "millions of humans, bound to brick and concrete cities" that deserve the benefits of respite, ignoring the people who actually owned land and lived there and their desires to live and work in the same landscape. The promotional booklet containing these essays also included formal portraits of the leading state and federal leaders, such as Pollock, Zerkel, and Carson, juxtaposed with snapshots of some local residents in their work clothes. In one such photograph, local resident Charles Edgar Hawkins stands on the edge of his property, which joined the fishing camp of then president Herbert Hoover (see figure 10). According to his granddaughter, Theresa Cook Angus (daughter of Virginia Marie Hawkins Cook), her grandfather was represented as only a working man, in his coveralls during the middle of a working day. What the photograph does not indicate is the Hawkinses' extensive flower garden, including many hostas that the family planted. These hostas are visible today among the overgrowth on the flat area near the Rapidan River where the Hawkinses had their home. The one-dimensional representation of individuals and of the populace as a whole served to set the stage for rendering residents displaceable. In another photograph in the promotional booklet, a woman smoking a pipe wears a scarf, likely to keep her hair pulled back and her head protected from the sun while she works. The caption for this photograph reads, "A typical elderly mountain woman in the Shenandoah National Park. Her homespun dress, pipe of tobacco and customary mountain headwear, are typical of the womenfolk of the sturdy people who have inhabited these

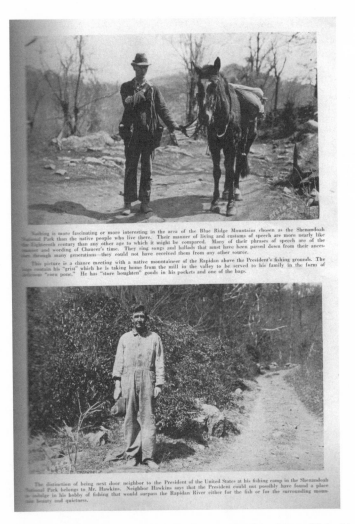

The distinction of being next door neighbor to the President of the United States at his fishing camp in the Shenandoah National Park belongs to Mr. Hawkins. Neighbor Hawkins says that the President could not possibly have found a place to indulge in his hobby of fishing that would surpass the Rapidan River either for the fish or for the surrounding mountain beauty and quietness.

Fig. 10. Reproduction of a page from a promotional booklet published in 1929 by the Shenandoah National Park Tourist Bureau. Mr. Charles Edgar Hawkins, pictured in the lower photograph in his work clothes, stands on the road on the edge of his property. This photograph, and many like it, was meant to represent mountain folks in a way that played to readers' assumptions about them. Park promoters used this one-dimensional representation against mountain families to justify the removal of residents from their homes. Mr. Hawkins owned 177 acres within the park's boundaries along the Rapidan River, and was compensated $1,844 when his land was condemned by the state of Virginia. According to Hawkins's granddaughter, Theresa Cook Angus (daughter of Virginia Marie Hawkins Cook), her grandparents always missed their place by the river.

mountains since the days when the pre-revolutionary adventurer advanced against this frontier. With the advance of modern customs into these wilderness places, this hardy pioneer type is disappearing." This caption contradicts earlier statements in the booklet that the mountain residents were completely isolated from modern society. Additionally, the caption implies that mountain families and their ways of life were disappearing on their own, and that modernization was inevitable. This rhetoric again trivialized (or romanticized) the lives of mountain families and diminished the impact that the park would have on the nearly five hundred families that would be displaced once the park was officially approved.

No mention was made in this promotional publication about whether or not citizens would be allowed to stay in their homes once the park was formed. It was not until a letter from NPS director Arno Cammerer in 1934 that it became clear that residents would have to move en masse. This change in decision was one of several factors contributing to a lack of organized resistance to resident removal *before* the process had already begun. Many park promoters had assumed residents could stay, that their property would become government property but that they could continue living there under special conditions, as was the case in developing the Blue Ridge Parkway, where property owners were given land easements. Even if promoters and state officials did not think residents could stay, the issue of removing families was minimized so as not to deter the federal government from accepting the proposed park in the region. Therefore, widespread community resistance did not exist in enough time to make a significant impact on the ways that the boundaries were determined or how families were to be removed.[2]

Therefore, the letters discussed in this chapter exemplify the ways that community action against the park was illustrated not through traditional protest but in the ways that people were represented and valued as their relocations became inevitable. It is important to discuss the term *community* here. In this chapter, "community members" refers to a diverse set of people of varying socioeconomic backgrounds and professional positions. The communities in each of the eight counties affected by the park's formation had multiple kinds of responses to residents' removals and relocation. Some were ambivalent, some were supportive with the hope that better living and education conditions would be a result, and some were patronizing in their views of mountain families. The community members discussed in this chapter, no matter their feelings about the park itself, were concerned with assisting mountain residents with the complexity of the removal process, and in convincing officials that the residents deserved their attention.

While concerned community members could not help residents keep their homes, they wrote on their behalf, using their knowledge of power structures and rhetorical strategy to gain access to certain services, and to have readers identify with residents' needs through their representation of them. Some of these citizens were experienced writers, and their letters present arguments about the responsibility of park officials to attend to the needs of the people displaced. Their letters also reveal recognition of status; that is, given the rhetoric of park officials and their subsequent actions, community members used their perceived connections to assist residents in their requests. In turn, some of the letters written by residents themselves reflected rhetoric reminiscent of advocacy and social action, indicating the mountain residents' recognition of status and power in positions of support. In adopting stances as advocates, they positioned themselves as people in a position to help, in equal social standing with others who saw themselves as advocates. In this way, residents reflected similar values as community members who wrote letters. These analogous rhetorical acts from seemingly different groups undermines the notion that all mountain residents were isolated; in fact, they shared systems of social values with their neighbors and surrounding communities and asked park officials to do what they saw as morally just based on those values.

Much of the correspondence between government officials and residents reveals a complicated network of communication in the mountains. Several letters refer to past verbal conversations with park rangers, local sheriffs, and social workers. In some cases, government officials wrote in favor of particular residents, such as persuading other government officials to grant various permissions, justifying residents' actions, and bending the rules given special circumstances. The line between advocating for a resident's situation and favoritism was fine indeed, as the culture of oral communication and being "neighborly" shifted to a culture of bureaucracy and regulation. The development of the park, its slow transition of authority from state to federal officials, and its many rules and procedures for living there until homesteads were available prompted a series of events that required written communication. The events of moving from the park and requesting materials from vacated homes, obtaining and following special use permits (SUPs), and continuing the daily trials of living are evident in the letters discussed in this chapter.

Letters Highlighting Transfer of Authority and Requests for Building Materials

As residents faced relocation, they began a process of moving that included requests for building materials, even when those buildings had been part of the appraisals and paid for by the state. Not all residents, particularly tenants, understood this, and whether they were to move to resettlement housing or found land on their own, they hoped to use the lumber from their existing buildings to build new ones. Because the granting of requests was *believed* to result from favoritism rather than because of confusions during the transfer of authority, many people writing to government officials consequently represented themselves and others as good citizens, as worthy of the requests they made, in the hopes of being granted their requests based on their character. Some of this perception certainly came from Homesteads Project Manager Ferdinand Zerkel (discussed in chapter 1) and how he encouraged residents to cooperate with officials during the relocation and homestead-approval processes. Long before the park was officially approved, several networks of missions, churches, and schools were located in the mountains, helping the families in need with food and clothing, spiritual needs, medical care, and education.[3] The process of family removal prompted a series of letters from missionaries as they tried to help residents remain in their homes for as long as possible, and when they were forced to leave, missionaries asked for lumber from the buildings. Janet E. Walton, a missionary with one of the several Episcopal missions located near the park's boundaries, St. Luke's Mission on Tanner's Ridge, wrote on behalf of one of the residents.[4] In her December 4, 1935, letter to SCCD chairman Hall, Walton requested wood from a building and said that the resident was "a very fine man. He lives a short distance from me and brings my water each day, as I have no water on the place. . . . I am writing to you to ask if you will not give him permission . . . to go there and tear down the buildings and put himself up a little house on his father in law's land outside the Park." Walton explained that while some people were taking materials without permission, she and the rest of the mission "encourage them to live up to the law and give the Park authorities no trouble of any nature whatsoever."

She concluded that the resident was "a hard working man [who] has never received one thing from the FERA [Federal Emergency Relief Administration]." Walton told Chairman Hall about how much the mission needed the help of this resident so that he might continue living near the mission. She professed that she did not know what the mission would do without his help and urged Chairman Hall to respond at once, before people without permission took the materials from the site. Walton's references to the resident's character and the mission's reliance on him indicated her assumption that she and Hall possessed the same values. By detailing the resident's hard work, Walton sought to inform Hall of the resident's worthiness of favor, positing him as deserving of the building materials requested.

Because of the imminent transfer of authority, Chairman Hall forwarded Walton's letter to Director Arno Cammerer at the NPS.[5] Although he forwarded her letter, Hall also responded to Walton, explaining the SCCD's position on the matter. He explained why her letter was forwarded and said, "You understand that we are merely undertaking to conform to the requirements of the National Park Service in the taking over of the Park." His letter explains that while the SCCD had previously made decisions about removal of building material and the like, the transition of authority from the state to the federal government dictated that Hall forward any requests to the Park Service. During this transitionary period, many residents and their advocates understandably were confused about what was permitted and whose permission to seek.

Once he received Walton's letter from Chairman Hall, NPS director Cammerer responded on December 11, 1935, explaining the complexity of the situation: "I do not know whether Mr. Hall has authority to grant permission to have this house dismantled while it is still State property. He may be up against the same legal prescriptions as I will be [when the NPS has jurisdiction over the land]. I will write to Mr. Hall and tell him that as far as we are concerned we have no objection to letting [him] have the lumber from the house if it has no historical or administrative value." His response to Walton indicates that until the land became federal property, distributing materials to residents was under the state's discretion. This kind of information became important to other residents and their advocates as they sought various materials. Many letters mimic the rhetoric of preservation in their requests, making sure that officials knew that the buildings they requested had no "historical or administrative value."[6] This use of the officials' rhetoric indicates an evolving framework upon which residents constructed their requests within their letters.

Cammerer's letter also reveals the confusion among bureaucrats about what their legal responsibilities were as they responded to residents' requests. This confusion then largely contributed to the kinds of requests made by residents. In the following letter from Cammerer to Hall, Cammerer addressed Walton's request by proposing a way to get around the legalities:

> Personally, if the place has no historical or administrative value, I would much prefer these oldtimers to have the benefit of the lumber from them. We would have to tear them down anyway and probably burn a lot after we took the land over. After we have taken the land over I would be forced to advertise for bids for this material. Until we take the land over, however, the actual jurisdiction of these houses is still in the State, and of course, you have extended one hundred per cent cooperation in endeavoring to save all these old places that might be necessary by keeping in contract with this Service. You may on your part be prevented also from disposing of State property but it occurred to me that you might be able to sell the lumber for $1.

Cammerer pointed out to Hall the restrictions that would constrain the NPS once the land was transferred. In the interest of residents, therefore, Cammerer suggested to Hall that he "sell" the lumber to the resident, as a way around state law and future federal legalities. Cammerer favored Walton's request on behalf of the mountain resident and his representation of the resident reflects his feeling about how to find some advantage for residents given the situation. Cammerer did support Walton's request, suggesting that park officials were not uniformly opposed to the requests of mountain residents. Walton's representation of the resident as one who worked hard and kept his word opposed what was generally accepted about residents and therefore constructed him as a person worthy of their attention. The letter between Hall and Cammerer reflects the thinking of officials as they were faced with the problems and concerns of the people living on the land. Because residents were not consulted and many promises were made by state officials but not able to be kept by federal officials, letters and conversations such as the one between Cammerer and Hall were common as officials figured out ways to answer people's concerns given the regulations that were in place.

While Cammerer's letter appears sympathetic to residents' requests for buildings, a response from Lassiter to Charles G. Leavell, the minister at St. Stephen's Episcopal mission, reflects how his negative views of mountain residents influenced his responses to requests. Leavell's letter, written on March 9, 1936, requested on behalf of one of the residents the removal of building materials, very similar to Walton's request. Lassiter's reply to Leavell on March 11, 1936, illustrates not only a shift in land ownership (from the state to the federal government) but also a shift in attitude toward adhering to regulation: "These permits were issued as an act of mercy in order that this *class of people* would not be evicted in the middle of the winter" (emphasis mine). Lassiter ultimately denied Leavell's request, implying that they should be satisfied with the ability to stay via SUPs. Lassiter's response to Leavell's request is much less sympathetic toward residents' situations than Cammerer's response to Walton. On the one hand, Lassiter's reference to residents as "this class of people" indicates his elitist views toward some of the mountain residents (the issue of class will be further discussed in chapter 3). On the other hand, Lassiter was aware of previous inconsistencies in granting requests before SNP had jurisdiction over the land. His various correspondences therefore reveal a strict adherence to Park Service policies, once he had authority to do so. While his rhetoric throughout most of his correspondence with residents seems unfeeling, he was committed to being fair and following park regulations. In addition, Lassiter's commitment to follow policy represents a shift from a word-of-mouth culture to a bureaucratic culture. Where neighbors and businesses had once made oral agreements, the federal government's presence began a shift toward paper trails and red tape. Throughout the mountains, word spread of Lassiter's strict adherence to the rules. Letters of request continued to be written, however, because of the perception that Lassiter would grant them as long as they did not violate federal regulation.

The requesting of building materials came not only for families seeking to use the materials as they rebuilt but also for use by service organizations such as churches and missions. The ministry governing St. Luke's and St. Stephen's missions was located in Charlottesville, and headed by Archdeacon Wiley Roy Mason. In the several letters he wrote to Lassiter, he requested building materials not for residents, but for the mission itself. In the following letter dated March 19, 1935, Mason said that he wanted to continue his mission work but sought permission to do so first:

> I need to find out some things right now. I understand that permission has been given the mountain people to stay on in the Park area for another year. I would like to have this verified so we can plan our work. If they stay on we would like to continue having services. . . . Do you think the Church could be there indefinitely or should it be taken down? I'm going to build a church this summer and would like to have those windows if that must be taken down. One window is a memorial and of course we would like to put it elsewhere. I am sorry to trouble you about all these small details but I don't want to do anything without permission. There are other matters I want to talk to you about but I will postpone those till I can see you.

Mason ultimately wanted to remain in the park another year, providing church and mission services to those remaining in the park until homesteads were ready. However, if the church was to be razed, Mason wanted to use materials to build a new church. Mason's rhetorical use of the phrase "sorry to trouble you about all these small details" highlights Mason's understanding of Lassiter's responsibilities. Like many residents who wanted to be seen as cooperative, Mason apologized for any trouble caused.[7] He asked for advice in proceeding and indicated his willingness to further follow explicit direction. Mason's representation of the residents, while he provided services for them, was that residents, if remaining in the park, deserved to continue to have their church and its services available to them. His tone is not patronizing, but rather practical in providing services should residents be allowed to stay for another year.

In addition to those located within the immediate vicinity of the park, others not close by became interested in the materials from destruction of buildings in the park as well. During the time after the park was approved, the Skyline Drive was being built, and people were slowly being moved from the park, more and more surrounding communities became aware of the various concerns of residents. Their stories prompted responses from around the state, such as the one from Walter Onslow, a journalist from the *Washington Post*. Onslow wrote a letter to Secretary of the Interior Ickes on behalf of Mr. and Mrs. R. E. Mims of Page County, previous landowners in the park. The Mimses (whose family members founded the prominent Mimslyn Inn in Luray, Virginia) were wealthy and powerful landowners who sold their land willingly and were strong park advocates. Onslow's letter suggested to Ickes that the buildings once belonging to the Mimses be saved rather than razed. In his May 28, 1934, letter, Onslow explained that the Mimses' six-bedroom cottage[8] had been condemned with other property in the park but that Mrs. Mims's Girl Scout troop still used the property for "weekend trips into the mountains." He pointed out that Mrs. Mims "wanted to write to Mrs. Ickes and to Mrs. Roosevelt because of their interest in Girl Scouts asking their help to have the cottage saved from razing so the Scouts could continue to use it, but decided it was too small a matter to bother them about." Onslow represents Mrs. Mims as an advocate for the park, one who understood the societal proprieties in troubling women of some standing such as Mrs. Ickes or Mrs. Roosevelt. Onslow, however, positioned himself as one of the good old boys who could help out the "girls." In his letter Onslow engages Secretary Ickes, and at the same time points to Mrs. Mims's character in not wanting to be a nuisance to women who might have some authority to help save her cottage. In addition, Onslow carefully distinguished the cottage from other homes being torn down: "As a mountain lodge it is supposed to be unequalled around there." In this way, Onslow suggested that while some of the buildings could be destroyed, this particular one should be saved, for Scout use and for general use by the secretary or, he jokes, as a place to "banish the representatives of the press." Onslow said later in the letter, "The Girl Scouts would get a hell of a kick out of your help," suggesting that Onslow was familiar with the secretary and that good-natured joking was acceptable in this kind of correspondence. While the Mimses were not fighting for survival in the same ways that some other families were, Onslow's request shows that maintaining building structures was a concern of many residents, no matter their socioeconomic status.

Secretary Ickes forwarded the letter to NPS director Cammerer, who in turn forwarded it to Lassiter, saying, "Let me have your report, including your own recommendations." Lassiter replied a day later, saying that the cottage was "not as large as Mr. Onslow's report would indicate" and continued by describing the cottage in detail. He said, "As there are three other summer homes in the immediate vicinity which will be demolished in accordance with your often expressed wishes to remove all structures along the

Lee Highway, I think this building should come down along with the rest." The Mims Cottage was torn down, despite Onslow and Ickes's letters of advocacy for Mrs. Mims. Ultimately, the secretary and the NPS director deferred to Lassiter, who for the most part thought many of the buildings that had no "historical or cultural significance" should be razed, in accordance with park regulation.[9]

Lassiter's commitment to follow the park's regulations about building materials can also be seen in his response to Madison County attorney Charles Ross, who requested that a resident be allowed to use material from an abandoned building. He said to Ross, "I am sorry to advise that it will be impossible to grant [this] request, as all salvageable material from the abandoned buildings in the park area is to be used by the Resettlement Administration in providing outbuildings, etc., in the homestead projects." Lassiter was careful to document his decisions, leaving a detailed paper trail and indicating how seriously he took bureaucratic policy. Lassiter's rhetoric places him as a transitory figure between the world of word-of-honor, valuing oral and handshake agreements, and the world of bureaucracy, valuing written rules and regulation in the form of letters, SUPs, and eviction notices. With the development and use of technologies such as typewriters and carbon paper, written literacy could be used to document more rules and regulations, the breaking of those rules, and the consequences for people doing so.

An important part of this story, however, is what actually happened to the building materials. While policy dictated that lumber from vacated homes would be used by the Resettlement Administration, the "CCC boys" occasionally were instructed to burn materials considered to be in poor condition, the very materials that advocates such as Walton, Leavell, and Ross requested. Residents within and outside park boundaries wrote to request materials, rather than see them destroyed. While many buildings were salvaged for administrative buildings, it was easier to destroy them than engage in a fair process of who should receive those materials. Once word got around the community that materials were being wasted, residents distrusted the government further, as seeming inconsistencies and contradictions in governmental decision making continued. The perception of the government's inconsistencies pervaded the community, and existing distrust was cultivated as residents felt further and further misled by park officials.

The contrast between Lassiter's responses to people such as Ross and to poor mountain residents is stark. He rarely used conciliatory or explanatory rhetoric with mountain residents. He seemed to do his best to follow federal regulations, once the NPS owned that land and once he had authority to do so, yet with residents of social standing he apologized for the given situation. While he tended to reply to poor park residents[10] tersely and largely without explanation, his responses to people of standing, such as Ross, were patient and explanatory, illustrating the ways in which Lassiter agreed with the unfavorable representations of mountaineers. Issues of class distinction and some official's assumptions about residents will be further discussed in chapter 3.

Letters Obtaining and Following Permits

While many residents willingly sold their land to the state of Virginia as soon as they were notified of the park's approval, some remained in the park under a special use permit (see figure 9, page 50). However, some landowners had tenant farmers living on their land who, because they did not own property, often did not have the means to move out of the park right away. In addition, depending on a person's eligibility for resettlement assistance, some were unable to obtain SUPs. In one case, Charles T. Melton was a Warren County landowner whose 92 acres were originally appraised at $4,450, and of which 89.7 were condemned and sold for fair market price of $3,920. However, Melton had sold his tenant, Edgar Merchant, 78 acres, and he continued to live and work on Melton's land once it was sold. On behalf of Merchant, Melton wrote to SNP to request that Merchant be allowed to continue living in the park until housing could be found for him. Only residents who had agreed to sign SUPs were given the option to remain in the park. As he requested special consideration for his tenant, Melton stated that Merchant "has lived there as a good worker, a good tenant, and a good citizen." Melton's emphasis on citizenry and work ethic mirrors Walton's. Both advocates implored officials to grant requests on the basis of what they believed to be shared values about what constituted special favor—good moral values.

Despite Melton's value of good citizenry, Lassiter denied his request to allow his tenant SUP privileges. Lassiter's letter explained his reasoning as based on the government's desire to move residents out of the park as quickly as possible. Once his initial request was denied, Melton was not deterred and wrote to Lassiter again. In his second letter, Melton asked that Merchant be able to remove the fence rails from the property Melton used to own. Like the requests for removing building materials, many of the requests for removing fence rails had been granted before transfer of the land from state to federal government. So by the time Melton wrote on behalf of his tenant in 1937, the park's policies were more concrete. Lassiter therefore denied Melton's request.

These requests and subsequent denials characterize what was to become a series of written requests. On the surface, this denial seemed arbitrary, since other residents had earlier been granted similar permissions. Lassiter explained to Melton that this kind of request had been ruled on and was official policy. In an uncustomary explanation, Lassiter said in his December 7, 1937, letter, "At a meeting held here Monday it was decided that all private property in the Park area not needed for Park development would be turned over to the Division of Subsistence Homesteads." Again, because of Melton's standing as a prominent citizen, he was afforded an explanation from Lassiter. While seemingly Melton adhered to and spoke of similar value systems, his requests were not granted because of rules and policy. That is, bureaucracy was gaining more value than a sense of a person's worth. To residents, though, the seeming inconsistency in granting requests was arbitrary and unfair. In truth, the denials of residents' requests represent bureaucracy taking hold, and the increasing bureaucracy resulted in general distrust of government officials. Despite this general distrust, residents continued to represent themselves and others as good citizens deserving of various requests.

In addition to obtaining SUPs, residents also requested consideration for life tenure. At the urging of state and local officials, Secretary of the Interior Ickes approved a list of forty or so elderly or infirm residents (the original list contained over seventy names, but many chose to move), granting them permission to live out their lives within the park's boundaries.[11] One resident, John T. Nicholson, appealing to Lassiter's emotions and ego, used quotes from the Bible to persuade Lassiter to grant his father, John Russ Nicholson, life tenure in the park (see figure 11). In his, letter of April 10, 1935, John T. pleaded with Lassiter to include his aging father on

Fig. 11. John T. Nicholson, son of John Russell Nicholson. John T.'s father owned 130 acres in Madison County and was compensated $1,638 for the land condemned by the state of Virginia. John Russ Nicholson was included on the "Secretary's List" of those elderly allowed to live out their lives in their park homes, but he opted to move from the park to live with John T., his son. (Library of Congress, Prints & Photographs Division, FSA-OWI Collection, reproduction number LC-USF34-T01-000360-D DLC; photograph by C. Arthur Rothstein; used by permission of the Nicholson family and Grace Rothstein)

this list. As was characteristic of Nicholson's several letters written to park officials, his handwriting was very neat, contained fancy swirls on the ends of characters, and generally consisted of flowery and formal language:

> Dear Sir: may these few lines please your honor to accept my heart felt thanks and appreciation of your noble kindness in authorizing me and my aged father (73) to continue to live in our present home until fall, or until such time as homesteads are ready for occupancy.
>
> This is felt more keenly and appreciated far more than you may imagine. I feel very much for my aged father, he will be 74 years old 15th of next Oct. He longs to remain the balance of his life in his present home.

If there is anything that you can do towards helping him to remain at his present home it will be greatly appreciated, and you will be blessed, listen, "blessed is he that considereth the poor" (Ps 41:1). We both belong to the Lord through faith in Him. We both as Christians, true to the profession of our faith, has carried out the order of the used permit so far to the very letter absolutely, and shall continue to do so as long as we are allowed to remain in the Park.

Nicholson's rhetoric illustrates that he continually positioned himself as unique among park residents. He repeatedly expressed gratitude, and as a preacher he quoted the Bible in order to persuade Lassiter of his honorable intentions. He referred to Lassiter as "your honor" and praised his "noble kindness" as the director, rhetoric typical of his others letters (see chapter 3). That is, Nicholson assumed that if a resident were in good favor with Lassiter, he may grant the request. Nicholson represented himself and his father as cooperative and good citizens, as they followed the regulations of the SUP. He closed the letter saying, "Very sincerely yours in hope of future favors." His explicit flattery for the specificity of favor indicates that he understood that his requests might be granted if he remained in good standing with Lassiter. Nicholson's religious rhetoric constructed him as a Christian man with corresponding values. Further, he informed Lassiter that if he fulfilled Nicholson's request, he too would be considered honorable. Nicholson's repeated use of "your honor" and "pleasant look and good disposition" indicate that he thought these adulations would persuade Lassiter. As was consistent with his ethos as a religious man, Nicholson wrote what he perceived would move Lassiter to action. Nicholson's strong belief in God was evident, to be sure, but his repeated use of flattery and religious conviction as rhetorical devices indicates his belief in their effectiveness in swaying Lassiter.

Letters Addressing Maintenance of Daily Life

In addition to the letters that addressed the issues of obtaining building materials, SUPs, and life tenure, in the early stages of the park's development mountain residents also sought to continue with the intricacies of their daily living, despite their impending removal from park land. In addition to people who had once lived within the park, letters of this type also came from people living close to park boundaries. Their routine collection of dead wood or berries from land, which was a communal understanding in the area, became a legal matter, one that prompted written permissions once the park owned the land. Missionaries and attorneys—as well as residents such as John T. Nicholson, who wrote for his father and brother-in-law—wrote on behalf of residents. In addition to advocating for individual needs, some residents wrote to park officials about issues that affected whole communities. For instance, Daisy Nicholson wrote to Lassiter several times, concerned about the fairness of distributing available resources. Daisy and her husband, Haywood, lived in Madison County as tenants.[12] Daisy implored Lassiter to allow the residents living near the Nicholson brothers' orchard to have fruit for their own "family use," a government phrase used in letters written *to* residents. Daisy's mimicking of the park's rhetoric shows her desire to follow park regulations literally. In her April 1, 1936, letter, she suggested that the residents remaining in the park needed fruit more than the wealthier orchard owners, who no longer lived in the park. She presented her argument to Lassiter by explaining that the people who lived right around the orchard had large families and could make good use of the fruit. She understood the nature of the SUP and reminded Lassiter of the rules within the permit—that previous landowners could no longer profit from their property. In this way, she argued, the previous owners of the orchard, who were selling the apples, were in violation of the park's rules, while Daisy Nicholson and the neighbors for whom she wrote were worthy of fruit.

While the Nicholson brothers no longer operated the orchard (as it belonged to the park), they did have an SUP to continue harvesting the apples. Since many residents were no longer allowed to gain commercially from their land, Lassiter often directed residents to share the fruit available from the many orchards located within the park's boundaries. Daisy Nicholson was aware of this practice, as shown by her use of the government's phrase "family use." She pleaded with Lassiter to let the people living near the orchard have the fruit, given that they were poor and had difficulty getting food and clothes. Daisy represented her neighbors as having need and therefore as being more deserving of the food than the wealthier orchard owners. In this way, she represented herself as community-minded, and as an advocate for her neighbors. As she directed Lassiter to visit Old Rag School (see figure 12) himself so that he might see their plight and agree

Fig. 12. Old Rag School, located in Madison County, was not only a school for local children but a central meeting place near the post office and general store in the small community of Old Rag near Weakley Hollow. The existence of this school, and several others like it, contradicts what promoters claimed about mountain residents' lack of access to education. (Courtesy of Shenandoah National Park Archives)

to let them have the fruit, she initiated a dialogue with him as someone who might also be concerned with the welfare of the community.[13]

Lassiter replied to Daisy Nicholson soon after, saying that "[I] wish to advise that I am not in a position at this time to turn over the apples on this place to anyone. Without bias to any of the people, not only your section but in all of the Park last year, it was my desire that all of you obtain sufficient apples from the trees within the area needed for family use, and it will be my aim again this fall to try to make a suitable division of the fruit." While Lassiter briefly explained that he tried to act in fairness in distributing the apples, his reply was vague. This ambiguous reply did not deter Daisy, who wrote again later the same year. In her letter dated August 29, 1936, she implored Lassiter yet again to allow residents in need to collect the apples. In appealing to Lassiter's sense of fairness, Daisy constructed herself as conscientious and concerned with justice. She expressed her opinion of what was fair, stating that the Nicholson brothers were not in as much need as the residents for whom she wrote. She constructed herself as a person who understood what was right and that the situation demanded Lassiter's immediate attention.

Lassiter, however, forwarded her letter to Ranger Hoskins, who responded to her: "Your letter of August 29 addressed to Superintendent Lassiter has been referred to me for an answer. If you recall on the same day that your letter was mailed, I called by to see you relative to a request that you had previously made to get apples from the orchards that were formerly owned by Peter and Paul Nicholson. The Nicholson Brothers have permission to get apples from these orchards through this season." Hoskins's letter was a formality, documenting in written form what he had told Nicholson in person, that because they had been issued a permit, the owners of the orchard would be allowed to collect the apples.

Daisy Nicholson's letters indicate what many mountain residents desired when they wrote to officials in the early days of the park's existence: that they be able continue with their daily lives while living on federal property. Her letter represents families in need, and who therefore were deemed worthy of her requests. The following letter, written by a much wealthier landowner, addresses a similar request to maintain one's livelihood. Marvin Mundy was a Rockingham County landowner from near Elkton, where he owned a tourist hotel with several cottages, a tea room, and a gas station consisting of three acres and selling for $5,100. When he wrote to NPS director Cammerer in 1935, requesting that his service station remain open to residents in the park, Cammerer replied that allowing him to continue his service station would violate park regulations.[14] Cammerer said, "Our handling of this situation is not whether the service is needed for the public in these various stations . . . but whether they are unsightly in the view." Not satisfied with this response, Mundy traveled to Washington DC (a ninety-mile journey) to speak with Cammerer in person. During their conversation, Mundy revised his request to include storing his equipment in buildings on park land until his new buildings were ready. Cammerer must have been impressed by Mundy's tenacity and success in business, and although he could not grant his request to keep the service station open, he did tell Lassiter that SNP should comply with Mundy's revised request. In his December 14, 1935, letter to Lassiter, Cammerer wrote, "I regard Mr. Mundy as a square-shooter and a good neighbor, and as he is willing to do the right thing I am glad to meet him more than half way." This judgment on Mundy's moral character reveals the values of the Park Service in relation to residents and granting permissions and favors. Because of his good moral character and willingness to "do the right thing," Cammerer felt Mundy should be granted his request. Those who were not in good moral standing, according to Cammerer, Lassiter, or the park's rangers, might not be granted the same. This kind of process allowed for the appearance of subjective decision making, which in turn led to confusion about policies and procedures, and hence led to the letters and the rhetoric within them. That is, much of the advocacy rhetoric in the letters written by residents is based on the assumption that park officials *would* bend the rules or grant favors given a resident's good standing in his or her community and with the government.

Despite their very different socioeconomic situations, both Daisy Nicholson and Marvin Mundy wrote to maintain a life similar to the one they had before the park was established. Their requests—such as those asking for building materials, SUPs, or life tenure—exemplify the tangible items that residents asked for from park officials.

Conclusion: Identity, Literacy, and Representation

The advocates of mountain families, whether inside or outside the park's boundaries, countered the monolithic representations posed by those in power. The gendered stereotypes wrongly constructed men as shiftless, lazy, and violent, and women as beggars looking for handouts for their children. Examining the complicated relationships of surrounding community members to park residents underscores the ways that residents identified with and often adhered to socially accepted values. While on the one hand positioning themselves as advocates of their neighbors who were opposed to the negative stereotypes accepted about them, their advocacy in some ways served to perpetuate stereotypes about mountain families. As these letters constructed mountain residents as good citizens, they simultaneously constructed them as unique among mountain residents. In these letters, residents argued for their distinctiveness among mountain residents as good citizens, and consequently asked for their special treatment. Their arguments were steeped, however, in terms of fairness and respect for the people, as residents encouraged the government to do the "right" thing by them.

Lassiter's strict adherence to regulation and attempts to be fair outweighed social standing and favoritism, as he placed more value on the bureaucratic procedures of the government. However, this did not deter residents from writing letters to park officials. Rhetorical strategies of out-lining moral character and work ethic were used by experienced and in-experienced writers alike, illustrating the dominant social values held at the time. Residents continued writing for their neighbors, indicating their tenacity and sense of citizenship in advocating for those in need and ulti-mately their resistance to bureaucracy. Their constructed subjectivities dif-fered vastly from Sizer's conclusions about residents as unlearned and un-tamed. Their sense of moral and social justice is evident in the letters as they presented their cases to Lassiter. The letters highlight that while one might distrust government and bureaucracy, it was better not to let it be known, so that through "knowledgeable resistance" some of their requests might be granted. The letters discussed in chapter 4, however, show their distrust of bureaucracy, making part of their identity a skepticism of gov-ernment procedure and the humans enacting and enforcing them.

The letters in this chapter and the next highlight the requests that res-idents made for tangible items, such as building materials, CCC trucks for moving, and permissions for maintaining their livelihoods. In addition, chap-ter 3 also discusses the kinds of disputes residents faced as their ways of life were challenged by relocating to vacant homes, removing materials, and cooperating with officials despite the situation and how they were treated. Some of the disputes between neighbors many have existed before the park was established, but as the next chapter shows, the longer residents lived under NPS regulation, the more their written documentation highlighted the park's responsibility for their management.

Historically, definitions of rhetoric have contained a male bias that emphasizes changing "people and things."[15] Of the letters discussed in this chapter, which includes letters written by community leaders as well as mountain residents, as many are written by women as by men, demonstrat-ing that women saw themselves as significant communicators. They par-ticipated in a discourse of change, attempting to persuade government leaders to answer their requests favorably. But while their discourse re-vealed a level of knowledge about rhetoric typically defined as male, women writers also emphasized rhetoric typically defined as female—that of com-munity and family. They discussed their family situations as a means to convince officials. Likewise, the men writing letters used multiple kinds of strategies to persuade officials to grant their requests. In this way, while many of the men and women held traditional roles (e.g., farmers, housewives), their written discourse crossed gender lines as they figured ways to influence government officials' decisions about their livelihoods. Women who were social workers and attorneys, entering the business world at a time heavily dominated by men, significantly participated in these discourses, balancing what they knew to be discursively powerful together with the community situation.

The contents of the letters crossed gender lines. However, issues of class and education are reflected in the form and style of these letters and in particular in the ways that government officials "saw" the people writing them. So while the letters' contents demonstrated careful attention to community, fairness, and justice, because the form and style did not always adhere to standard code, readers might not have reacted favorably. In the following chapter, issues of class and education become important ways to view the letters as mountain residents continued to live on federal property and while they continued with their daily living.

The letters written by missionaries, social workers, and local attorneys contained various rhetorical strategies that were acceptable in business correspondence at the time. Likewise, the letters that mountain families wrote advocating for each other contained similar expressions of socially accepted codes, indicating their knowledge of the rhetorical situation despite their lack of formal education. Adopting the stance of an advocate placed residents in a position of certain social standing, in a position to help others. Several residents showed a mutual support for each other and requested assistance for each other, as they urged the government to consider their neighbors' situations. The form of a business letter typically does not reveal personal information. But in these letters men and women wrote about their personal and communal situations. This revelation of identity, however, does not mean that people were ignorant of the "proper" forms or styles. Rather, the situation of being displaced from their homes and their livelihoods was so significant as to trump following form. In addition, the government's apparent favoring of those who were cooperative therefore called for people to address *who* they were when making requests. Their private lives were then scrutinized, and perhaps "judged to be inadequate or inappropriate," based on a set of values dictated by those in power.[16]

3

GENRE KNOWLEDGE AND ASSUMPTIONS ABOUT CLASS AND EDUCATION

[Rhetoric is] . . . the use of language as a symbolic means of inducing cooperation in beings that by nature respond to symbols.
—Kenneth Burke, *A Rhetoric of Motives*

When we speak, our utterances fly by as events like any other behaviour; unless what we say is inscribed in writing. . . . This too is not different for action in general: its meaning can persist in a way its actuality cannot.
—Clifford Geertz, *Local Knowledge*

Rhetorical forms that establish genres are stylistic and substantive responses to perceived situational demands.
—Karlyn Kohrs Campbell and Kathleen Hall Jamieson, *Form and Genre: Shaping Rhetorical Action*

In his letter to Episcopal Minister Leavell (see chapter 2), SNP superintendent James R. Lassiter referred to the people remaining in the park as "this class of people." Throughout his letters, though he maintained a strict adherence to fairness and to following park regulations, it is clear that he had little respect for some of the people living in the park. As he and his park rangers worked toward establishing trails and administrative buildings, they were also faced with the management of people—management that they did not expect, as it was assumed that families would be moved before park officials took over from the state late in 1935. Lassiter's resentment toward this aspect of his job is clear in the letters he wrote to other officials and to residents themselves.

Lassiter's written responses adhered to government restrictions, and therefore largely denied the requests asked by mountain families. However, even though the mountain residents' letters often did not elicit the action they desired, the lasting effect of their written documentation illustrates their action: their action to demand being seen differently, to show Lassiter that they were not to be resented, and that the circumstances of their lives were worthy of his attention. Furthermore, their letters demonstrate that Lassiter's assumptions about class and education were erroneous. The residents' letters mirrored accepted conventional forms and styles of letter writing, even if their nonstandard spelling and grammar indicated less formal education, and likely was "seen" by those more formally educated as an indicator of value systems. Assumptions about their standards and morals were reinforced by their letters. However, by closely examining the content of the letters, we see that residents shared values of education, justice, and responsibility.

The recurring phrases used frequently in mountain residents' letters invoked broader social and institutional patterns, thereby illustrating mountain residents' knowledge and use of rhetorical strategy. The use of the rhetorical conventions of the letter also illustrates residents' discursive knowledge about value systems and modes of communication esteemed by government officials.

While their nonstandard spellings and grammar did reflect little formal education and/or a particular socioeconomic status, their letters also provide important insight into their resistance to the park's establishment. What they resisted in their letters was the corresponding assumptions about their morality that came from those in power. So while their grammar and spelling may have been nonstandard, their adherence to the generic form of the letter indicates their rhetorical knowledge not only of the genre but of the power of writing such a genre. They knew that rules about the genre existed, even if they were not "schooled" in enacting those rules.[1]

The letters discussed in this chapter reflect the ways that residents became more and more familiar with the regulations imposed by the park on their daily lives. As many residents continued to vacate their homes and move elsewhere, those remaining were issued special use permits (SUPs). Some were given permission to move to vacated homes that were in better locations or in better repair. This process led to several disputes among residents, as people who had moved found out that their homes were occupied by someone else. This set up a resentment not only with the park but with neighbors and families, as people felt they would have stayed in their homes longer if they had known others were going to move in. The letters in this chapter, as in chapter 2, also discuss the requests for building materials, but these letters contain a heightened sense of the awareness of rules and regulations dictating residents' actions, together with a more sophisticated use of the letter to incite action from the government. In addition, the letters reflect a growing tension between residents and what the park had come to symbolize for some residents and some of their descendents: a government entity with little knowledge of or respect for the locals.

Knowledge of Rules Influences the Ways Requests Are Made

As residents lived under the auspices of the park for a longer period of time, their knowledge of the park's rules and regulations become evident in the letters they wrote and the ways in which they made their requests. When residents requested building or fencing materials, in essence they were asking for materials that the state had paid for when purchasing property for the park. However, their perception was that the material would be wasted or destroyed, as they saw the Civilian Conservation Corps (CCC) dismantling and burning some homes. As Lassiter says in one of his letters, the salvageable material would be used in building resettlement homes. All other material would be destroyed. However, residents would use material deemed "not salvageable" and thought it rational that they be able to use the material rather than see it burned or destroyed by CCC.

Rebecca Jane Powell Baugher's letters show how residents requested building materials while highlighting their knowledge of the developing workings of the park. Rebecca and her husband, Lloyd, and their three children lived on a small farm in Swift Run Gap in Rockingham County.[2] By SUP they lived on landowner Henry Shifflett's vacated property from 1934 to 1936. Rebecca's first letter was written February 19, 1936, to her congressional representative, Charles H. Taylor. His office forwarded her letter to NPS acting director Arthur E. Demaray, who responded to Rebecca Baugher that the Resettlement Administration (RA) "desired to secure the salvaged material from the buildings in the park when they are demolished for use in the construction of homesteads for some of the former residents of the park." Armed with this information yet not deterred from her request, she then wrote to Lassiter on March 31, 1936, explaining that while she had written to Taylor, she directed her request to Lassiter.

Like many of the residents' letters, Rebecca Baugher's letter adhered to standard letter-writing practice, even though she had little formal schooling (according to the 1930 census). Her request reveals a person interested in salvaging what she could from the property she lived in, as she sought to persuade the superintendent to allow her to use the materials from her current house to build another when she moved outside the park's boundaries. She first appealed to Superintendent Lassiter's logic, saying, "The house I live in is 3 small room and they are not one piece of it plain lumber all rough." She continued by saying that because the wood was rough, it was not useful to the "CCC boys" who would "burn it up and I hope you Had rather give it to me then for them to burn it up."[3]

Baugher's letter suggests that residents were well aware of the activities occurring during the relocation process. It also suggests that she assumed that the CCC employees had been directed to burn any lumber that was not deemed useful to the RA. Rather than burn and waste the lumber, she argued, give it to her to use in a modest rebuilding of her home. Baugher also appealed to Lassiter's emotions: "My Husband was a Vutirn in the World War and He never has got a thing."[4] Because her husband was a veteran, but did not receive any aid from the government, she suggested that it was not too much to ask for this lumber. As her letter continued, she commented on her own character: "I wouldn't go ahead and take thing and not ask you all for them." As she assured Lassiter of her integrity, she referred to CCC camp superintendent Bert, who she said could vouch that she was a good citizen who helped him save windows for other residents. While her tone at times was pleading, she was assertive in her postscript: "Answer at once." Baugher's letter reflected the pathos and ethos that many of the other letters did—the hope that the resources could be used rather than destroyed. Because of her previous cooperation and good citizenry, Baugher felt she should be granted her request.

Lassiter denied her request, stating that "I can not grant anyone permission to remove anything from the park area." Lassiter's response is different from Demaray's, who explained how the park planned to use the material. In addition, those who had been landowners were sometimes allowed

to remove materials from the park. Lassiter's response to Baugher, however, did not explain this to her. This lack of communication with residents
led to a lack of understanding about what materials could be removed and
by whom. However, Rebecca Baugher's letter illustrates that growing
knowledge of the park's activities and regulations affected the ways residents constructed their requests.

Joseph Wilson Baugher, a Rockingham County landowner whose eight
acres were condemned and sold for $1,935, was a distant relative of Lloyd
Baugher. Joseph Baugher was also interested in making sure that he was
seen as trustworthy in making his request. In his February 14, 1936, letter
to NPS director Cammerer, Joseph wrote, "Kind sir, Just a few lines in regard to the Park land as I am living inside the Park . . . when I move out if
they do as usual it will be robbed away. . . . And I am asking you if I can have
any of my buildings. . . . If tore down by the CCC boys it is mostly all burnt
up if I can get it honest I will appreciate it as I need it to build my little
place I have got." Like Rebecca's, Joseph's letter reveals his knowledge of
the plans for the RA's use of materials, yet residents believed, indeed saw,
that before these materials could be salvaged, they would likely be stolen
by other residents or burned by the CCC. Baugher explained this to Cammerer, suggesting that his request was justified given what actually occurred in the park rather than what was planned for the materials. Baugher
was certain to tell Cammerer that he wanted to request the materials hon-
estly, that is, to obtain them through written permission rather than stealing them as did some other residents. Baugher, aware of the park's stance
on such stealing, requested the materials in written form and set up an
ethos of trustworthiness so that his request might be granted. Like his relative Rebecca, Joseph Baugher also appealed to Cammerer's logic, suggesting that his use of the materials made more sense than for it to be destroyed.

Moving building materials and putting them to good use was a source
of many requests from residents to park officials. Several residents wrote
about the needless burning of materials, though it is clear that many buildings were to remain in the park. What residents wanted was to use those
materials that would be deemed unusable by the park or RA and consequently destroyed. Baugher employed a logical argument similar to those
in many of the letters; residents felt it did not make sense that they could
not make good use of the materials. However, park officials were in a bind.
While they often did not use the "plain" lumber that most buildings were

made of, distributing the lumber equitably was a difficult task. CCC workers burned the materials deemed unusable for the homesteads; the residents, however, could not see the logic in allowing any of the materials to go to waste, especially with so many families in need. Wasting materials, especially on the heels of the Depression, was considered by residents to be foolhardy, if not immoral; however, because rules and bureaucracy took precedence, many requests like these were not granted.

In addition to explaining what was happening to the materials as buildings were razed, some residents added to their requests their knowledge of the park's goals in conservation and taking care of the land and remaining property. This construction of assisting the park in its goals revealed a different dimension of discursive knowledge. As letters and oral communication to and from park officials accumulated, residents added to their understanding of the situation and the park's value of conservation. Joseph Baugher's letter, for instance, stated that he "would move all and clean up old scraps," recognizing the park's goals for clearing the landscape. When the CCC did raze a building, they also removed trash and cleared away debris. Baugher was aware of this, and by stating that he would clear away old scraps, he made clear he understood the process and purpose of the CCC's coming through. He not only constructed himself as understanding this purpose but also suggested he was one who would help with this process, even as he was requesting the lumber for his use.

Similarly, Elmer Hensley (step-grandson of Victoria Meadows Hensley, discussed later in the chapter) identified himself as helpful in the park's goal of conservation. He said in his December 5, 1936, letter to Lassiter, "I have decided not to take a Home Stead. If I can get these old Buildings here I can have a place. . . . I will tear them all down & clean up the place. Fences & all & burn all the waste. Free of charg for what good is in them & I will move in a short time. You could have some body look the place over & see what good is in them. Please let me know soon." Hensley assured Lassiter that he was so reliable that someone could inspect when he was finished. Because Hensley decided not to take a homestead, he needed the lumber to build another home. Whether residents signed (or were approved) for a homestead or not, the lumber in their houses was considered park property; and, for the most part, Lassiter did not grant requests for the lumber in accordance with federal regulation. However, Hensley reasoned, he would clean up the place in the same way that the CCC boys had been instructed to do, thereby completing work for free that would otherwise have to be paid for.

Ben Meadows (Victoria Meadows Hensley's first husband's nephew) wrote a letter similar to Elmer Hensley's in that he felt he did not cause trouble and therefore should be granted his request. On February 7, 1938, Meadows wrote, "i have cash money in the buiden i bought lumber and re-bard the house and barn and bought windows." Like many residents, Mead-ows spent his own money making improvements on the (now government-owned) property while he lived there under a special use permit. He hoped, therefore, for reimbursement from the park. Meadows's letter shows a growing sense of tension among residents as they moved to and from vacated homes and salvaged building materials, all precipitated by the park's establishment. As he asked for the materials, he said, "i have not never reseved[5] no hell at all since i have been here so i thank you ought to let me have the building . . . so i hope you will study over it and say yes." Meadows separated himself from those who caused trouble for park officials and there-fore thought the park ought to let him have the building materials he re-quested. In so doing, he emphasized the government's responsibility, doc-umenting through written discourse his stance on the government's culpability in the situation. He seemed certain that once Lassiter consid-ered the matter, he would see the logic in his request and let him have the building.

Revelations of Daily Life:
Written Permissions for Cultivation and Firewood

While residents such as Rebecca Baugher, Joseph Baugher, and Elmer Hensley wrote for permission for building materials, other residents wrote requesting to plow land so they could cultivate crops and to collect timber for firewood. One of the regulations of the NPS was that federal park prop-erty could not be cultivated or harvested without permission. As the home-steads were delayed because of multiple shifts in administration, it became clear, however, that because residents were forced to remain in the park until their homesteads were ready, they would need to continue cultivating and harvesting in order to subsist; hence the issuance of SUPs. Park officials granted permissions to residents, ensuring that they cultivated only for their "family use" and that they use only dead trees for firewood.

Some residents broke the rules, however, which created further problems among residents and with park officials. William A. "Buck" Dodson, a Madison County landowner whose six acres were condemned and sold for $231, anticipated problems with his plans to plow his land. He wrote on March 24, 1936, "I am writing to ask about plowing for a corn crop. . . . Why I ask you about this is some folks here say I can't do this. And most likely report this to you." Talk among neighbors about what was allowed within park regulations must have been confusing. Since the rules shifted between the SCCD and the NPS, and since it seemed to residents that Lassiter granted requests based on favoritism, residents were often confused about whether or not they could cultivate what was once their property. So while they attempted to follow rules as they understood them, the bodies of authority shifted, thereby rendering their previous discursive knowledge and interactions seemingly powerless. Dodson also made clear that his neighbors would report him for plowing, so he wrote to Lassiter first to ensure his permission. This letter reflects what many residents realized about park officials: as long as residents asked for permission first and conducted themselves in the spirit of cooperation, they were likely to be granted their requests. Those who broke the rules without written consent often faced eviction notices for not adhering to their SUPs and, consequently, to federal regulation. This understanding of regulation that required a written letter also suggests their knowledge of genre and of the potential power contained in letters.

Several other letters revealed residents who desired cooperation with the park and saw that cooperation as evidence that they deserved the requests they sought. For instance, Victoria Sullivan Meadows Hensley (stepgrandmother of Elmer Hensley), who lived outside the park when she wrote her letter of March 9, 1936, suggested that because she willingly sold her property and moved promptly, she should be able to collect wood from the park. She wrote to Lassiter, "May I get some dead wood off the place where I moved from for my own use. I will appreciate it if I could. I moved out of the Park November 8, 1934 and didn't cause you all any trouble. Answer at once." Because she had not caused trouble when asked to move, Hensley saw herself as deserving of the park's permission, and by saying "Answer at once," she demanded and expected response from officials. Many people did cause what the park deemed as "trouble," by taking materials from vacant homes, refusing to move, and allowing their children to beg from tourists on Skyline Drive. Since these acts were viewed as un-cooperative, the people doing them were seen by park officials as causing trouble, as a "class of people" not able or willing to cooperate. These con-clusions were consistent with the overall view of the mountaineer, and let-ters such as Victoria Hensley's sought to counter that view. Therefore, the residents who did not engage in these acts saw themselves as worthy of their requests, and made sure in their letters that Lassiter was made aware of the ways in which they cooperated. By saying she did not want to bother Lassiter, Victoria Hensley recognized his relative authority and displayed her discursive knowledge of her place in relation to the park. She set herself apart from those who were uncooperative, using written literacy to do so.

Requests for dead wood also came from residents who lived nearby but who did not necessarily own land in the park. Collecting dead wood from the area had been a common occurrence, though not necessarily a legal one, but with imposition of federal regulation and preservation of natural habi-tat, collecting wood without permission was strictly prohibited. Only those remaining in the park under SUP were allowed to collect wood, and only if they wrote for permission. Mary Elizabeth Jenkins Gray, a Page County resident living close to the park's boundaries but who did not own land, requested that she be allowed to gather wood from within the park's boundaries. In order to persuade Lassiter of her request, she highlights her status as a widow and the needs of her children. She wrote to Lassiter October 25, 1937: "Mr. Lasader, Mr. JW Weakley told me to call your at-tention for a load of wood that he was shore you had forgotten that was my mother down to see you if there would be such as for me to get wood i am a widow with four small kids of Elbert C. Gray deceased ilive just below ED Weakleys store pine grove ihate to be so much trouble to people but that is the only way for me Just come and see my condition." Gray's letter mentioned oral communication between her and a fellow neighbor who had given her advice about her situation, indicating the communication among neighbors about the proper ways to correspond with park authorities. To be sure Lassiter understood who she was, she mentioned his previous con-tact with her mother, who her husband was, and where she lived. Like Daisy Nicholson, Gray encouraged Lassiter to come see her in order to prove her trustworthiness, to prove what she said about her condition. Lassiter, how-ever, denied her request, because it was not legal to allow people who did not hold SUPs to gather wood (or any material) from the park.

After the official land transfer, SNP authorities were not in a legal position to allow the collection of wood. Gray's request, however, is a poignant example of the multiple ways the park affected the lives of many, including those who did not live within park boundaries. People like Gray previously collected dead wood or berries, but at the impetus of the park, they were compelled to write letters of requests, and in turn were denied. According to Reed Engle, requests like these continue to be made today, but the park, due to conservation regulations and liability issues, cannot grant such requests. From the beginning of the park's establishment, local residents have been baffled at the various rules and the ways that the park's existence changed their livelihoods. Those forced to move were impacted greatly—yet those who lived close by were also affected as previously common practices became illegal.

John Jewell did not request wood, but his request for apples reflects sentiments similar to those expressed by Elmer Hensley and Joseph Baugher about caring for park property. Jewell wrote to Lassiter on March 23, 1936, to request permission to collect apples. He explained that in return for caring for the property, it was only fair that he be able to collect the apples where he lived. He also explained that the person who collected the apples the previous year did not care for the place. Jewell said it was morally right for him to have access to the apples, and in this way, like many others, Jewell appealed to Lassiter's sense of justice.[6] Because he took care of the orchard, he felt that he—not someone else who did not cooperate with and assist the park—should be able to collect the apples.

The residents' construction of self-worth, of deserving Lassiter's consideration, was a recurring theme across the letters archived at SNP. Men and women alike represented themselves as sharing values of conservation. Men volunteered to care for the land and women evoked a sense of community values. A constant reestablishment of themselves as worthy citizens indicates their continual battle to be seen by those in authority as citizens with valid concerns and requests, and who deserved some semblance of acknowledgment from the government.

A letter by William Zebedee Lam, a Page County resident, shows how the park itself caused certain kinds of negotiations between neighbors. In his letter written to Zerkel on April 17, 1936, he requested permission to cut the grass from a particular seed he planted on what was now park property. His letter, much like the letters of others who requested the harvests from their land, reveals an interesting occurrence among neighbors resulting from the appearance of SNP. Lam explained that a friend of his planned to plow that land with the permission of SNP. However, Lam said that "it is a new kind of grass an i dont want it plowd up" and his friend "has plowed mar ground than he could farm last year." He asked Zerkel not to tell his friend of his request, as he felt sure his friend would become angry. Lam's letter illustrates the ways that the park allowed some to cultivate vacated land and some to move into vacated properties. Lam's request for Zerkel not to share his request with his friend highlights the way new procedures unwittingly pitted neighbor against neighbor. In several instances, Zerkel's letters to residents encouraged a sense of secrecy. For instance, Zerkel wrote a letter to Greene County landowner Marcellus Breeden on January 21, 1935, in which he informed Breeden of his approval for an extension of his SUP, and stated that the permission was "for your PERSONAL and CONFIDENTIAL information only and positively not for your passing this idea to others." This level of secrecy, and a sense that only certain people would be granted certain permissions, established a pattern of distrust among residents and between residents and officials. Keeping moves or SUP extensions or any other information secret was unlikely in the local communities, as many neighbors and relatives were in constant communication over their status of relocation.

The amount of communication among neighbors is evident in the ways that residents moved into homes as they became vacant when homesteads were available or when housing was found elsewhere. Some residents moved into these vacated homes without permission as soon as they knew they were vacant, even at the risk of being discovered by park officials. But other residents, such as Lilly Pearl Nicholson Campbell, requested in writing permission to occupy a vacated home, in a manner similar to those who sought written permissions to remove materials or harvest crops. Lilly Campbell, wife of James R. Campbell of Nethers (a small community in both Madison and Rappahannock counties), wrote several letters to officials from 1936 to 1938. Her letters ranged from eight to fourteen pages long, and in them she took great care in explaining to Lassiter her situation and her rationale. In November 1936, Campbell wrote to Lassiter to request permission to move into a home where the current resident was "getting ready to move out pretty soon." Campbell explained that she "would like to get that house for this winter as its more comfortable than mine an also it is down off of the mountain." She told Lassiter to "bee sure an tell them [the current residents] not to up set the house none or move none of the fence from the place." Campbell's letter shows that people were often aware when neighbors or relatives were moving. Letter's such as Campbell's also show that residents knew the goings-on around the mountains and that Zerkel's suggestion to keep anything secret was unrealistic. In any case, as residents vacated and others moved into their homes, disputes arose as families negotiated the uses of their property.

Growing Tensions among Neighbors and with the Park: Using the Letter to Cite the Park's Responsibilities

As people continued cultivating land, moved into vacant homes, or requested dead wood or materials, tensions among neighbors began to grow as the fairness of the government's responses came into question. On May 8, 1935, for instance, Rebecca Baugher's husband, Lloyd Lee Baugher, wrote to Lassiter explaining that the family who had vacated the home he now lived in continued to burn fences on the property. Once some families had vacated their properties, families awaiting services, such as the Baughers, were allowed to move in with an SUP. This change of housing often caused dissension among residents because they felt other people were living on their property, although legally it belonged to the government. Baugher stated that he wanted Lassiter to "write me a notis and send me so I can give it to the chief to serve on them." Baugher's complaint letter prompted a letter from Lassiter to the family who had vacated, advising them of Baugher's SUP and telling them "not to be bothering us with all your petty quarrels and scraps." Several of Lassiter's letters to residents with disputes reflected his frustration at having to play the role of mediator between residents. They also reflect the way that Lassiter disregarded their dispute and the way that the imposition of the park in fact exacerbated (if not caused) the disputes. By labeling the situation as petty, Lassiter showed the residents that their concerns over their livelihoods and losing their homes were not worth his concern.

Another dispute over vacated property occurred between George Robert Herring and John Wesley "Boss" Morris, both landowners in Greene County (see figure 13). George Herring vacated his property to move his family into another vacated home, and Boss Morris moved into

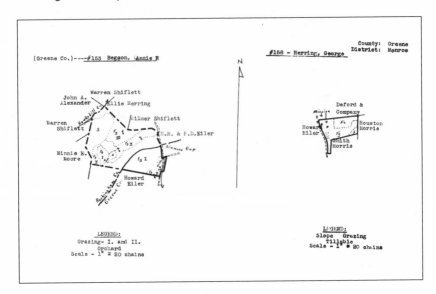

Fig. 13. Reproduction from a Greene County plat book. This plat page shows several of the land tracts in Greene County that were surveyed for the park and ultimately condemned. The right side of the page shows the tract belonging to George Herring, husband of Lillie Herring and neighbor of John Wesley "Boss" Morris. Deed Book 25.

the Herring property. In this March 10, 1935, letter, Boss Morris reported to Zerkel that George Herring continued to return to his previous property, even though Morris lived there under SUP, which he referred to here as "the contract": "I have moved to the George Herring place and under the Contract was to use all buildings an be responsible for them. Mr. Herring have been to the CC Camp no 3 trying to get the store room from them. this room would be of use to me as the roof is bad on the corn house. He also has it locked and orders me not to touch it. Also has a few hundred pounds of hay in the barn. Would like for him to move it out so I will have room for my cows. If you desire me to hold all buildings please let me no at once so I can show the foreman my permit when he comes to tear them down." Morris reported Herring's actions not only because he wanted the buildings but also because reporting Herring's rule breaking was a way to show officials that he wanted to cooperate and that he knew what the rules of the permits were and how to follow them. His communication with Zerkel pointed toward the park's responsibility in administering and honoring his contract.

As residents argued over property and as tensions grew, some became fearful of their safety. Rockingham County landowner Columbia Frances Hensley (wife of Nicholas Wysong Hensley, whose 138 acres were condemned and sold for $10,410) wrote to Lassiter on March 26, 1936: "I am writing you to find out if I can put Ben Hensley and family out from here and if you will help me if I cant get them out myself? Please sir write me up a vacation [eviction] nitice that I can have served on them to get out of the house that I am occupying now. let me hear from you real soon Mrs. NW Hensley p.s. I am being treated so bad I just cant stand it and stay here. they are staying here under my permit. you ask me to stay and take care of the house." Hensley asserts that because she was cooperating by taking care of the house, she wanted Lassiter to uphold her contract by evicting the family imposing on her. With Ben Hensley's family living in her home, she was unable to enact her duties. Aware of the system of evictions, Hensley requested that the park require the family to leave, so that she could remain in peace and to continue following the park's rules. The B. F. Hensley family was served with an eviction notice in March 1936 and asked to vacate the residence of Mrs. N. W. Hensley later that year. In writing this letter, Hensley points to the park's responsibility in keeping her safe under their administration of the property.

The sense that the park had a duty to attend to residents' various situations is also illustrated in a letter by James Lam (son of Ardista Lam). He wrote on April 27, 1936, "I am writing to you in regard to Mr. Roy Taylor grzing his cows in the Park Land He is now grazing in the place that my mother lives on Ardista Lamb and they give me trouble at times he lives out side of the Park and I wish you would attend to this." In reporting the matter, Lam wanted to ensure his fair use of the property under his permit, but he also wanted it understood that he felt Lassiter should attend to it. The disputes between neighbors were in part caused by the park itself, and letters such as Morris's and Hensley's indicate a growing tension with the park's authority and the management of the land.

In the following examples, residents become so distraught over their living situations that they ask the park to buy their property, a request impossible to grant as the surveys and purchases through the state were completed by the time they wrote their letters. The requests, though, indicate how desperate some residents felt because of the results generated by the park. For instance, Page County resident Fannie Baugher Comer (wife of

Frank P. Comer) wrote to park officials requesting that they buy a certain tract of her land. She said in her December 16, 1935, letter that one of her neighbors had, "bought wood of me last winter and did not pay for it. He has treated me dirty and cut timber large enough for saw timber. My land joins this land and I am afraid he will cut over on me. And if he does I can't do nothing as he does not own any property or real estate. Will you try and get the Park people to take over my tract that joins the Kelsey Line no 504— 65.2 acres Price $4960. Since the death of my husband it would help me so much. . . . If the Park wants someone to over see the Co. land I will keep people from cutting the timber if they will appoint me. I've told you the truth and every one is best off not to have any dealing's with [him]. He cut a couple of acres over on us when my husband was liveing." Comer's concern comes from managing her land in relation to the park's boundaries. By revealing her status as a widow, Comer emphasizes the ways in which her neighbor had acted badly and made her feel unsafe. She further suggested that she be appointed by the park to ensure that no other wood would be cut by her neighbor, that she would assist the park in enforcing the rules. She also proposed a solution to her dilemma with her neighbor: the park should buy her tract of land so that she would no longer own land adjacent to his. Even though Comer did not live in park boundaries, the park had so permeated residents' lives that she felt officials were responsible for her troubles.

In a second letter later that month, on December 24, Comer informed Lassiter of her fear for her safety and Lassiter's responsibility for it: "What I told you about [my neighbor] getting wood was the honest truth. But I did not know that you was going to tell him. He came to my place last evening with a big rock in his hand expecting to knock me in the head with it. I did not go out and he threw it against the hen house as he left. He knows I have no men folk to protect me. He is two big a coward to go where there is men folk. I did not want him to cut over on me is why I written. But I did not know that my name would be mentioned to him. I am all alone except my little girls. And his is sorry enough to do something to my property." Most of Comer's distress came from the way Lassiter handled the situation, suggesting that he further compromised her safety by telling her neighbor that Comer had reported him. She castigated Lassiter and warned him of her neighbor's volatile nature. Comer reminded him of the violence that could be inflicted on her, invoking the violence toward women that occurred in the mountains during this time and suggesting the vulnerability of women alone and caring for children. Several other women writing to officials, while not mentioning their marital status, were also afraid of the repercussions of reporting the infractions of their neighbors. In cooperating with the park and following procedure, and furthermore by documenting that choice on paper, they risked their safety with some of the people living around them.

In the same way that Comer asked the park to buy her land because her living situation had deteriorated because of the influx of the park, so too did Bluford H. Lam make such a request. Lam's letter resisted the notion that mountain families did not care about education. His letter, in addition to demanding that the park act on its responsibility, also candidly stated his desire for his children to go to school, a school that existed in the park long before the park was established. Lam said in his December 10, 1936, letter:

> I don ever thing I could do to get the Park in the first place I gave 10 acres of land and went around with the men and showed them the conors [corners] and did not receive a penny last winter the CC boys came and blasted my road full of rocks and went away. and left my road in such a bad shape we couldent get a doctor in the whole winter. and the children had to stop school as the buss could not get in. and this winter they have ben out of school a week on account of bad roads every family is close to the school but the ones living on the blue ridge mountains that have to go over this road on account of the CC leaving the road in such a bad shape. asking you kindley to take my place for the next ones as we hafto meet the doctor about 2 miles on horse back I have don all I could to get the Park thinking it would take my place you no it has took all around me just leaves room for us to go out over the Park. hope you will be kind enough to take it and help me that much as the children isent getting any learning.

Lam's five-page letter alluded to the complexities of activities in establishing the park while families remained on the land. He argued that while he had done everything that had been asked of him, such as "donating" land to the park, the park had not made good on promises made by state officials to maintain roads. While those promises may have been made by the SCCD or park promoters during the early days of proposing the park, Lam felt it the NPS's responsibility to fix his impassible road. Furthermore, Lam explained, because the road was destroyed by the CCC, the land he still owned (which was outside park boundaries) became less valuable. He explained that because the surveyors originally intended to include his place within park boundaries, their plans for the road created problems for his property when they did not include it. Lam was therefore concerned about his children's access to school. Without sufficient road maintenance, his children would not be able to get to school. This concern for the literacy and education of his children countered the assumptions that mountain residents were not interested in education or that it was not available to them. In fact, in this case the park's road prevented Lam's children from going to a school that already existed before the establishment of the park. Through his letter, Lam recorded the history of the decision-making process, as it was detrimental to his family's access to medical care and education. His letter demonstrated the value he placed on people keeping their word, highlighting the tension between the spoken word of the SCCD and park promoters and the written policies of the NPS. Lam's letter, like several others written by those whose lands were not condemned and bought for the park, illustrates that the establishment of the park affected even those whose lands were not "condemned." Furthermore, Lam's letter, like Dodson's oral history (see chapter 1), speaks to the ways that the complicated process of forming the park and the changes in authority made for broken promises and seemingly unjust procedures.

Similarly, Madison County landowner Ida O. Lillard's letter shows how the park's establishment adversely affected her livelihood and how some residents demanded that the park take action on their request (see figure 14). She wrote to Lassiter, "I want a little information and I know you can give it." Rather than the typically polite request that many residents used (for example, "just a few lines," and "I hate to bother you"), Lillard plainly stated what she wanted and informed Lassiter that she was aware that he had the information she needed. The distinction between requesting and demanding is that Lillard positioned herself as making a legitimate request and precluded Lassiter's refusing her that information for any reason. The information she needed pertained to a neighbor's cattle wandering on her property. Lillard's land was adjacent to the park and some of the fence line extended into the park's boundaries. In her letter she asked, by using a hypothetical example[7] (that is, she did not name specific people), whether or not "the party that sold the land [can] still claim that fence and move it

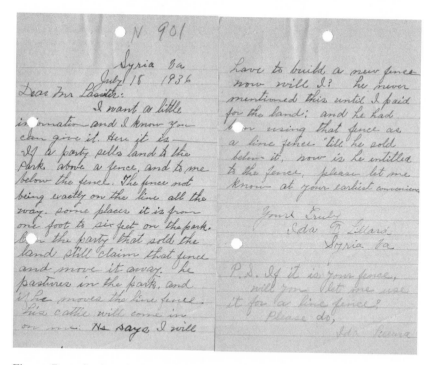

Fig. 14. Reproduction of Ida O. Lillard's letter. Lillard, who never married, lived in Madison County. She owned 64 acres and was compensated $1,236 for her property when it was condemned by the state of Virginia. (Courtesy of Shenandoah National Park Archives; used by permission of the family)

away." The "party" apparently still lived on park property and continued to pasture cattle there. According to her letter, the party informed Lillard that he was going to move the fence, since it was his. The result, complained Lillard, would be that his cattle would "come in on me." In her letter, Lillard insisted that Lassiter settle her dispute with her neighbor. This insistence functions as resistance to the park's inaction, and as a way to identify as a person deserving of his attention.

Page County landowner James Buracher similarly insisted that the park do its part in assisting him. He not only asked for materials but also suggested that SNP pay him to do their work for them. He said in his February 27, 1935, letter to Lassiter that his neighbor used "to fix the fence but now you all have bought the land and now it is in your alls place to fix your part of the fence. It would be four (4) or five (5) days work to fix your alls part of the fence so by causing you all the trouble of hireing someone, I'll fix it for six dollars ($6.00) so this work must be done at once so just as soon as I receive the $6.00 I'll fix your all part of the fence and everything will be all right then." He reminded the park of its responsibility, but also suggested that in order to be helpful and to have the work completed in a timely manner, he would make the repairs for a fee.

In a similar instance, Lilla Meadows explained to Lassiter in her November 19, 1938, letter that CCC workers had destroyed her potato crop and that she should be reimbursed for it. She said, "Camp 3 destroyed them I planted 2 dollars worth seed and they was very good. If you want to you can send some body to eastamate about what it would been worth I am a widdow and worked hard for them I feel like you or willing to get me sompling for them." Like Joseph Baugher's letter, Meadows's reflects the common interaction with CCC workers. In asking for reimbursement, she mentioned she was a widow, yet she did so quickly before arriving at the crux of her argument: that she worked hard to cultivate her crop and she felt sure Lassiter would see to her reimbursement based on her work ethic. In addition, in order to show her trustworthiness, she told Lassiter to send someone to check her accuracy in estimating what her crop was worth. In this last sentence, she did not ask Lassiter to send someone else; rather, she told him to check her story, confident in her assertion that she should be compensated for her loss.

Madison County resident Lizzie Nicholson Dyer, wife of Charley Dyer (who was paid $717 for his sixty-four acres) and relative of Teeny Nicholson, complained to Ranger Hoskins, "Will you plese come Down and git [my neighbor] to put His Hogs up all Drop Him a letter we Been wating all the spring and He want put them up We hovent put out a Bit of girden yet they aer sraying the green zaud[8] Dawn Here we aer Both living on the zame Farm you come Dawn at once." Dyer's request insists that officials send her neighbor *written* notice, indicating her understanding of the generic power that formal letters from the park documented the infraction and incited (some) residents to follow the rules. Her neighbors hogs were "sraying" the sod, therefore preventing Dyer from planting her garden, a serious problem for most residents as a garden was often their primary source of food. Like Lillard, Dyer demanded that the ranger visit her immediately to settle the dispute, suggesting the park's responsibility in helping residents.

Fig. 15. Photograph of Teeny Florence Corbin Nicholson, taken in 1935 by WPA photographer C. Arthur Rothstein, in front of her home. Teeny was known to have an extensive flower garden. This photograph and approximately 250 others were taken to document rural America and are currently available at the Library of Congress. (Library of Congress, Prints & Photographs Division, FSA-OWI Collection, reproduction number LC-USF3301-002173-M2; used by permission of the Nicholson family and Grace Rothstein)

In another example, Teeny Florence Corbin Nicholson (see figure 15) also wrote to Ranger Hoskins to settle a dispute. She told him in her March 13, 1937, letter that her neighbor's "family just keeps milking my cows and I give them milk every time they come after it. . . . They done my cows bad last year they would milk them and take thire bells off and pull thire tails and made other threats." She asked Hoskins to move her neighbor as soon as possible because "if you leave it to him he wont move at all"; concerned with her safety, she urged Hoskins not to mention her complaints to her neighbor "or any one that would tell him Because if he knew it no telling what kind of private injure he would do to me and please have my house fix up as soon as you can for it is in sorely bad shape. Remember me to your wife." Nicholson was sure to tell the ranger that though she had been neighborly in sharing milk, her neighbors stole her milk anyway. She suggested to Hoskins that he take action to move them; otherwise they would not leave on their own. Nicholson's letter departs from others reporting disputes in that she insisted the park use its authority to maintain residents' safety. Like Dyer and Lillard, Nicholson recognized the park's authority and therefore demanded response to the threats to her livestock and herself through protection from the park's employees. While she was insistent that they help her, her letter reflects a familiarity with the ranger. She said, "remember me to your wife," positioning herself as one who knew him personally and one who followed the conventions of an informal letter.

Each of these examples demonstrates the ways that residents, through their insistence that the park fulfill its duties as administrators of disputes, resisted the notion that they did not have fully realized lives. As the park had infringed on their way of living, they seemed to be saying, it must now take responsibility for the disruptions it caused. Many letters in the archived collection describe instances where neighbors' stock grazed on others' land. These kinds of disputes were common before the park was established, and local law enforcement presumably settled them. But once the park assumed authority, local law enforcement no longer had jurisdiction. Residents came to know that one way to get the park to act on their disputes was to register their complaints in written form. In their letters, they expressed fears of bodily harm, yet not positions of helplessness. Rather, their letters exhibit a recognition of and insistence on SNP's responsibility to remedy the various situations that occurred on their property. They not only recognized the park's authority, they demanded that the park exact that authority fairly. In each of the letters, there is an urgency and directness when they demanded that Lassiter or Hoskins attend to their matters. As with many letters, the grammar and diction were not necessarily advanced; however, the authors' sense of the situation, their sense that it deserved a government official's attention, is evident. These residents were not afraid to inform government officials of their duties in providing assistance. So while they were inexorably forced off their land, within that situation they made demands, in the written form deemed appropriate, for the various resources they thought should be available to them. As social action, their letters serve as their participation in the typified actions of this newly realized SNP community. In the next chapter, residents begin not only to call for the park's responsibility but also to question the park's authority overall.

A Growing Sense of Frustration

Like Rebecca Baugher, many of the letter writers reflected a desire to cooperate, and a desire to be seen and acknowledged as persons with moral standing. The writers discussed in this chapter constructed themselves as having this desire, and as being the kind of people who followed the law and would do what was expected of them. Constructing identities of cooperation, however, was more complicated than simply acquiescing to rules and exhibiting moral behavior. The residents constructed identities that showed that while they understood the rules and wanted to follow them, they equally expected park officials to act in fairness; that is, to participate fairly in an agrarian culture's system of bartering. In this way, residents documented their expected participation and in turn expected park officials to respond accordingly.

In some letters, they placed themselves in positions of little authority, apologizing for taking up an official's time with their simple requests. In other letters, writers assured officials that they would clean up the land around the buildings they asked to remove. Indicating their perception that many buildings were being razed, residents wrote that they would participate in the cleanup if they could have their request granted. In this way, they constructed themselves as deserving of services and on equal footing with officials, a different rhetorical move than positioning themselves as troubling the park officials. Some of the women who wrote letters specifically mentioned that they were widows, appealing in some cases to the male officials' sympathy.[9] Finally, while some of the letters reflected conflicts with other residents, they reported their disputes in a spirit of cooperation with the park. Their construction of their requests within their letters reflected the middle-class values of propriety and morality at the turn of the century.[10]

By invoking these values in their letters, residents countered what was assumed about them: that they were illiterate and isolated. Residents often reappropriated the discourse of power into a familiar discourse, translating government rules and discourse into a common language, demonstrating a sophisticated manipulation of language. Their letters demonstrated their knowledge of the rhetorical situation, their relative position of power, and their enactment of a productive identity within their power relationship with park officials. They showed park officials that they were literate in social values and attitudes. However, because their written (and, in some cases oral) skills did not adhere to standard learning, their social literacy was often overlooked. While residents themselves illustrated literacy "as an integral part of social events and practices," government officials conveniently separated their skills from the given social context.[11]

While their letters adhered to socially accepted codes of conduct and moral action, their use of phonetic spelling and nonstandard language caused those in power to detach their skills from their worthiness as humans. It is this process of separation that had (and continues to have) enormous implications for those who were judged as illiterate.[12] These power dynamics involved in separating skills from contexts had devastating effects on individual lives, and (as I argue later in the book) on the culture at large, as people's assumed literacy, and therefore moral, capabilities were misunderstood. Letter writers repeatedly constructed themselves as adhering to social code through cooperation and rule following, but government officials did not *see* them because of their so-called lack of skills, which was assumed to indicate something about their morality.

As the letters in chapter 4 show, the disputes among some residents began to escalate as residents lived multiple years under the auspices of the park and as their displacements loomed. These letters point toward a more explicit sense of resistance to officials as residents demanded that the park assist them in settling their disputes. Both chapters 2 and 3 illustrate ways that residents tried to do what those in authority wanted them to do as it related to socially accepted values and morality. The next chapter, however, addresses how mountain residents resisted that authority and consequently the values placed upon them. Though the residents who saw themselves as advocates and cooperators seemed to play into dominant social codes, they also worked within the system as it existed, resisting with a knowledge of how the system worked. That is, through what I call "knowledgeable resistance,"[13] mountain residents used their literacy to construct alternative identities. Park officials saw working with mountain families as difficult, yet these letters illustrate that accepted stereotypes could no longer work for park officials. While this chapter discusses the ways that literacy can be used to reflect and reify social values and hierarchies, in chapter 4 we see that the writers do not reproduce accepted discourses. Rather, they assert identities directly counter to those prescribed for them, thereby stepping out of the boundaries in which they were expected to remain.

As chapter 4 demonstrates, mountain residents' varied use of rhetorical strategy, use of genre, and representation of identity within genre suggest the complexity of the community on the land that comprised the park. This complexity contradicts assumed notions of the mountaineer, and elucidates that mountain residents were active agents in their responses to the imposition of the park. Finally, the letters discussed in this chapter illustrate social attitudes and assumptions about literacy and what literacy reflects about an individual's worth. Who the letter writers were *perceived* to be seemed a crucial part of determining whether they were worthy of the services they requested. While these attitudes were already present in the minds of government officials, they were reinforced by the letter writers themselves. Who they were perceived to be becomes even more of an issue in the next chapter as residents participate in discursive negotiations of power and resistance.

RESISTANCE, NEGOTIATION, AND SOCIAL ACTION

Genre, in this way, becomes more than a formal entity; it becomes pragmatic, fully rhetorical, a point of connection between intention and effect, an aspect of social action.
—Carolyn Miller, "Genre as Social Action"

Discourse can be both an instrument and an effect of power, but also a hindrance, a stumbling-block, a point of resistance and a starting point for an opposing strategy.
—Michel Foucault, *The History of Sexuality*

The disputes among residents discussed in chapter 3 prompted some to politely ask for assistance from Shenandoah National Park officials. As several disputes escalated, however, letter writers' stance of resistance was more apparent as they demanded, rather than requested, the park's intervention. The previous chapters illustrated ways that residents exhibited what I call "knowledgeable resistance," recasting the identities constructed for them while at the same time working within the value systems honored by park officials. This chapter, however, addresses how mountain residents more explicitly resisted the inscriptions placed upon them. By not reproducing accepted discourses in their letters, they asserted identities that defied those prescribed for them and thereby pushed against the boundaries they were expected to uphold.[1] Clear hierarchies were instituted and enacted specifically because there were people living in the park who would resist the park's management of their lives. Without resistance "there are no relations of power."[2] The transgressions that residents committed were only transgressions insomuch as their presented identities came in contact with those defined for them. Ultimately, there was no "transformative encounter with authority," because the power structures "rapidly close[d] up behind" them.[3] That is, the power structures were so entrenched that concrete action was nearly impossible. The letter writers, especially the ones who countered SNP, knew these power relations were in place, yet they wrote the letters and engaged those power structures anyway. When they questioned under "what 'a thorite'" the government acted, their inquiry was more rhetorical than when residents asked for tangible things such as harvests or fence rails. The differences between the letters in this chapter and the ones discussed earlier are that these letter writers moved beyond asking for literal goods and services. Rather, their letters asked more abstract questions, challenging government officials and questioning the very power structures that affected their lives. By questioning authority, they invite readers to critically examine the power structures of SNP.

Some mountain residents used literacy as a way to resist the identities constructed for them by those in power. From the letters written to government officials in the 1930s to the letters written to government officials by the Children of Shenandoah at the beginning of the twenty-first century,[4] literacy as resistance is an historical legacy. Some of the tension between the park and its surrounding residents has not diminished, nor have these strategies of resistance disappeared. Contemporary advocates, including those now employed by the Park Service, seek to fairly represent the mountain families whose lives were changed in the 1930s.

The people discussed in this chapter wrote letters that represented themselves as deserving assistance, questioning authority to ensure fairness and fair play, willing to bypass authority in order to find answers, willing to write to high-powered state and federal officials, and finding offense by false characterizations yet also finding it important to rectify those false allegations. Unlike letters employing strategies of advocacy and cooperation, these letters more plainly countered characterizations made about residents. Their stances may have gestured[5] toward accommodation and politeness; however, their letters are more assertive, demanding not only that the park grant their requests, and not only that the government acknowledge them as people, but also that the government acknowledge that their requests were valid and important, that their letters deserved some kind of action.

A Sense of Honor: Disputes, Tension, and Resistance

Several of the letters in chapter 3 discussed the ways that the imposition of the park exacerbated disputes among neighbors as residents moved from the park and others moved into their vacated homes, and the ways that residents pointed to SNP's responsibility in handling those disputes. Letters such as Fannie Comer's and Teeny Nicholson's suggested a fear for their safety as they asked for help from Lassiter and his rangers. Lillie Coleman Herring, wife of George Robert Herring, also felt threatened. However, her letter does not indicate that her safety was threatened, but rather that she was threatened by the way that Zerkel *saw* her. Her letter further explains the dispute between her family and Boss Morris (as discussed in chapter 3). However, the emphasis of her letter is not her dispute with Morris but rather Zerkel's assumptions about her.

Some letter writers were polite and adhered to accepted social codes and values. Lillie Herring's letter, however, was a vehement attack on the government officials, particularly Zerkel, who had written her a notice of infraction. Herring fervently defended her identity as an upstanding citizen, and her letter is one of the most passionate letters contained in the SNP archives, written by a woman whose family was finally forced from their land in 1936. Like many of the letter writers, Herring did not offer resistance to the takeover of her home and property, but rather resistance to the procedures of administering the land and the people living there. In this letter in particular, Herring was angry and insulted that Zerkel had assumed some misconduct on her part. She said in her four-page letter, written March 17, 1935:

> I'm now answering your letter I recived from you. so called a Copy to
> Boss Morris. I'm very mutch suprised to get a thang like that. I have not
> said or even thraught of tearing dawn any thang up there . . . and I do
> know the CCC boys has been giving a way the buildings. and I can prove
> this to you [she lists four or five people CCC boys had given buildings
> to] and I wretten to W C Hall Chairman Richmond [of the SCCD] and
> he said you all had no right to give a way the buildings. and I say if you
> were a goning to give them a way wouldent it be more nicer to give it to
> the one who awned the property.

In her frustration, Herring seems to make sarcastic reference to the copy sent to Morris, because she maintained that he lied about the Herrings' tearing down buildings. Her anger is evident throughout as she explained the activities of stealing from the park, and asserted that she was surprised that Zerkel would assume that she had participated in those activities. In her letter, she chastised Zerkel for "sending me your harble letters" and for believing the lies of others in the community. She set herself apart from her neighbors who took windows and lumber, and angrily let Zerkel know that she would inform members of the community of his discrepancies. Her letter suggests that she was aware of the power of written literacy, in that it could change Zerkel's assumptions about her and consequently the decisions he might make about her and her family.

The passion and vehemence with which Herring wrote in this letter starkly contrasted with her second letter to Zerkel. She wrote to ask him a "favor" on November 26, 1935, eight months after her first letter: "When Boss Morris Moves out of the house I used to own. Will you please give it to me. My Husband George R. Herring is dead and left me Six children and no home. And I could get the house out of the Park and it would be some help to the children. You all gave the mission people severl buildings and they have moved them out so I would be awfull thankfull if you would help me some. So let me Hear from you at once thank you." While her first letter contained four pages of details defending her honor, her second letter, only a paragraph long, contained a defeated tone, simply requesting Zerkel's assistance. In her new position as a woman caring for children on her own at the end of the Depression, Herring's tone shifted to the practicality of caring for her family rather than defending her honor. In addition, both her letters provided further information about how building materials were handled during the transition of authority from state to federal government. Herring knew that the Episcopal missions had been given some of the lumber to move churches, and in her second letter she asked for the lumber from her house, vacated by her and lived in by Boss Morris, so that she could use it in a new home.

The passion in Herring's first letter was generally absent from the letters of the park's archives. Herring's letter, however, does reflect some general sentiment about the officials' attitudes toward mountain families. It was assumed they were lazy and not to be trusted. Lassiter's letters to other government officials (particularly to social workers) contain disparaging comments about the mountain residents remaining in the park, as we saw in chapter 1. Herring's letter, though written to Zerkel, contains rhetoric that heatedly resists that construction. Through her complex rendering of events, she refused to be called a liar and demanded that Zerkel cease his wrongs toward her and her family.

Herring's letter is an example of several of the letters written by residents wherein they resisted how they were seen and began questioning authority, shifting their emphases from requests for tangible items to rhetorical resistance. John T. Nicholson (see chapter 2) also defended his honor when he was accused of stealing windows from his father's vacated home. Nicholson, a famed preacher in the area and known locally as a colorful character, wrote a long, ornate letter to Park Ranger Hoskins explaining why he took the windows. His is one of the most interesting and strategic examples of a resident very transparently constructing himself as knowing the rules and wanting very much to follow them. He began the letter by saying, "Dear Chief Ranger, may this please your honor to carefully read and consider every word of this letter." As in his earlier letter to Lassiter requesting his father's life tenure, Nicholson referred to Hoskins as "your honor," placing him in a position of authority. This rhetorical positioning recognized authority and at the same time asked for acknowledgment of his morality. Nicholson said to Hoskins in his four-page letter, written January 28, 1937:

> I humbly beg of your honor to say that I certainly do regret that I took those windows, but it was like I told you. I did not want to do so, before I seen you or my friend, Mr. J. R. Lassiter, but had wait untill I could see you I would not get them because some other folks came the next day to get them. I needed the windows had in my house, and that is the only reason why I went and got them. I had no thought as to stealing, I abhor, and shrink from the thought of such of thing small or great in value. . . .
> Dear Chief, since I have learned that this displeased you, I have been hurt and troubled over it for more than you may imagine, and I have been on my knees before the Lord Jesus Christ—my Saviour, Judged and confessed to him.

As he did when advocating for his father and for a neighbor, Nicholson constructed himself as honorable and trustworthy. He clearly tied his own identity to the way he wrote about this identity, as a man knowledgeable of

God and the Bible, and a man who detested the thought of stealing and further of displeasing his friend Ranger Hoskins. Nicholson later stated that he removed the windows before someone else stole them, but despite his honorable intentions, he would return the windows. John T. Nicholson was very interested in working with park officials (as when he pleaded with officials to see him as cooperative, as discussed in chapter 3). In subsequent letters, he continued his rhetoric of cooperation but with attention to defending his honor, to making sure Hoskins and Lassiter saw him as he saw himself. His rhetoric was very polite and very strategically catered to the egos of Hoskins and Lassiter. In his January 28, 1937, letter, Nicholson explained to Hoskins, for the second time, why he took windows from a house, and he offered restitution. He stated that as a "real Christian [who] should live before God and man," he would "buy you as many windows as I took from that house and will put them where ever you say." More important than returning the windows was the possibility that he offended Hoskins. He said, "I sincerely mean this because I am grived and hurt very much over it since I saw that you were displeased because I did so, but I hope you will gladly pardon me for doing so, as I humbly assure you that I will be very careful from now on in obeying the rules and regulations of you Park Officials. Indeed I have obeyed the special use permitt to the very letter and have nothing to regret as to this, and shall continue to do so as long as it please you Park Officials to permitt me to remain in the Park." While on the one hand he apologized for taking the windows, he was also clear that in fact he had followed all the rules of the park. He assured the officials of his honor, stating that he would be more careful and that his intentions to follow the rules never wavered.

Nicholson's posture of humility continued in his letter: "Please excuse poor writing and all mistakes as I never had the opportunity of going to school as much as one day in all my life so far to learn to read and write. What little education I have, I picked it up here and there." His commentary on his literacy skills suggests humility, yet he resists what Hoskins may think of him either in terms of stealing or in terms of his ability to write a letter. His defense of his honor and literacy assert a human agency and dignity contrary to common stereotypes of the mountaineer. His rhetoric demonstrated his ability to discern moral values, even while recognizing the ways his actions might be misinterpreted by officials.[6] As he did when publishing his poem in the local newspaper (see the epigraph at the beginning of this book), Nicholson was careful to be seen as cooperative and agreeable, lest his actions of writing letters be misinterpreted. The poem addressed park officials overtly, condemning the appraisers and boosters for promises made and not kept. He said to officials, "If by chance this you read / Be assured I do not oppose the Park." He continued to construct himself as supportive yet also expressed his deep sadness and concern over how the park's land was obtained. Nicholson's resistance to the park, while remaining subtle and indirect, was enacted through his sophisticated use of literacy, both in letters and in submission to the local paper. How to resist and make his views known yet also remain agreeable was a tightrope that Nicholson walked throughout his dealings with park officials.[7]

Nicholson's questioning of the park in his poem in the local paper, and the following example from Lula A. Haney, represent early examples of residents questioning authority, a questioning that would increase throughout 1936, 1937, and 1938. In several cases, when mountain residents were not successful in their various requests to SNP authorities, they wrote letters to other officials, either within the state or federal government. For Lula Haney, writing to President Roosevelt was her first action. Lula Haney, Nellie Haney Sims's aunt and John K. Haney's wife, lived in Rockingham County (seventy-four acres condemned, paid $5,065). Haney's house was scheduled to be razed because of its proximity to the proposed Skyline Drive.[8] In an effort to save her home, Lula Haney wrote to President Roosevelt on January 13, 1936, saying, "We had a 100 acres here on top of the 'Blue Ridge' now the entrance of the 'Park' on Swift Run Gap. I am not ashamed of the old house, tho it does look kinda weather beaten. I always loved my 'mountain home' and never wanted to sell it, but as you know how it all happened, guess it is 'gone' now." Haney's letter suggested that if he knew her personal attachment to the house he would do something for her. She told him that her family's choices for moving, choices provided to her by the government, were unacceptable. She explained that she had signed for a homestead, but that their current home would be torn down before the homestead was ready. She therefore asked Roosevelt where her family, including her son's children, was supposed to go during the interim. While she realized she would ultimately lose her home to the park, she requested to remain there longer until her homestead was ready. She concluded her letter to Roosevelt, "I know there is some other 'authority' perhaps I should have asked, but I did not know to whom to go, so in humble simplicity I come to you for directions and information. May I hear from you at an early date? May God bless and keep you as one who leads our 'nation.' Fraternally yours, Lula A. Haney." Haney's use of quotes around certain words perhaps indicated her sarcasm about the so-called authority of the park, especially if she saw them as having no authority. Her use of quotes around "authority" itself indicated that she knew the chain of command; in fact, she mentioned earlier in her letter that she had written to SCCD chairman Hall about keeping her general store, which had been shut down by state officials in order to donate lands for the park, and indicating her early correspondence with other officials. She said, "I understand a few people will be allowed to stay, so you see a little store here would mean convenience for them. If in any way you can permit me to occupy this place for any period of time, I'll appreciate same." Though she appeared to be aware of the chain of command and park officials' positions in it, her knowledge led Haney to bypass them and write directly to the president, a poignant rhetorical move given the president's marketing of SNP and Skyline Drive as a prime example of the ways in which Works Progresss Administration (WPA) programs could benefit the poor. Like many letter writers, she reflected humility in "bothering" the president, yet simultaneously she also deemed her situation, and the situation of the park as a whole, as something with which he should be concerned. She asserted her authority and right to bring her situation to the attention of the president of the United States. The letters of Herring, Nicholson, and Haney further tell the story of people losing their homes, and their desires to salvage what they could from their lives. Their letters, however, shift from a mere request for tangible goods. Rather, their writing represents the ways that some residents moved toward a questioning of authority, a questioning that was seen in more and more letters as residents continued to live in the park under special use permit.

Questioning Authority

When mountain residents requested certain assistance and building materials, they participated in the discourse expected by government officials, following the rules and providing written documentation of their requests. When mountain residents wrote letters that questioned officials' authority, their literacy served as resistance, using the letter as a means of social action. While the writers discussed earlier recognized the park's authority and demanded that officials act on that authority, the writers in this section moved toward questioning the park's authority. While many residents conceded to the power enacted by the federal government and by the rangers and superintendent acting under the federal government's auspices, many others neither participated in nor reinscribed the order of discourse dictated to them. The park and its mandates did not hold power for them, and they resisted their neighbors, the assumptions about them, and ultimately the park itself.

Lilly Nicholson Campbell, in one of her later letters to Lassiter, began questioning the way the park had handled certain situations. The wife of Madison County landowner James R. Campbell, whose twenty-five acres were condemned and sold for $503, Lilly Campbell said in her January 15, 1938, letter, "I sold my land to the Park at their on price an I feel at they ought to help me out on getting me a home where I would like to have as its no big place but I feel like if I ever get it pd for I could live on it so I hope you can advise me what to do for the best I would like for you to rite to miss humbly house for me an see at she helps me out."[9]

Campbell directed Lassiter in his responsibility, telling him to work with the welfare agents, such as Mabel Humrickhouse, on her behalf. Families had been promised that if they sold their property they would receive assistance. But at this late date, welfare agents presumably deemed the Campbells as being at risk for assistance, thereby denying what had been promised them. Part of her problem was that she had been accused of removing lumber without permission and therefore was seen as not deserving of aid. Campbell assured Lassiter that she had been told verbally that they could have some of the lumber, "so after all this happen it was marked up govement Prop I don't feel at this is a bit fair to treat no one about their children when its not one man out of a hundred but what hasent broke the Rules in the Park area ever since the govement has excepted this land." Campbell similarly defended her actions as legitimate given the situation and questioned the disparity in the way the government seemed to overlook some residents removing materials, but not her.

This inconsistency in who was able to remove materials was also questioned by Walter Lee Cave, Madison County resident and nephew of Gordon A. "Gird" Cave and son of Miley H. "Click" Cave (see figure 3 on page 6). He wrote to Lassiter on March 24, 1937, telling him he wanted to know who gave another resident "permission to tear down Walker Jenkins building and move it off of the Park end Mr. Hoskins tol me that no one living out of the Park was not alawed to came in and take eny thaing out and them that lived in side was not alawed to take eny thaing out so I want to no whear [he] get his a thoritie from. As ever W. L. Cave." Initially this looks like a dispute with the person who removed the building materials. However, Cave's concern is not with his brother-in-law (Walter's sister Leslie, also known as Lessie, was married to Walker Jenkins), but rather with the authority given him by park officials. Cave was probably concerned in the same way that Lillie Herring was, about how buildings were distributed and which residents were granted permission to remove them. Cave made clear that he was knowledgeable of the rules and reminded Lassiter of them—that no one was officially allowed to remove any building materials or wood cuttings from park land. His letter suggested, however, that another resident had removed something from the park, and Cave questioned whether Lassiter had given him permission to do so. Implicit in Cave's letter is an accusation that Lassiter's system of permissions was unfair, or at least inconsistent. If Cave or family members were not given permission to remove anything from the park, then other residents should not be allowed to remove anything either. In this way, Cave resisted the park's seemingly random system for doling out permissions. Further, Cave challenged Lassiter's values: if Lassiter did not act on these values, then he was a fraud. However, this is another instance in which Lassiter was bound by federal regulation. As his response letter indicates, while the SCCD might have provided certain permissions to residents, once the NPS took over the land, park officials were bound by federal policies.

James R. Campbell, Lilly Pearl Nicholson Campbell's husband, questioned a different source of authority in his November 30, 1937, letter to Lassiter. He said, "I have letter from the welfare workers at Elkton Va stateing I could not get home stead as I need one thousand dollars for my place I am oweing a few hundread dollars and I want [won't] have nothing like that amt after I pay my debts I would like to get a home stead and hope to hear from you why I cant as I am sure you will give me the propper information." As explained in chapter 1, the Department of Public Welfare, the Resettlement Administration, the SCCD, and SNP had varied and complicated relationships, making consistent policies for residents nearly impossible. Representatives from the Department of Public Welfare had visited Campbell and informed him that he was not eligible for a homestead because he did not have enough money. Campbell's letter further suggested the complexities of the relationships among the large government entities. He questioned the authority of the social workers, stating that he hoped to hear from Lassiter the reasons he could not receive a homestead. In this way, he signaled Lassiter's authority, placing Lassiter in a position to make a more favorable decision for him. In fact, Campbell's letter directed Lassiter in his authority, telling him that he was positive of Lassiter's ability to provide him proper information.

Residents used their literacy skills not only to interact with powerful government officials but also to question the authority with which those officials were making their decisions about families' lives. As in most of the letters, there is an undertone of hopelessness, a recognition that most likely their letters will not incite the desired action by the government. The letter writers often did not have formal educations, yet they used the literacy they did possess as "control over one's own life."[10] They had no say in losing their homes or obtaining the information they demanded, yet they chose to participate through literacy anyway, as a means of controlling their personal responses in an uncontrollable situation.

Gird Cave, the preacher at Dark Hollow Church, and cousin to Click Cave, was passionate about making park officials understand who he was and what he believed in. Cave wrote an unprecedented seven letters to park officials, all dated in 1937 and 1938, late in the process of removal. Only Lillie Herring's passion rivaled Cave's, but Cave's tenacity was unparalleled. In his letters[11] to Lassiter and Hoskins, he meticulously described his situation and his desire to "live right." Cave had been seen as disagreeable by officials initially because he had refused a homestead and would not sign a permit earlier in 1935. Like several other residents, Cave's refusal of a homestead was a way to resist losing his home. Letters from Lassiter to Cave and between Lassiter and Zerkel indicate that Cave's initial refusal was viewed as "uncooperative" and he was seen as ungrateful for the assistance offered him. Therefore, when Cave began writing to park officials, his letters contained assurances that he wanted to "do the right thing by every body and not be contrary." The right thing in this case was to cooperate with the government, take their charity, and not cause any trouble; that is, not to assert himself in a way that was disagreeable to the government.

Once it became clear that losing his home was inevitable, Cave requested that he be able to remain in the park through a special use permit. In his

March 26, 1937, letter, he stated, "Tell mr Hoskins to come around I will sign it as I have allready found out many hard feelings and troubles can be stopped and still as I have lived hear all my life and tried to live right and be at peace with my fellowmen and I want to continue to do so and to cooperate with you people and still let me say I need your assistence to try to get me located elsewhere." Cave finally agreed to sign an SUP in 1937, as many residents did when they realized it was a way to remain on their land as long as possible. He indicated that he understood the "hard feelings" that Lassiter and Hoskins had toward him for resisting the process of permits and homesteads, but explained that his behavior resulted from living in the park all his life and wanting to stay there. His demeanor in the letter seems to acquiesce to the situation, telling Lassiter that because he wanted to be at peace, he would "cooperate with you people."

However, Cave did not acquiesce completely. In an undated letter that arrived at SNP after the one written in March, Cave articulated his dissatisfaction with the way the park had treated him. He had not heard from Hoskins since he had first written to him, and he now wrote to remind Hoskins that he wanted to do what was right. He had done what was instructed, but because the park had not responded to him, he said, "It seems that we have ben laid aside." Cave poignantly suggested what many residents asked for in their letters: they wanted acknowledgment, recognition that as people they deserved responses and that further, their requests, because they were prompted by the intrusion of the park itself, also deserved response. Castigating Hoskins for ignoring him, Cave reiterated, "So as i understand you told some parties iff they would stay off you would see that they would get some help." Here Cave referred to residents and their children begging[12] from or selling paper flowers to tourists on Skyline Drive.[13] Cave said that he had kept his children "off the road" and in turn thought Hoskins should keep his word and help his family. As Cave's letter indicated, the reason for selling flowers to tourists was that "we at present are in need the children have no way to get them any clothes." This negotiation with Hoskins denotes Cave's understanding of the system underway in the park: as long as people followed the rules and cooperated, they would get the services they needed. However, because Cave had not been responded to, he wrote to Hoskins to remind him of *his* responsibility. Cave ended his letter by suggesting that if the park did not help his family as they promised, he would have to do something: "i dont wont to give you people no trouble but iff we cant make no arraneements the children will have to try and make something someway." Essentially, Cave suggested that if the park did not make good on its promises, it consequently forced families to break the park's own regulations. That is, Cave stated what many residents intuited: the park's complicity in leaving people with little to no options often left them little choice in breaking from regulations.

While this first letter reflects a man succumbing to the park's authority, and his second letter reflects frustration at the park's administration, his subsequent letters illustrate his continued resistance and insistence that the park do right by him. On November 3 of the same year, Cave wrote to Ranger Hoskins to remind him of a doctor bill. He explained to Hoskins that "i have gotten hell from Dr. Ross that it has never been settled." He reminded Hoskins of his promise to pay the bill for Cave's family, and that Cave has "had no work for a long time," presumably because his church had been closed by the park. Cave's sixteen acres, including the church building, had been condemned and sold for $755. Cave's letter served as a reminder to the park to keep their word in helping him, "as you said you was going to." In this way Cave documented in written form their verbal agreement, mimicking what the government had also done in tracking decisions made.

Soon after in December, Cave wrote another letter to Lassiter, this time explaining that the Department of Public Welfare had informed him that he did not qualify for a homestead. His frustration with the system, especially since he was persuaded to cooperate in a system that continually did not meet its promises, is clear in this letter. He said, "They say we have to rent for our selves so you know that this is not fair or there is people lots younger than i that they have bought homes for. . . . i cant see that this deal is any ways right." While the park did not administer the homesteads (confusion such as Cave's over who made certain decisions is evident in several residents' letters), Cave again reminded officials of their responsibility and accused them of not living up to their promises. In this way, Cave fashioned himself as a legitimate source of criticism and resistance to authority. While on the one hand he was a recipient of the services provided, he also saw himself as being able to assess the park in its actions. By establishing his knowledge of the generic conventions of the letter, he was able to resist how he was seen by park officials and to document his protest of their handling of the situation, while at the same time negotiating with those in power to get whatever services he could.

While the letters written to park officials waned in 1938 as the last of the remaining families were moved to either homesteads or other locations, one last letter of resistance arrived at park headquarters in 1945. During the 1940s, after most residents had moved out of park land, a series of letters were written to Virginia senator Harry Byrd in which several people petitioned to move back into the park. Richard Nicholson, the son of Teeny and George Bailey Nicholson, wrote one of these letters to Senator Byrd:

> A number of mountain people have asked me to write and ask you if it would do any good or be a chance whatever of the people getting their homes back to have petitions wrote out and lay these petitions before Congress on the grounds that the mountain people was badly misled when they sold their land for a Park believing that they could stay there and not be forced to move. Almost every man or woman who moved from the Park would sign such a petition. There is those who live in different homestead locations and 9 out of 10 would much rather go back to their old home in the mountains. Because they were born and reared in the mountains and they will never be satisfied otherwise. . . . Also if the move mentioned above would do any good send me a sample as to how such petitions should be wrote or fixed up. The mountain people and myself will be awfully thankful for anything you can do or suggest in this matter.

Richard Nicholson's letter is yet another record of the confusion about the rules of the park and the transition of power from the state to federal government. Nicholson's letter referred to the former residents' sense of place and region as part of their identities. His letter was prompted by their coming to knowledge of the "Secretary's List," where others had been granted life tenure. However, the life-tenure list was meant for those who were sixty years or older or infirm. Therefore, Richard Nicholson was not necessarily aware of this, but he thought it fair that he and others too be able to live out their lives in the park. To most people like Nicholson, the list seemed purely subjective, and they thought that if they were "good" people, they too would be added to the list.[14] According to Reed Engle, "The list was essentially for those over 60 years of age and or infirmed." While the list was generated to help older or infirmed residents, the perception by many residents was that it was for those with good standing with the park, and they made their cases accordingly.

Byrd wrote to Secretary Ickes about his receiving several letters from Richard Nicholson, who wished to petition that he and others be able to move back into the park. In the response by the Department of the Interior's assistant secretary to Senator Byrd, he stated, "Private occupancy of the lands is incompatible with [the park's] administration in accordance with the fundamental purpose of a national park, which has been defined by Congress to be 'to conserve the scenery and the national and historic objects and the wild life therein and to provide for the enjoyment of the same in such manner and by such means as will leave them unimpaired for the enjoyment for future generations.'" This reiterated what has been formalized in federal law regarding the formation of national parks in general and SNP in particular, where families living on land would be seen to "impair" the land.[15] However, while the park's policies stated that people were not allowed to remain, the Secretary's List was, at least in the minds of many residents, a clear indication that the rules could be bent. While Richard Nicholson's advocacy letter reflected his knowledge of the list and the bending of procedures, those very procedures were quoted in order to refuse Nicholson's (and others') requests to live in their homes.

One resident, Matilda Breeden, is an example of an older resident provided life tenure in the park. Her letter illustrates the way that the park became responsible for the residents remaining through life tenure. In her letter she said, "i am asking a favor or you, i have a hog to kill and hav no place to salt my meat i would be aful glad if you would put me up just a small bilden to put my meat in." Breeden's letter, which does not question the park's authority in the ways that Nicholson's and others' letters did, nevertheless does remind us of the enormous impact that the park had on individuals' lives as they were compelled to continue interacting with government officials as they proceeded with their daily lives.

Conclusion

The patterns identified in the letters include simple requests, advocacy for "nabors," demands for assistance, and resistance to park authority. But these rhetorical patterns, across the three-hundred-letter collection archived at SNP, are not the only features of mountain families' letters. In fact, the men and women living in and near the park engaged in a complex negotiation of identity with those in power. Their sense of values and morals is reflected in the letters, a sense of what is right, a sense of sharing the wealth, a consciousness of using materials wisely, and an awareness of literacy and its power. Indeed, their letters are constructed much like the instructions contained in turn-of-the-century composition texts. According to Lucille Shultz, letter-writing instruction not only taught students "how to write business and social correspondence," it also "inculcat[ed] children with the manners and morals of polite society in 19th century America."[16] While this sense of manners is contained within most of the letters, many simultaneously broke from the accepted codes in order to stand against the tacit assumptions made about them. Shultz also suggests that while in some cases letters were an occasion to reflect these classed values, they were also an occasion "for resisting dominant social codes."[17] The anger, passion, sarcasm, frustration with misunderstood bureaucracy, and shrewd understanding of the situation in some of the letters were in frank opposition to what was expected of polite society in the 1930s.

The rhetorical and literacy skills in the letters suggest that mountain residents believed in the rhetorical power of letters and that they could change NPS and SNP policy. The literacy of mountain individuals was more complicated than representations of them by those in authority, those who had the power to make decisions affecting their lives. Reading the letters in this way suggests that those living in the mountains of Virginia or adjacent to the proposed park were not innocent pawns or primarily victims manipulated by the park. Indeed, the people inhabiting the park were, as a group, as complex and as diverse as any community.[18] Their use of savvy rhetorical strategies in conversing with government officials suggests that mountain residents were engaged citizens actively using the rhetorical skills in their possession. Given the fact that many of their requests were not granted, and that they often knew that they would not be granted, the act of writing a letter at all indicates a significant act of social resistance and participation. "Limitations with literacy skills did not mean that people were cut off from using literacy in powerful and moving ways," and certainly in these letters power is evident in these texts.[19] The so-called success of the letters lies in their very existence, the act of writing them, and the act of engaging those in power to acknowledge who they really were, not whom officials presumed them to be.

Furthermore, the fact that residents wrote to those in authority meant they were willing (at least rhetorically) to enter a bureaucratic world to make an argument or express a need. That they seldom accomplished their original purpose is not the point: it is the long-term legacy of these letters that reveal crucial aspects about the residents themselves—about their literacy (we can indeed decipher the letters and they are often poignant and rhetorically complex) and about their values and ethics—a very different picture from the one presented in publications such as *Hollow Folk*, park brochures by early promoters, and officials' letters.

The rhetoric in these representative letters from residents resists the dominant definition of people living in the Blue Ridge Mountains. They were primarily represented as ignorant, illiterate, and irresponsible. How mountain residents represented themselves through their "skills" often served to reify what those in power assumed about them, in terms of their intelligence and in terms of their values. However, when we study the letters in depth and with attention to underlying rhetorical awareness, a more complex picture emerges. Their letters illustrate a speaking out, a dialogue with authority that challenged inscribed identity. My analysis suggests that when identity is challenged in such a way as to threaten their homes, livelihoods, and characters, they resisted those identities and wrote letters despite their lack of formal education, to enter into dialogue with those in power. Their literacy is not the literacy of the genteel southerner. Rather, the literacy reflected in these letters is a challenge to identity. They did not challenge the "state apparatus" as it existed, but rather worked within that system.[20]

In each of these letters, the writers used their literacy, their knowledge of the situation as well as their specific letter-writing skills, to resist the prevailing attitudes about them. The letter writers foreshadow the kind of resistance and activism that comes later in the disenfranchised region, and they tell a story important for any person trying to participate in a discourse of power.

While many of the attitudes about mountaineers were espoused by those other than NPS employees, SNP officials became the primary recipients of the letters that contained resistant rhetorical strategies in defending character and honor. Some SNP officials did hold stereotypes about some mountain residents, but much of the resistance, while justified, was in some cases misdirected. This resistance has continued through the descendents of mountain residents and others interested in the dramatic story of families losing their homes. For instance, Harold Woodward, whose grandparents were removed from the park, felt as though the park purposefully prevented him from accessing his family's records in the park's archives. As a family and local historian, Woodward requested access precisely when the records were away from the archives being cataloged. In a 2000 *Washington Post* article entitled "Anger in Appalachia," Woodward explained that he felt the park was roadblocking families' access to their ancestors' artifacts.[21] In truth, the park was in the process of caring for the records, professionally cataloging them for record maintenance and accuracy. Woodward has since visited the archives and the recently cataloged records, conducting research for a large project about his family's history.

Within the last ten years, SNP has created several exhibits that highlight the multi-varied stories of the residents within the park's boundaries (see figure 16). These exhibits, together with a short film, *The Gift* (developed in consultation with folklorists Charles Perdue and Nancy Martin-Perdue and the Children of Shenandoah), have sparked a renewed interest in the cultural history of the park. A similar exhibit of the mountain families is on display at the James Monroe Museum in Orange, Virginia. According to an article in Charlottesville's *Daily Progress* in 2004, local historian Liz Lonergan created the display to counter commonly accepted stereotypes about park residents. She said, "The park made them out as uneducated, poor and ragged, and the majority of them weren't.... We're hoping the exhibit tells that side of the story."[22] The displays at the James Monroe Museum and the park's visitor center recently created by park historians suggest a new public openness to and interest in hearing the multiple layers of the stories of the mountain families' experiences. However, Lonergan's quote perpetuates the dichotomous relationship between the park and its inhabitants. Many of the stereotypes were generated well before park officials were administering the land.

Today's SNP officials continue to work with the public as they administer the landscape, hiking trails, and campsites within the park. For instance, local residents living near the hiking entrance to Old Rag Mountain in Madison County have long complained about hikers parking on their prop-

Fig. 16. A former exhibit at the Harry F. Byrd, Sr. Visitor Center, Shenandoah National Park. This exhibit painstakingly describes the history of Shenandoah National Park and the dramatic way it changed mountain families' lives. The photographs and words from the families highlight their opinions about the park and the complicated processes they went through while being relocated. A new exhibit, which opens in spring 2007, includes interactive displays that involve visitors as they follow the park's history and individuals' stories. (Photographs by the author)

erty or on the small roads, blocking residents' access to their homes. In order to alleviate local concern, the SNP officials proposed purchasing land for a new parking lot, providing increased access for visitors to the park. This proposal has prompted further community debate, documented in several letters to the editor in the *Madison County Eagle* about the "wrongs" of the park. Although the parking lot was in direct response to local residents' concerns, some other local residents contest the park, invoking its history and using the "unjust" formation of the park as arguments against the new parking lot.[23]

The activist group the Children of Shenandoah, formed in the early 1980s, is another way descendants and interested people work to counter the misrepresentations of their ancestors.[24] The Children of Shenandoah's very existence was rooted in their resistance to the park and the ways that they continue to work toward re-representing the story of the park—and recognizing the effects of the past on the present and the ways that public memory is constructed. Before it disbanded several years ago, the group was consulted in the making of the park's interpretive film *The Gift*. In addition, members gathered yearly to tell stories about their ancestors and to collect documents about family life in the mountains. They also wrote letters to their congressional representatives opposing various contemporary actions of the park. Members also wrote letters to their representatives and to local papers to increase awareness about this "injustice" and "further attempt[s] by the park to desecrate our families' lands." In this way, their identities were significantly tied to SNP, its existence, and their resistance to it.

Many people who lived in the park lost their homes and were misinformed or mistreated by government officials. However, not all of those wronged were compelled to write letters. Some simply moved away. Some blatantly stole property. And a few took their cases to court. The choices available to them, and the choices they ultimately made, were linked to class, literacy, and education. But the letter writers discussed here chose to use literacy, no matter their "skill level," as a means of resistance, as a means of asserting what they thought of themselves, contradicting what officials assumed about them. Furthermore, the resistance relationship is reciprocal. Today, the visitor's centers at SNP display new cultural histories of the park existing in conjunction with the resistance of the surrounding community and its insistence that the park address past wrongs.

Finally, while the resistance of the mountain families through their letters reflects a different kind of resistance than protests and picketing, their identities as persons engaged in their communities are well documented in these letters. As they re-envisioned how they were seen by those in power, mountain residents constructed a counterhistory, recording a significant yet untold portion of the narrative of Shenandoah National Park.

5

SOCIAL PARTICIPATION AND
RESISTING CULTURAL CODES

The writing of letters enters so much into all the occasions of life,
that no gentleman can avoid shewing himself in compositions of this
kind. Occurrences will daily force him to make use of his pen, which
lays open his breeding, his sense, and his abilities to a severer exami-
nation than any oral discourse.
—John Locke, quoted in William Roberts, *The History of Letter
Writing* (1843)

The only thing that sometimes redeems stupid paragraphs—that
makes clever wording irresistible—is a reason to act at once, a subtle
demand that must be met now.
—*How to Write Letters That Win* (1910)

The letters written by mountain families illustrate the broader social and
institutional processes that continuously exclude those whose access to literacy is in question. As we have seen in the previous chapters, some mountain residents, though misrepresented and often mistreated, chose to use
literacy as a way to "talk back" to those who were affecting their lives. The
mountain residents were not asked to participate in the discourse that surrounded the formation of the park. Yet their letters are on the threshold of
public and private: they represent an intervention in public discourse, where
they used both schooled and indigenous forms of literacy. As we continue
to expand our understanding of literacy and its multidimensional nature,
we might also ask how a local study such as this one can have broader implications for studies of language and literacy.

One of the implications for this study is the way that texts, power, and identity are inextricably linked. Jacqueline Jones Royster's recent study of nineteenth-century African American women's writing makes this conclusion about literacy: "Literate practices are constrained, if not defined, within the hegemonic order, and for those who are not members of that order (women, nonwhites, members of lower socioeconomic classes), using literacy to accomplish their own purposes creates adversarial relationships and conditions. The effect, of course, is that people without social position, or political power, or economic power typically experienced problems in accomplishing their sociopolitical goals through literacy."[1] The problems Royster refers to are the actions or the effects solicited by African American women's writing—it tended to be ignored in the nineteenth century. That is, though their writing was rhetorically innovative, *who* the writers were perceived to be affected how the writing was received. Rhetoricians such as Royster are therefore reexamining the writings of many nineteenth-century African American women, publishing and studying them for their important contributions to literacy and the rhetorical tradition.

Those remaining in the park after the transfer of lands from Virginia, and those who wrote letters during this time, included "members of lower socioeconomic classes." Their socioeconomic status caused some park and other government officials to refer to them as "that class of people" whom they believed did not hold the same values, literacy, or economic standing as those in power. Their texts, however, challenged these assumptions, using literacy, despite its limitations, as a means of confronting their identities.

Therefore, when mountain residents came in contact with documents such as the special use permit; disparaging, curt, or accusatory letters from Lassiter; or eviction notices, their sense of who they were in relation to literacy and the government oftentimes had devastating effects. However, as Denny Taylor concludes in her work, the unsolicited contact with "toxic" literacies, such as those found in the documents written to mountain families, was an occasion for mountain residents to become active agents of their situations. They created counter-narratives about themselves, using their letters as a way to participate in the situation even though they knew that the playing field was not even. Residents such as Rebecca Baugher, who advocated for her neighbors, exhibited a critical consciousness, in the Freirian sense, of her circumstance, her position, and the position of her neighbors in relation to officials. According to Royster, this kind of participation means going against the grain. She says African American women writers in the nineteenth century "reenvisioned their context, reshaped their sense of reality, charted courses of action, including rhetorical actions, that would lay the foundations from which a tradition of literacy and social action would emerge."[2] While the women Royster discusses were African Americans with some social standing, the poor, white, mountain residents also lay foundations for participating in the situation as it was handed to them. Their courses of action were limited; that is, they were not allowed to remain in their homes. But their rhetorical actions, through letters, contradicted what was expected of them and therefore reshaped how they were seen, if not by the government officials reading the letters, then by themselves and by future readers. In this chapter, I highlight the letters written by mountain families to government officials as a way to theorize the inextricable link between identity and literacy, and the ways in which the study of individual literate practices can reveal complex institutional and systemic factors contributing to individuals' sense of themselves. The letters served a powerful function: they responded to the discourse generated by park promoters and officials by creating an antidote for it, using literacy, steeped in its tradition, but for the purpose of remedying the poison used to harm them.

Counter-Narratives and Rhetorical Resistance

The mountain residents' letters show that they understood the form of the letter and had a growing rhetorical knowledge of the discourse of the park. Insomuch as residents were "educated" in the discourse of the park and ultimately the federal government, they used that discourse to create counter-narratives about themselves.[3] Remember, the residents writing letters were primarily those who remained in the park because of difficulty in finding alternatives or because they saw remaining in the homes as long as possible as a form of resistance. Of those who left right away, some willingly sold their land and had or found the means to move immediately. Of those remaining, many worked to follow the regulations of the park, but because of the confusion in transfers of power, following the rules was no easy task. Residents had to educate and reeducate themselves on the various discourses of power, adjusting to administrative changes and transfers and new directions in policy. Using their literacy as resistance, some were able to write from varying positions in order to negotiate the multiple discourses of power, using complex rhetorical approaches.

Literacy serves as a means of cultural capital, and the mountain residents used that capital to gain access into the discourses circulating in the park. The linguistic strategies they used were "oriented (except in rare cases) not so much by chances of being understood or misunderstood (communicative efficiency or the chances of communication), but rather by the chances of being listened to, believed, obeyed, even at the cost of misunderstanding."[4] The evidence of their education exists in the recurring accepted conventions used throughout their letters. In this way they re-envisioned the situation so as to create a place for their sense of who they were, rather than others' senses of who they were. The repeated uses of rhetorical devices, and how they functioned for individual residents, illustrate the complexities of rhetorical construction available to them.

For instance, a significant number of the letter writers mirrored the park's rhetoric in its official documents, as well as its correspondence, representing themselves in ways they believed park officials would "deem appropriate."[5] The special use permit stipulated that families were allowed to gather enough wood or apples "for family use." Many of the letters echoed the park's rhetoric for collecting apples and berries, directly quoting from documents such as the special use permit or letters from Lassiter or Hoskins. Other recurring letter conventions included the phrases "just a few lines," "I hate to bother you," and "Answer this at once," each indicating the various ways that residents adhered to standard letter-writing practice, yet in turn highlighting the ways that they resisted those codes. Despite their adherence to certain forms and rhetorical devices, their linguistic variances and phonetic spellings most likely were perceived as a general lack of knowledge by those reading the letters at the time.

Recent literacy scholars contest this one-dimensional approach to reading texts. For example, in her discussion of rhetorics of resistance, Min-Zahn Lu states that when various cultures appropriate the English language, their nonstandard language use is most often seen as "linguistic imperfection." Lu, however, suggests these moments of linguistic variances as acts of resistance to the standardized English that often works against marginalized cultures and language users. She explains that scholars such as Lyons, Canagarajah, and Anthony, among others, are interested in the ways that language users resist standard English by "code-switching, code-mixing, style shifting, and borrowing." She concludes, "The range and vibrancy of englishes that African Americans and Native Americans have developed throughout U.S. history prove that English owes its life to the peoples' [*sic*] refusal to be submerged by situations designed to keep them down."[6] Lu's conclusions imply that this refusal is an active occurrence, whereby minorities recognize the forces keeping them down and then work against it. Appalachian sociolinguists Kirk Hazen and Ellen Fluharty draw similar conclusions about language use in Appalachia. They "bifurcate the term Appalachian English into two separate terms: *Appalachian Englishes*, referring to varieties of English spoken in Appalachia, and *Appalachian Drawl*, the popular language stereotype." Drawing on the work of Appalachian linguists Clare Dannenburg and Walt Wolfram, among others, Hazen and Fluharty conclude that "future studies contributing to sociolinguistic knowledge about Appalachia should include a more detailed account of inter- and intro-ethnic differences in Appalachia . . . and ethnographic study of the identity issues surrounding the sociogeographic split between Northern and Southern culture in Appalachia."[7] The kind of language study they recommend shifts contexts of language use to the forefront of understanding discursive construction.

Lu's argument, as she points out, extends to many marginalized groups. She says, "Attention to the interplay between and across one's language expertise, affiliation, and inheritance, along with attention to individual writers' understandings of different aspects of their selves and lives, can help us interpret and depict one another's discursive resources (and by extension, language needs) in terms of not only the 'actual' (lived experiences) but also the 'possible' (possibilities and prospects) and the 'imagined' (desire, hope, aspiration), so that we may represent one another's actions as grounded in the realities of our lives by never predetermined by them."[8] Lu urges us to reexamine multiple linguistic practices in the ways that writers see themselves. She suggests the necessity of documenting literate practices, understanding historical, political, and social contexts, so that then we can attend to the "language needs" of various groups. By doing so, the actions taken by groups such as the mountain residents in Virginia can be understood through the contexts of their lives, rather than by the ways others defined them. The documentation process Lu proposes is crucial for those cultures that we typically define as dispossessed and marginalized, and for the historical record about displacement processes in general.

A recent issue of *College English* further highlights Lu's argument about world englishes. In July 2006 several composition theorists, including Lu, extended the notion that writing teachers should attend to the ways in which international students engage the English language and the ways that such engagements can inform our conceptions of learning to compose and learning standard English. Their assessment of the history of the English language as varied and changing, though many Americans see "standards" of English as rigid and set, has implications for the ways in which some Appalachian Americans use language. In the same ways that international language users can be dismissed as not understanding language because of the variant forms they use, the letter writers discussed here were dismissed by Lassiter and other officials because their language use did not always conform to standard usage. According to the theorists writing in the 2006 *College English* issue, this nonconformity does not necessarily mean lack of knowledge of the complexities of language. Rather, they see "multilingual language" as a capability of "communicating with one another in a number of languages, code-switching as appropriate to the rhetorical situation."[9] Similarly, I see the language use of the mountain families as a way of incorporating their cultural language use together with the rhetorical conventions expected from officials in positions of power. However, their writing was not viewed this way by officials because of the accepted "privileged varieties of English."[10] As a result, officials' negative perceptions of mountain residents resulted mostly in ignoring their protests or requests rather than working with them to resolve various problems or disputes.

The resistance exhibited by mountain residents can also be seen in the contents, as well as the language use, of the genre of the letter. While Shultz argues that learning to write letters "inculcated" learners with accepted middle-class values of nineteenth-century America, she also suggests that while in some cases letters were an occasion to reflect these classed values, they were also an occasion "for resisting dominant social codes."[11] Many letter writers, while adhering to the rhetorical and social conventions of the letter, also broke from those conventions by making statements such as "let me hear from you" and "answer at once." They exhibited their knowledge of formal convention and standard letter writing, yet at the same time challenged officials' actions. Their demonstrative statements placed residents in positions of deserved response.

The regularity with which letter writers used the formal features of letters such as "Yours truly," "Sincerely," "Just a few lines" demonstrates their knowledge of the genre of the letter. Their participation in writing letters and the ways that they wrote them illustrate the social image of the genre within the community. Writers and their readers had particular expectations about the letter. Because letter writers paid attention to both social and rhetorical convention, we can deduce their active participation in the rhetorical situation.

As mountain residents were forced to enter into (Dell Hymes's conception of) the speech community of the National Park Service, they exhibited their knowledge of shared rules for constructing rhetorical arguments. So while their individual "skills" (such as spelling, grammatical structure, and syntax) do not necessarily adhere to standard forms, their speech acts (in Austin's sense) indicate larger social understanding of language, genre, and rhetorical structure. Their interactions with government officials are evidence of their abilities to engage in complex language use. In other words, close attention to the contextualization of the language used in the letters reveals "how constituent messages are understood" and used.[12]

In addition to the use of the letter to document their participation of the events, the mountain residents used the genre of the letter to document their identities. The conventions of the letter prompted them to include the name of the town where they lived (in some cases where they received their mail), and to sign their names. But they also included identifying information such as whether they were widows, war veterans, farmers, mothers, or fathers. They named who they were and the places they came from. Their letters quietly said, this is who I am, not who you imagine me to be.

As has been documented in several Appalachian studies over the last twenty to thirty years, resistance has taken many forms in the Appalachian region. The United Mine Workers of America striking in Kentucky in the 1970s and the Save Our Cumberland Mountains group organizing in Tennessee in the 1980s are examples of the highly visible ways that Appalachians have struggled to "fight back" against power structures taking advantage of the region. However, as the letters in this study illustrate, in Appalachia there are various kinds of fighting back. Forms of resistance "often assume forms far less visible than picket lines and mass movements and include such behavior as gossip, backtalk, holding onto one's dialect, moonshining, open violation of game and fencing laws, and migration."[13] In Great Smoky Mountains National Park, residents in Cades Cove refused to sell their homes. Similarly, residents along the Tennessee River refused to sell their land to the Tennessee Valley Authority.[14] Several residents in the proposed SNP also refused to sell their homes. Still others brought suit against Virginia or contested the assessed values of their property. For instance, Addie Pollock, the wife of avid park promoter George Pollock, sued the state through Page County in 1930 to pay her more than the "fair market value" that was determined for her property. She claimed that her property, Skyland Lodge, was worth $8,000. The claim form stated, "This house is expensively built. . . . Stone was especially quarried and dry outside with solid cement inside. Between inside of side ceiling, is a heavy coat of Cobots[,] Quilted grass expensive; then comes metal lathing with waterproof painted." According to Reed Engle, documents such as this one were "another type of written process that resident's used. In spite of all her pull and influence she did not get what she wanted."[15]

A dramatic occurrence of resistance is documented in a photograph of Leslie Cave Jenkins, wife of Walker Jenkins and sister of Walter Lee Cave, who, while seven months' pregnant, was carried away from her property by two government officials, forcing her family's eviction. While Jenkins's forced eviction was considered an "embarrassment" by local authorities, her defiant act can be seen as a woman standing her ground in the midst of losing her home. Courageously she faced law enforcement as she made others *see* her as a person literally carried off, not just figuratively on paper.

Perhaps some of the residents could not (or did not) conceive of another way to resist, but no matter what they thought their alternatives were, they *did* choose literacy as a way to resist, particularly as a way to resist what others thought they knew about them. Their letters consequently serve as testimony, a way to tell their story, because few, certainly not those in the government, were listening.

Yet while these residents chose to write letters, the letters were the direct result of the park's establishment. The Commonwealth of Virginia, through its Public Park Condemnation Act in 1928,[16] enacted a system whereby residents were supposedly forced to sell their land, leave the proposed park boundaries, and find housing elsewhere. And many did. Original planning did not account for the Great Depression and the ways that fair market value would not provide them enough to finding housing elsewhere. And the 1928 Act made no concessions for those who lived there but were not landowners. Those who wrote letters were (largely) the ones bound by their material conditions—they were trapped by economic forces, forces that resulted from "blatant political and economic oppression."[17] Their existence within the park, on land that no longer legally belonged to them, following new (and sometimes ambiguous) rules enforced by the government, was not unlike being in a prison. Their letters served to unmask the power relations imposed on them.[18] They had to monitor the language they used in the letters and were administered in their discursive practices.

The act of writing the letter, together with the employment of certain rhetorical strategies of resistance, indicated their ability to resist discursive knowledge. The power relations imposed on mountain residents reflects the way that Virginia's move to establish a national park in its mountains sponsored the literate act of writing letters. That is, these letters did not necessarily reflect residents' "everyday" literate practices.[19] Both the letters they wrote and the documents they received from government officials were the result of a traumatic shift in their livelihoods. Their letters represent a reaction to the "toxic" literacies forced upon them and the ways that they created counter-narratives within them.

Toxic and Violent Literacies

In order to understand mountain residents' use of literacy as an antidote to prevailing assumptions about them, it is important to delineate the ways that literacy has been theorized as potentially toxic and violent. Both Denny Taylor's and Elsbeth Stuckey's recent works on the toxic and violent natures of literacy are important to understanding the ways residents constructed their letters. Like the people Taylor describes in her study, the mountain residents and neighbors of SNP were subjected to the documents of bureaucratic agencies such as Virginia's SCCD and the Department of Public Welfare, the Department of Agriculture's Resettlement Administration, and the Department of the Interior's National Park Service. The documents produced by these agencies contained information in them about the residents, "facts" that described their home lives, their financial situations, and their "abilities" to make judgments about themselves.[20] However, according to Taylor, "Facts are *never* value free. What is written and not written recasts people's lives. Print is used quite literally to decide who lives and who dies. Very often, violent acts are legally sanctioned through paperwork that is required by federal law. None of this is true, of course, if you are privileged by society. If you have status—money to pay for a lawyer . . . then the 'rules' do not automatically apply. What is written becomes open to interpretation and professional manipulation."[21] For the mountain residents of SNP, the facts written about their lives often had adverse effects on their living conditions. If Lassiter wrote them a letter admonishing them for their alleged violations of park regulations, they were then less likely to be able to move to other (better) housing within the park. If social workers found families uncooperative, illiterate, irresponsible, unwilling, or "lazy," then they were deemed not eligible for homesteads or any other government assistance.[22] For the subjects of Taylor's study, "*Without exception,* there were times in the lives of these men and women with whom I worked when they could have reconstructed their lives. *Without exception* all genuine opportunities were denied them. Invariably, denial occurred through the use of official texts. Through the language of domination. The language of humiliation."[23] For the most part, the mountain residents of SNP were bound by the documents written about them first by some of the other Virginia residents who were park promoters, by some in bureaucratic agencies such as the public welfare and school systems, and by Miriam Sizer and the subsequent *Hollow Folk,* who defined them as "types." However, the literacy in mountain residents' letters illustrates a different kind of "reconstruction" that places their fate in their own hands, rather than in the hands of bureaucracy. They acted out, particularly if written literacy was not a routine part of their everyday lives. By constructing counter-identities in their own written texts, they resisted the "language of domination" and "humiliation." In this way, the literacy contained in mountain residents' letters suggests that literacy is dynamic. That is, literacy is *both* liberating and constraining.[24] The mountain residents enacted a literacy in which they became "active agents in the construction, negotiation over, and transformation of their social worlds."[25] On the one hand, their lives were drastically changed and they often had no control over where they lived or the assistance they received. On the other hand, through literacy they were able to control how they represented themselves to those in power.

As the studies conducted by Royster, Lu, Taylor, Cushman, and Stuckey suggest, documenting the "texts, the participants, the activities, and the artefacts in their social contexts" highlights the inextricable link of identity and literacy, and the ways that the study of individual literate practices can reveal complex institutional and systemic factors contributing to individuals' sense of themselves.[26] The mountain residents who wrote letters enacted some control through their knowledge and manipulation of a genre, the letter. In the following discussion, I suggest that letter writing, as a form of autobiography, is a crucial aspect in any documentation of an historical event.

Personal and Public History: Letters, Autobiography, and Testimony

Oral historians have been interested in placing narratives of personal history alongside the accepted narratives of history in order to gain a fuller account of particular events.[27] Sylvia Salvatici, for instance, writes about the individual and collective memories of displacement in Bosnia and the role of testimony in telling the psychosocial story of trauma in war-torn Kosovo. She says there can often be a "gap between the normalizing public discourse and the intensity of the popular experience of war, displacement and return," and therefore it is important to collect multiple "narratives and discourse of suffering and healing." She highlights the ways that "non-remembering" actually becomes a resource for refugees, a coping strategy for the trauma.[28]

Similarly, in her review essay of several historical texts about the psychological effects of enforced displacement, Wendy Webster discusses the implications of refugees who are forced to cross borders as they are displaced by war. Specifically, the studies she reviews examine refugee camps and the feelings of alienation experienced by refugees. Webster says, "Such liminal spaces have usually been experienced as acutely oppressive rather than liberatory, and used to reinforce rather than unsettle ideas of 'otherness.'"[29] The mountain residents facing displacement to homesteads and resettlement housing in Virginia similarly experienced oppression. The interim period where people lived on land that was no longer theirs was one of the liminal spaces Webster describes. As Webster argues, when border crossings have been enforced, "such displacement may breach the boundaries of self."[30] SNP residents thought of themselves as mountaineers, land- and homeowners, independent; but with their displacement to resettlements in the lowlands, their entire identities were forced to shift as they faced leaving their homes. What might be the psychological and lasting effects in terms of regional and national identity tied to this displacement? How have individual and regional memories of the park been collected and recounted? According to Lois Cave Hurt (Walter Lee Cave's daughter and Walker Jenkins' niece), her mother Gertie "had a hard time" being away from her family when she was forced to move from her home and extended family.[31] Similarly, Larry Baugher said of his grandparents, Joseph Wilson and Sarah Elizabeth Baugher, "Their spirits were totally broken—they never recovered."[32]

The private memories of families such as the Caves and the Baughers have increasingly become a priority in documenting the past, combining them with the constructions of public memory and memorializing past events and places. The studies Webster discusses have a "common concern with memory, and the process of forgetting and remembering, underpins these contestations of official versions of history."[33] Similarly, the letters written by SNP residents add dimension to the version of the story, contributing to the collective memory of who they were and who they were not as they were displaced from their homes.

Webster, like other oral historians, argues for the inclusion of individual voices in collective histories and says that to "incorporate oral history" as a "way of restoring humanity to refugees" emphasizes "the ordinariness of those affected, and mak[es] evident the complexities of individual lives and identities to ensure that they are not represented simply as undifferentiated and helpless 'victims.'"[34] Letters, though generically different from oral histories, serve a similar function, as they add dimension to the story of the park. Similarly, the voices in the letters of mountain residents indicate complicated people with complex rhetorical knowledge. While they had no choice in their displacement, they did choose to interact with park officials and to make their voices heard. The plight of families displaced to form a national park is certainly different from the various displacements due to racial genocide or war; however, the connections in terms of rhetorical history and identity are important.

In the same way that historians have argued for the inclusion of oral histories to tell community stories, literacy scholars have also suggested the importance of including individual literacy narration in order to understand a community's literacy history. Individual literacy narratives shed light on the political and socioeconomic contexts of individual literacy. Furthermore, literacy narratives of communities, gathered in part through individual literacy histories, are important for understanding the political and socioeconomic contexts of historical events, events like the formation of Shenandoah National Park.[35]

Literacy Narratives, Critical Inquiry, and Issues of Genre

In Beth Daniell's discussion of literacy, she invokes Lyotard's conception of "grand narratives" to examine composition and literacy studies. She says that studies of the "little narratives" assume that "literacy is multiple, contextual, and ideological."[36] Similarly, the history of Shenandoah National Park needs to include more of the "little" narratives. This work has already been in process, as SNP's cultural historians construct exhibits and publish new books, and as archaeologists and folklorists conduct new research and interviews. During the 1960s just over one hundred oral histories were collected by a local journalist who in turn donated them to SNP (they are currently held at James Madison University). In addition, SNP cultural resource specialist Reed Engle has conducted several oral histories to enhance his historical projects. While this research and the research presented here add to the story of SNP, there remain many stories to be told by descendents of residents and neighbors of SNP.

The letters of the mountain residents serve as a partial literacy narrative of the communities and of the individuals in the mountains of Virginia. This project has examined the broader community issues, only partially attending to individuals' stories. Many questions remain about the individuals who were affected by such an enormous change in land ownership and community. What caused particular people such as Rebecca Baugher and John T. Nicholson to write letters? What else did they write? Besides what the census data can tell us about their literacy and education, what might their individual stories tell us about the history of literacy in the region? The fact that many of these stories are unattainable now underscores the importance of collecting individual literacy narratives. The letters show that understanding the literate practices revealed in the letters provides us with a fuller understanding of the history of the park, further emphasizing the importance of literacy within historiography.

As oral historians and literacy scholars have suggested, individual pasts are crucial, legitimate narratives to include in our historical narratives. The letters of the mountain families of Shenandoah National Park illustrate the political implications of literacy in this large displacement. Forced displacements will probably continue to occur as the world continues to develop and as cultures continue to clash. Despite this inevitability, the diligent (and publicly funded) recording of individual literacy could retain the histories of our cultures and the changes and developments within.

Questions for Further Inquiry

In addition to the oral histories that could supplement the story of SNP, there are other questions that could be asked about this historical moment. The work of Brandt, Cushman, and Barton and Hamilton, among others, has been documenting the literacy practices of persons who are still available for interviews so that we can hear from them their thoughts on their literacy knowledge. This project studies people who lived long ago—their daily literate practices are not documented (as far as I know), so the letters they wrote and their relation to their daily literate practices are mostly unknown. Consequently, several questions remain about the individuals who wrote letters to SNP officials: What other literate practices did they engage in? Did they already know how to write letters or did they have to educate themselves (as John T. Nicholson did) so that they could write to officials? How much was letter writing a community activity? The answers to these questions might very well affect the conclusions and interpretations drawn in this study. Because the letters cause me to ask these questions, this project reiterates the importance of documenting the ways that literacy is or is not a part of individuals' lives. Understanding their lives and understanding their literate practices helps us to realize the cultural and historical implications of the establishment of SNP. To ask the question of the New Literacies Study Group, however, how do the people of the Virginia mountains (and their descendants) benefit by doing so? And further, what do we learn about broader issues of literacy and rhetorical strategy?

In the foreword to *Situated Literacies*, Taylor describes a meeting of the Literacy Research Group at Lancaster University, facilitated by David Barton. Taylor recounts the conversations among the researchers and scholars, summarizing a recurring question of the group: "Who benefits from our studies of literacy"?[37] What difference does it make that we study the literacy event of letters written by multiple mountain residents in the

1930s? The letter writers in this book are all deceased—how might an academic book about their writing be beneficial to others besides scholars and researchers in literacy? How might a study like this one effect social change?

In "Literacy Practices," Barton and Hamilton's chapter in the same book, they explain that New Literacy Studies emphasizes the social and historical contexts of literacy and the ways in which literacy can be studied to account for these factors. Scholars in the United States, the United Kingdom, and Australia are in general agreement about the importance of contextualizing a literacy event in order to fully understand the social and historical dimensions of literacy acquisition, in addition to understand the implications of particular literacy events.[38] Where New Literacy Studies takes an important turn in the study of literacy and language use is asking about the social and ethical responsibility of scholars conducting such studies.[39]

As we consider who benefits from our scholarly work and how our work might have implications for writing instruction, we can simultaneously consider the forces driving the literacy practices in the first place. The letters written by mountain residents in Virginia reflect the social mechanisms that were already in place in the state of Virginia and the federal government's Department of the Interior. Yet at the same time, the letters illustrate the ways that the economic/material condition of the park was affecting the literacy practices of the region. As Brandt suggests, "Individual literacy exists only as part of larger material systems, systems that on the one hand enable acts of reading or writing and on the other hand confer their value."[40] By examining the letters in "relation to the social institutions and power relations which sustain them," we begin to understand the implications, both positive and negative, of SNP as a sponsor of literacy.[41]

Deborah Brandt's concept of a literacy sponsor is an important tool in investigating the ways that a government entity and large displacement in turn affected the education and literacy in the region. For Brandt, sponsors of literacy "are any agents, local or distant, concrete or abstract, who enable, support, teach, model, as well as recruit, regulate, suppress, or withhold literacy—and gain advantage by it in some way."[42] The formation of SNP was one of the "dynamic sources of literacy and literacy learning" in the Virginia region. The park's presence prompted this series of letters, but it also contributed to a growing access to public education, albeit one fraught with its own disparities in access. In addition, the creation of SNP sponsored a new and lasting political discourse of resistance to what has been perceived about the park, and where it serves as an "incubator" for the kinds of debates that continue today (such as disputes over accessing the archives, building new parking lots, and information contained in historical displays).

In addition to these acts of sponsorship, however, forming SNP also brought an end to the small mountain schools located within park boundaries, an end that may have been inevitable due to public education, but that nevertheless was perceived as a result of the park. According to Theobald, the disintegration of community education has significant impact:

> The celebration of urban industrial progress in the pages of our history books contributes indirectly to the stereotype of rural places, and therefore rural people, as unimportant. Indeed, rural dwellers have been told time and time again that the disintegration of their communities . . . the closed-up schools, and the growing sense of isolation are all a part of the prices of progress. They are all somehow or other unavoidable or natural, and therefore those who make the decisions (and profit from them) that create these circumstances are blameless. It is necessary, I believe, to keep these issues in mind as we work through some rural history that most historians, apparently, have considered unimportant.[43]

The formation of SNP, though not in the name of progress but fueled by bureaucratic agencies and business promoters, affected the community networks established in the mountains, including their small schools. Communities were dismantled when Virginia condemned people's property in the Blue Ridge. As Nellie Haney Sims, Lula Haney's niece, suggested in her oral history, "Everyone was sad and standing around crying and hugging one another." She said that the children were upset about leaving their school in Fern Hill and were not sure where they would go. The institution of SNP brought the promise of a better life, both in terms of the homesteads and in terms of education, for the mountain residents. Without a systematic study of the individual families displaced, it is difficult to determine whether or not this was true for them. Some of the residents moved did gain access to literacy, but at the expense of a community's "unsettling," diminishing one kind of literacy for another. Its advantage has been the park itself, its beauty and enjoyment, and, in an odd way, the resistance to it. With the various kinds of resistance and "bad press" the park has gotten over the years, employees have sincerely engaged in retelling the story to account for the residents' sacrifices and for the injustices of government officials, re-envisioning the park's history.

As we consider the literacy event of mountain residents writing letters, and other literacy events like it, how might we consider the formation of SNP as a literacy sponsor? Certainly, the Virginian letter writers examined in this study would not have written these letters, would not have recorded their requests and lives in this way, without the arrival of the park and the officials managing the park. What is the role of a large-scale displacement effort in the education and literacy of the surrounding communities? That is, how did literacy education change as a result of the displacement once the mountain people moved to the lowlands?

Finally, the importance of understanding the formation of SNP as a literacy sponsor lies in the ways that the dominant discourse touted great improvement for the mountain families. Further inquiry into the literacy narrative of individuals, and consequently their communities, would shed light on the ways that communities were affected in the long term. Furthermore, understanding letters as autobiography, as testimony to the history of the communities dismantled to form a national park, places literacy as a key to "identity formation."[44] Participating in this literacy event of writing a letter to a government official does not simply involve forming an identity. The consequences of engaging discourses of power as participants re-see themselves in relation to the world around them.[45]

Autobiographical acts such as writing letters and participating in oral histories can be an uncomfortable (and sometimes violent) process. Often the stories are ones that the genteel do not want to hear. Stories might make some uncomfortable, especially when discovering that an event (such as establishing a park for conservation) can be the cause of violent disruption in people's lives. Despite this discomfort, it is from past experience that broader social critique can begin.

However, the last thing that should be done, attractive though it may be, is to romanticize the displaced (or to demonize the displacers). Doing so would make them passive and uncomplex. The fact is, the people displaced from their homes to form Shenandoah National Park were complex and intelligent and worthy of the country's attention. What should be done, however, is to assume the displaced have stories to tell, and that their stories are crucial to broader historical narrative and understanding.

The process of studying "situated" literacy events has represented an important shift in New Literacy Studies. However, the letters highlighted in this study challenge the notion of "situated." Persons in the process of being displaced are on the move—their individual and community identities are in the middle of enormous change. Examining literacy through the lens of processes of displacement asks us to consider the concept of a situated event, and the ways we might define literacy and identity within those events. I turn now to traditional discourses of displacement to recognize the fallacies in traditional rhetorics of displacement, consequently arguing for the inclusion of the voices of the dispossessed in displacement rhetorics. If we are persuaded that there is an inextricable link between literacy and identity, then we might also be persuaded that "displacement" rhetoric should include the rhetoric of the dispossessed.[46] By elevating the mountain residents' story to the historical record, we add their voices to that history.[47] In the following chapter, therefore, I trace the rhetorical legacy of displacement and its multifaceted effects on the histories of communities and individuals.

RHETORICS OF DISPLACEMENT
AND THE POLITICS OF
EMINENT DOMAIN

Subject to the provisions of this act, the commission is hereby expressly vested with the power of eminent domain to condemn for use as a public park or for public park purposes, and to acquire title to all or any part of the lands described in sections three and four hereof, including dwelling houses, outbuildings, orchards, yards, gardens, and other improvements on such lands, and, all or any right, title, or interest in or to all or any part of such lands, and the improvements thereon, by the exercise of the right of eminent domain in condemnation proceedings or by gift, devise, purchase, or any other lawful means for the transfer of title.
—Public Park Condemnation Act of the General Assembly of
    Virginia, March 22, 1928

The words "for public use" do not realistically exclude any takings, and thus do not exert any constraint on the eminent domain power.
—Former justice Sandra Day O'Connor, Dissenting Opinion, *Kelo v.
    City of New London*

On June 23, 2005, the United States Supreme Court decided in a 5 to 4 vote that the federal government's right of eminent domain included "public purpose," essentially extending states' power to condemn land in order to foster economic development by private businesses. In the case of *Kelo v. City of New London,* residents of the Fort Trumball neighborhood of New London, Connecticut, argued that their rights as property owners were infringed upon as the state supreme court voted to allow their property to be "condemned" and sold for "just compensation" to private economic developers. These developers planned to raze existing structures in order to build office space, hotels, and new residences, for the "public purpose" of enhancing the local economy.

The news surrounding this story generated a media stir around the issue of eminent domain and the states' various condemnation laws. The *New York Times*, the *Washington Post*, and National Public Radio have devoted numerous articles and radio programs to discussing the broader implications of the Court's recent decision. This recent attention to the constitutionality of eminent domain highlights what individual landowners throughout America's history have faced when their property was condemned by local or state governments.

Condemnation laws like Connecticut's exist in nearly every state, though with varying rules regarding what can be condemned and for what reasons. Most often, condemnation suits are handled within the states' court systems, and other states (such as Illinois, Michigan, and Washington) have ruled to protect property owners' rights in similar cases. After the Supreme Court's decision, Connecticut governor M. Jodi Rell was quoted in the *New York Times* as saying that her state's legislature "'ought to consider' the state's eminent domain laws," implying that she disagreed that New London should be able to transfer property owned by one private owner to another private owner. Because the Supreme Court's decision essentially left condemnation decisions to the states, Rell said that the state of Connecticut should rethink its laws regarding what can be "taken" for public use. She also stated that there is a "need to strike a proper balance between economic development concerns and the rights of property owners."[1] Rell's concern for a "balance" between the public good and individual rights has been a concern for many states as they have debated various land use cases. Indeed, Justice John Paul Stevens, in the Court's published opinion of the case, explicitly states the disparity in definition of "public use" and the lack of certainty in predicting economic gain and for whom. Justice Stevens said that "while many state courts in the mid-19th century endorsed 'use by the public' as the proper definition of public use, that narrow view steadily eroded over time. Not only was the 'use by the public' difficult to administer (e.g., what proportion of the public need have access to the property? At what price?) but it proved to be impractical given the diverse and always evolving needs of society." The Court recognized the difficulty in determining public use and therefore accepted the notion of "public purpose" in order to determine the constitutionality of "taking" private citizens' land. This recognition adheres to case precedent where there is a "longstanding policy of deference to legislative judgments in this field." Justice Stevens's opinion cited *Berman v. Parker* in 1954 as precedent for the U.S. Supreme Court to defer to states' decisions on public purpose. In making those decisions, states' assessments about "community redevelopment need not, by force of the Constitution, be on a piecemeal basis—lot by lot, building by building." That is, it is not up to the Supreme Court to determine individual housing or land determinances. Therefore states are able, if they so desire, to condemn entire communities, even if some of the homes or land or businesses are not necessarily blighted. In doing so, the Supreme Court upholds states' rights in making these determinations for themselves, because needs and values and definitions within communities and states shift over time. Justice Stevens further said, "For more than a century, our public use jurisdiction prudence has wisely eschewed rigid formulas and intrusive scrutiny in favor of affording legislatures broad latitude in determining what public needs justify the use of the takings power."[2] The Supreme Court's decision, therefore, upholds previous decisions in part to avoid the federal government's involvement in determining local and state governments' economic and development needs.

Condemnation laws have been enacted by the states based on the Fifth Amendment to the U.S. Constitution, which states that an individual's private property may not be "taken for public use, without just compensation." The first case brought against the United States under eminent domain was *Kohl v. United States* in 1876, which clarified that states could not rule over the interests of the federal government. However, "Because the Constitution offers no clarification of these three quoted terms, the courts have been compelled to fill the void: Which uses of property are 'public'? How much compensation is 'just'? What amounts to a 'taking'? The thousands of court decisions that have grappled, and will continue forever to grapple, with these terms make up much of eminent domain law."[3]

Until the adoption of the Fourteenth Amendment, the states were not held to the same standards of just compensation as the federal government. But in the late nineteenth century, two cases, *Davidson v. City of New Orleans* (1878) and *Chicago B.& Q.R.R. v. City of Chicago* (1987), determined that just compensation *and* due process were the responsibility of the states. Many of the subsequent cases brought against states by landowners include either or both. Cases such as *Robert Via v. Commonwealth of Virginia* (1933) and *Tennessee Valley Authority v. Welch* (1946) included issues of due process, as private owners felt their property owners' rights had been infringed upon. In these and other cases like them, the U.S. Supreme Court reviewed states' various definitions of public use and left those definitions up to the states, ruling that issues of public safety, public health, morality, peace and quiet, law and order, and the like are abstract concepts, better regulated by local governments. These concepts, however, are steeped in value systems that change as society changes, particularly as those in power shift. In the *Berman v. Parker* case, the Court concluded, "The concept of the public welfare is broad and inclusive. The values it represents are spiritual as well as physical, aesthetic as well as monetary. It is within the power of the legislature to determine that the community should be beautiful as well as healthy, spacious as well as clean, well-balanced as well as carefully patrolled."[4] This case among many others set the precedent for the recent New London case, whose plaintiffs focused on the constitutionality of transferring land from one private owner to another. Justice Stevens's opinion stated, "The public end may be as well or better served through an agency of private enterprise than through a department of government," ultimately leaving states the burden of determining benefits and public purpose.

While the Virginia condemnation law of 1928 is not directly similar to Connecticut's, and the controversy of SNP is different from the economic development of Fort Trumball, some of the issues of displacement and individual land rights are similar.[5] Virginia's Public Park Condemnation Act was approved by the General Assembly on March 17, 1928. This act gave the State Commission on Conservation and Development and its chairman, William Carson, the authority to survey the land and determine its value for "just compensation." Chairman Carson persuaded the state legislature to pass the act as a way to condemn the land in the eight counties all at once, in order to avoid the delay of individual cases. When Albemarle County farm owner Robert Via brought suit against Virginia for condemning his land, the U.S. Supreme Court essentially upheld Virginia's condemnation law when it refused to hear the case.[6] Like the case brought against New London, Via's case questioned the constitutionality of Virginia's act of condemning his land. The U.S. Court's refusal to hear the case reasserted that states had the right to condemn lands as they saw fit, essentially upholding states' rights in determining what constitutes condemnation and what constitutes public use.

Issues of land use and land tenure have a complicated history in Appalachia and the United States in general. According to economist and Appalachian scholar John Gaventa, "Timber extraction for wood and paper, tourist development along the coasts and in the highlands, agricultural land use—all have shaped the history, culture, and, most essentially, the power and politics of the region."[7] Large, absentee corporations own mining rights to much of the land, and the inequitable land tenure has contributed to a history of poverty in the region. Gaventa's research on land tenure in Appalachia and the South suggests that power and politics play central roles in determining such abstracts concepts as public use, beautification, or peace. The most recent New London, Connecticut, decision reiterates the politics involved in defining public good versus the needs of individuals living in the area. Indeed, private property—anyone's private property—is subject to "taking" by local and federal governments. Hence, former justice Sandra Day O'Connor's dissenting opinion, which is concerned with the ways that states and local governments might go about defining public purpose and public good and a tendency to ignore individuals' situations and concerns.

In a *New York Times* article the day after the Connecticut ruling, Fort Trumbull resident Susette Kelo said, "I am sick . . . Do they have any idea what they've done?"[8] Kelo's statement indicates the gravity of her situation and the situation of any individual whose property is taken. Decisions like this, where people are forced from their homes, have the figurative (if not the physical) effects of making people ill. The effects of losing a home are profound. The second part of her statement is equally telling. She implies that those in power, those who have the power to make such a decision of devastating consequence, have no idea of her situation, have no inkling of her particular circumstance. She implies that if they did, they would not have voted they way they did.

Justice Anthony Kennedy, who wrote an additional concurring opinion on the New London case, recognized the potential for discrepancy in making condemnation decisions and warned states that "a court confronted with a plausible accusation of impermissible favoritism to private parties should treat the objection as a serious one and review the record to see if it has merit." Justice Kennedy recognized the possibility of favoritism and unfairness in rendering condemnation decisions. His urging for states to be aware of favoritism is a sober reminder of the potential for political power to overshadow individual ownership and concerns.

The Virginia Public Park Condemnation Act, SNP, the TVA, and Fort Trumball—none were free from politics, power plays, favoritism, or corruption, even if the ultimate goal was for a viable public purpose. All have various circumstances and degrees of classism and racism, but the process of rendering individuals "displaceable" has a history in this country, and is a topic of global concern as well. In the fields of rhetoric, anthropology, sociology, conservation, urban development and planning, humanitarian aid, and natural disaster, issues of displacement have become of primary concern. Some are historical examinations of moments of displacement while others are contemporary studies of the ways developers or conservationists are attempting to work with the displaced. Several of these projects are interested in displacement rhetorics and their analyses have important implications for using local and historical approaches to understand literacy.[9] In the remainder of the chapter, I will briefly describe several instances of displacement rhetoric in this country, and the ways displacement rhetorics are similar to and different from displacement rhetorics used across the globe as groups of people are displaced because of civil unrest, war, and genocide. In each of the following instances, identity, literacy, and representation become crucial issues as communities, local governments, and policymakers are persuaded that particular groups are displaceable in order to further the "public good."

Internal Displacement in the United States: Three Examples

Malea Powell's recent work on Native American rhetorics has been crucial to understanding the rhetorical complexities of the dispossessed. In her analysis of Susan La Flesche Picotte's work, for example, Powell says, "At every rhetorical turn in her writing and in her life, La Flesche presents us with a complicated intertwining of reform agendas and desires and her own need to heal and build the Native community into which she had been born." Powell describes La Flesche's negotiation of survival through alliance and adaptation, intertwining complex rhetorical arguments about her people while also using the discourse of the white community. Powell concludes that it is La Flesche's "sense of equal and shared responsibility that offers, I think, the most promise for a new disciplinary story . . . [,] an acknowledgement of that history and respectful efforts to redress its wrongs is an absolute necessity for the survival of any alliance."[10]

These notions of "shared responsibility" and "reciprocal relationships" have become important issues for some contemporary displacements and, as I will argue later in the chapter, a necessary element in literacy, identity, and displacement. Indeed, Malea Powell asserts in an additional study (on Sarah Winnemucca Hopkins and Charles Alexander Eastman) that "the space of absent presence is the space where the rhetorical tactics of folks like Winnemucca and Eastman can be put into conversation with Euroamerican 'oratorical culture' as a way to complicate its so-called transformations."[11] She argues for recognizing the displacee's rhetoric as a necessary aspect of understanding processes of displacement in general. Similarly, the letters of mountain residents contain complex rhetorics necessary to include in the conversation, to include in rhetorics of displacement. In Powell's conclusions referencing other Native American scholars, she suggests that understanding individual stories of survivance is crucial in understanding the past and, more important, in recognizing with an "honest sense" the responsibility for the kinds of enforced relocation like that of Native American communities.

For Malea Powell, this kind of investigation, where individual stories are woven into documented history, is of moral imperative for rhetoric scholars. She sees La Flesche's work of respectfully engaging the past as work rhetoricians should do as well: "If we engage in this work as Susan La Flesche did, in order to work for our people, our community, our discipline, then maybe we should begin our negotiations toward alliance."[12] Her notion of alliance includes a negotiation, a dialogue between past and present. Malea Powell's conclusions about alliance are similar to my conclusions about the Shenandoah residents' "knowledgeable resistance," where residents recast their identities but within existing power structures. What Powell does in analyzing La Flesche's rhetoric is place her knowledgeable resistance in relation to the rhetoric of the whites who sought to displace her community. Powell's conclusions are also similar to discussions occurring among history scholars, as oral historians argue for the legitimacy and location of life stories in historical narratives. As I argued in chapter 5, documenting individual stories is crucial to the historical narrative as a whole.[13] Letters, life writing, testimony, and literacy narratives are vital to literacy learning and acquisition. Placing La Flesche's rhetoric within Native American rhetorics and displacement rhetoric as a whole creates a fuller history. However, Powell's notion of survivance rhetoric is meant as dialogue, not as a dichotomy between the displacer with the power and the displaced with no agency. Placing these rhetorics in dialogue asserts that the displaced are actively engaged. Our projects both suggest that the displaced are not solely acted upon but had agency in their situations as they engaged power structures in their rhetoric.

Native American forced removal in this country began a legacy of displacement, and the many studies surrounding Native American history have provided much insight into the injustices of displacement. The land that is now SNP was first inhabited by the Monacan and the Manahoac Native American communities. Similarly, before families were displaced to form the reservoir of the Tennessee Valley Authority (TVA), "The Cherokee village Tanasi, which once thrived on a bend of the Little Tennessee River, gave the two rivers and the state their names. The site of Tanasi now lies under the TVA's Tellico Dam reservoir."[14] As we discuss displacements like those of SNP and the TVA, it is important to remember that the people living there then were not the first.

Like SNP, the Tennessee Valley Authority was designated to serve the public good. When the reservoir was created, nearly 3,000 families were displaced in order for the TVA "to provide navigation, flood control, power generation, reforestation, and economic development in a region touching seven states. The TVA today provides electric power to over six million people, principally in Tennessee, Mississippi, Alabama, and Kentucky."[15] The TVA displaced many more families than SNP, but the effects were similar. As families' homes were assessed for compensation for their land, "Reactions were mixed. Some sold quickly and were glad to get the price; others, convinced they should get more, had to decide whether to sell eventually or go to condemnation proceedings. A small number (96 families of a total of nearly 3,000) did nothing, and were forcibly evicted when the rising waters behind the dam make their continued presence dangerous."[16] Except for the number of people and the rising waters, this exact sentence could be used to describe the mountain residents facing the relocation out of the park.

The rhetoric used to persuade the communities of the value of the TVA and its plans for resources and rural electrification mirrors that used to form SNP. As development continued and the TVA faced continued criticism, the board presented the positive aspects of the TVA: "In tens of thousands of farmyards and farm homes you can see the change this power has already wrought. There are refrigerators in the kitchens. The water is carried by an electric pump instead of by the women, young and old, with their water pails."[17] What the TVA failed to mention was that these services were "for those who could afford it" and that many in the area did not have access to these benefits.[18]

TVA director Lilienthal also said, "In one decade the agency helped convert eroded, uneconomical farmland into lush dairy farms."[19] Based on his economic analysis, Chandler says that this simply was not true. Lilienthal's paternalistic attitude toward the people living in the valley and "benefiting" from the TVA is clear. He said that their farms were "eroded, uneconomical" and therefore not worthy of living in. No matter what their living situations, the benefit of the TVA and rural electrification were better than their current way of life, which he described as "backward."

Not only were the attitudes of some TVA authorities toward local people similar to those promoting SNP but there were also many changes and battles surrounding the ways that people would be displaced. TVA chairman Arthur Morgan and board director Harcourt Morgan had many disagreements about land condemnation policies. Arthur Morgan "believed that farmers who misused their land should have it taken away from them by state governments and given to someone who would take care of it."[20] Lilienthal, Arthur Morgan, and Harcourt Morgan battled over the establishment of procedures as families faced displacement and losing their homes.

Since its inception and development, the TVA has undergone much scrutiny over its purpose, its funding, and its overall success in providing economic development for the outlying areas. Its original conception included conservation efforts, but according to Chandler, "While TVA became the nation's largest utility, its regional development and resource conservation efforts largely atrophied." Chandler's discussion traces the TVA's historical development, its original proposals and purposes, and the subsequent economic and political impacts of the utility. He states, "Both TVA's purposes and its politics are complex. Supporters and opponents of TVA have historically divided along a liberal-conservative axis running through the New Deal." The TVA was originally conceived to generate economic development and was supported by Roosevelt in order to lower the costs of public utility. Countries such as Mexico, China, Brazil, and Russia have emulated the TVA's approach. Chandler's study discusses the implications of this emulation, as it is based on the assumption of the TVA's economic success. In fact, argues Chandler in his economic analyses, the TVA's "investments performed poorly," and he questions the cost benefit analyses of contemporary efforts to mimic the TVA's development. Chandler is careful to also explain the TVA's successes, but is highly critical of the ways that the TVA is not regulated in the same ways that other utility companies are because of its unique relation to the federal government. He says that the

> TVA experiment suggests that when resources are allocated by persons who answer neither to the marketplace nor to the electorate, they are not allocated efficiently. The TVA experiment thus bolsters the notion that democracy is good not only for purposes of equity and freedom, but for economic growth as well. This should be noted in developing countries where, as in the Tennessee Valley during the economic emergency of the Great Depression, people were willing to sacrifice democratic control for the expedience of faster progress. Economic decisions are also political decisions when they involve condemning one family's land to provide flood control for another, strip-mining one family's land against their will to provide slightly cheaper power to another, or building unnecessary power plants and billing the cost to consumers who had no voice in the decision to build.[21]

The TVA's mediocre economic success is reason to take pause over the recent Supreme Court decision about economic development "counting" as a justified reason to "take" individual land. The economic forecasting involved in community development is no guarantee that the proposed project will bring about successful or sustainable economic development. Indeed, the TVA has recently been selling the land originally condemned because it needs to generate funds.[22] As Chandler concludes, "Hundreds of farm families were dispossessed of their land and livelihood in order to make way for a reservoir that is not cost-effective and will provide one recreation and second-home development."[23]

Whereas the TVA's public purpose was much different from SNP's, the development of Great Smoky Mountains National Park (GSMNP) in Tennessee had much in common with SNP's formation in Virginia. When GSMNP was formed at the same time as SNP, the National Park Service faced very similar issues of building roads, razing houses, and condemning land. Durwood Dunn's *Cades Cove* is a detailed account of a particular community in the Smoky Mountains of Tennessee removed from their homes for the development of the park. According to Dunn's account, the people of Cades Cove, who were organized in their concerns, were continually reassured by state and federal officials that their community would be untouched by the park. Tennessee's condemnation laws, like those in Virginia, allowed for the taking of private lands for the park. The state sued a prominent landowner, John Oliver, for his 337 acres when he refused to "sell," and the ensuing court battle made both sides realize "the stakes were far greater than Oliver's small farm." Oliver's contention with Tennessee's condemnation act was that it condemned some owners' property and exempted others, forecasting the concern of favoritism and politics that Justice Kennedy stated in his recent Supreme Court opinion. After a series of appeals, Oliver eventually was forced to sell his property to the state so that it could donate it as federal park land. Approximately 110 families were displaced from Cades Cove. According to Dunn, "The harshness of tenancy or sharecropping had always been mitigated in Cades Cove by the fact that most rented land from relatives or friends who felt some personal obligation for their well-being. Now these families, often with numerous children, were thrust out of the cove into a hostile environment with absolutely no personal resources and practically no prospect of any employment."[24] Characterized as victims here, many, like John Oliver and others, resisted in interesting and innovative ways.

The various stories of survivance, resistance, and alliance of SNP, the TVA, and GSMNP are just a few of the examples of the kinds of displacement experienced in this country. As Malea Powell's work with Native American rhetorics suggests, understanding the rhetorics used by the dispossessed calls for the inclusion of those rhetorics in broader representations of those events. Her work, and the consequences of SNP, the TVA, and GSMNP, among others, point to a revision of the way future displacements are handled. The displaced often do not characterize themselves as victims, even if the displacers do. The lessons of previous displacements are evident in current conservation efforts, where planners have made efforts to include community participation.

Contemporary Conservation:
Community-based Management and Global Projects

Part of the controversy surrounding the New London, Connecticut, project is that commercial developers seem to have no interest in working with the individuals who currently own housing there. Similarly, when SNP, the TVA, and GSMNP were formed, consideration of residents' opinions and concerns seemingly had little value in setting up processes and procedures. However, contemporary conservation efforts have seen an enormous shift that incorporates cultural resource management. According to geoscientist Stan Stevens, this recent global shift has come about after years of international conservation efforts working under the "Yellowstone Model" of land preservation. Stevens points out that Native American removal from Yellowstone was the result of reservation efforts, not necessarily park policy or Yellowstone's conception by George Catlin. However, because Native Americans were displaced, Yellowstone's management as a "wilderness" became the International Union for the Conservation of Nature and Natural Resources' (IUCN's) "ideal . . . conception of national parks." As a result, "During the first half of the twentieth century, national parks became instruments of colonial rule in many areas of Africa and Asia." However, Stevens says, "Over the past several decades, concern has increased over the injustices caused by Yellowstone-model protected area policies, leading to calls for greater regard for human rights and cultural sensitivity in creating and managing protected areas, and warning that policies of eviction and confrontation are often ineffective as conservation measures and even harmful to the long-term viability of protected areas." This "rethinking of protected area principles" occurred in the NPS during the 1970s, as ecologist Raymond Dasmann encouraged the recognition of the human rights of indigenous people.[25] Indeed, the NPS hired cultural resource management specialists such as Reed Engle (who came to SNP in 1994) during the 1970s and 1980s to document the cultural histories of the regions surrounding the parks. Consequently, interpretive educational exhibits accounting for human contribution are in place in park visitor centers across the country (see figure 16 on page 122).

Studies such as those in Stevens's edited collection and Dawn Chatty and Marcus Colchester's *Conservation and Mobile Indigenous Peoples* focus on international conservation efforts where new parks are being established in such places as Indonesia, Africa, Australia, Nicaragua, Syria, and Thailand, among others.[26] Conservation rhetorics have shifted from idealized wildernesses to the integration of the protected areas and the indigenous people living there. According to Chatty and Colchester, "The overriding goal for mountain protected areas" is for "environmental conservation and the maintenance of landscapes," where "an essential and integral part of this goal must be recognition of the knowledge, rights, lifestyles, and cultural values of people living in and near mountain protected areas, including *identity* grounded in places."[27] This attendance to those who currently live in areas slated for conservation illustrates the ways that protection from development can coincide with existing inhabitants.

The Blue Ridge Parkway, which was approved by the Virginia legislature and authorized by Congress in 1936, connects Shenandoah National Park and Great Smoky Mountains National Park. In the 1930s and 1940s, land was acquired in similar ways for the two national parks, and in some cases scenic easements were established. When landowners agreed to a scenic easement, they agreed that no building or development would occur within a certain distance of the scenic highway.[28] Over the years, however, more development has occurred, causing park administrators to develop ways to work with the public in maintaining the tourist benefit of the scenic highway. According to Charles E. Roe, park administrators are working with a nonprofit company, the Conservation Trust for North Carolina, to obtain conservation easements along the Blue Ridge Parkway. These easements are tailored to individual landowners and "designed and written to satisfy a variety of conditions and future uses. Some easements may reserve forestland as nature preserves; others will allow existing uses such as timber management, livestock grazing, or active farming."[29] This contemporary effort at working with landowners represents a major shift for park administrators as they continue to preserve the scenic beauty of the Blue Ridge Parkway.

Conserving the beauty of an area, offering shelter for animals and plants, and providing for enjoyment of a region's natural beauty can be seen as benefiting the greater public good. However, the global efforts at establishing parks while working *with* residents is evidence of the ways in which the greater good can be accomplished while simultaneously attending to individual rights and regional and resident identity. The question remains, then: Could the same attention to individual rights in contemporary conservations efforts be extended to economic development?

Analyzing human capital together with manufactured capital when examining community and economic development is fraught with politics, particularly in a place like Appalachia. According to Appalachian economic theorist John Gaventa, "Political economists often analyze the ownership and flow of capital (and its links to power) to explain development. But increasingly, sociologists, community developers, economists, and others have begun to understand development not only in economic terms but in human, environmental, and social terms as well."[30] The rate of land ownership among the poor and minorities is disproportionate in Appalachia and today contributes greatly to the region's lack of economic development.

Gaventa states that "communities characterized by vertical social capital tend to be ones where dependency, patron–client relationships, and corruption prevail. Horizontal social capital can strengthen participatory democracy. Vertical social capital works against it." Citing several economists and environmental sociologists, Gaventa explains that, despite the many factors working against development in Appalachia, "reciprocity and mutual exchange" are crucial for economic development that ensures integrity, fairness, and civic engagement. In an earlier study, Gaventa concluded that lack of civic engagement (the resistance discussed in chapter 1) occurs when those in power promote "patterns of paternalism, patronage, and dependency."[31]

These patterns, which result in rhetorics of victimization, are precisely what concerns contemporary humanitarian efforts. The importance of making the displaced "beneficiaries rather than victims of development" is of primary concern for the organizations associated with the World Bank and the Displacement Network. Removal of Native Americans from their land, economic development in Appalachia, rural electrification, national parks, and forced displacement—each has its own unique layers of politics, economics, racism, and paternalism. Despite the obvious differences in each of these situations, the following discussion illustrates the ways that displacement rhetorics function in these situations and the ways that they are eerily similar.[32]

Lessons from Conflict-induced Displacement

According to the Displacement Network's Web site, "The World Bank estimates that over 10 million people are displaced by development projects each year, resulting in substantial, multifaceted risks of impoverishment. Outnumbering political refugees, development-induced displacees have become a concealed, global human rights and development problem. The International Network on Displacement and Resettlement (INDR) is composed of professionals working to assure that people who are forcefully displaced become beneficiaries rather than victims of development."[33] Agencies interested in individuals' needs during displacement work to ensure that those displaced retain some sense of control in their lives despite whatever conflict has induced their displacement. The World Bank's concern with avoiding dependency and victimization echoes Gaventa's conclusions about Appalachia, and recent humanitarian efforts for conflict-induced displaced persons are highly sensitive to the human capital involved in such situations.

For instance, in a study sponsored by the World Bank, Holtzman and Nezam examine the "characteristics of displacement-induced vulnerability" in several countries in Europe and the former Soviet Union. Basing their observations on fieldwork, surveys, and poverty assessments, Holtzman and Nezam comment on the notion of "dependency syndrome," where displaced persons have feelings of inadequacy, entitlement, or "an unwillingness to work or to seek work due to long dependence on external assistance."[34] These feelings are sometimes real or sometimes perceived by surrounding communities hosting the displaced persons.

Holtzman and Nezam's study concludes that "psychological impacts of displacement—alienation, socioeconomic dislocation, and feelings of loss and hopelessness—perhaps accompanied with a nostalgia for a semi-mythical past, are in certain ways similar to the types of impacts frequently heard" among various countries with varying circumstances for displacement.[35] Their study includes those internally displaced and those who have been forced into other countries.[36] They are careful to distinguish between types of displacements and types of traumas, yet they also recognize that "even a few weeks or month of conflict is sufficient to create memories and effects that may linger for long periods of time." While displaced SNP residents did not face war trauma, Holtzman and Nezam's recognition and study of the psychological effects of displacement are important in light of SNP residents and residents facing displacement in recent eminent domain cases. Psychological effects of displacement are traumatic, no matter the circumstances, because of the "wrenching of closely held ideals and faith in a nation, an ideology, or the value of friendship among neighbors."[37]

Because of these long-lasting effects on individuals and communities, studies such as Holtzman and Nezam's recommend community-based initiatives (similar to Stan Stevens's assertions about establishing national parks) in planning for shelter and economic development. While their study is in the interest of eradicating poverty resulting from conflict-induced displacements, their study has important implications for any communities displaced from their regions, homes, and livelihoods. They conclude that "populations affected by displacement have specific patterns of vulnerability" and face significant problems with unemployment, poverty, housing, and future sustainability.[38] Similar to Gaventa's conclusions about community empowerment, their conclusions highlight promoting self-reliance while at the same time providing sufficient relief funds. Their study provides for humanitarian agencies' specific "parameters of action" as countries work to sustain displaced populations, including extensively interviewing the displaced and documenting their concerns and needs.

While Holtzman and Nezam's conclusions value empowering displaced communities and encouraging self-reliance, some of the rhetoric used in their "action" strategies could be interpreted as perpetuating rhetorics of paternalism. While their study sensitively identifies the particular needs of displaced populations, one of their specific actions includes "poverty diagnostics," evoking a sense of mission work (and in many cases it is).[39] But this places the displaced in a certain hierarchical relation to the "diagnoser" that further disempowers them. On the other hand, the action plan is a very detailed assessment tool for analyzing particular individuals and particular communities and how to assist them. The effort here is extensive in assisting humanitarian agencies in figuring the appropriate kinds of assistance to provide depending on the persons interviewed.

Similarly, Gaventa's conclusions about Appalachia's economic development suggest that "research on land tenure and social capital therefore must involve understanding the culture of communities affected by the relationship to the land and the indigenous knowledge that has been drawn from it."[40] Understanding cultures, through extensive research and interview processes, ensures a greater chance of communities feeling some sense of power despite their displacement.

In countries that are war-torn and where racial and/or religious tensions incite displacement, the rhetoric of the "other" is used as a means of rendering certain residents displaceable. The rhetoric used by those committed to economic development is often similarly laden with constructions of the other, even if that economic development or land conservation could serve the public good. Being critical of the rhetorical processes involved and aware of the abuses of power that can occur in such developments is important as individuals' rights come into question. Justice Kennedy's warning that states treat seriously any accusations of unfairness is a recognition of the potential for unequal power structures. Historically, certain individuals with either influence or money have been able to bypass the system and have boundaries changed to their advantage.[41] This unequivocal unfairness is exactly why rhetorical and historical understanding is so crucial to contemporary decisions about property and land use. So that those rhetorical processes used in genocide and war are avoided, and so that the dispossessed can be empowered, processes of land condemnation must take into account the individual.

War and conflict-induced displacement may seem separate and certainly of a different caliber than the displacement of mountaineers from their homes in Virginia. Many Americans have a hard time recognizing the country's similar acts of enforced displacement, such as those of the many Native American communities or the Japanese internments. There are examples more directly similar to that of the park, such as the Tennessee Valley Authority's removal of families in order to form a water reservoir, or the states' highway departments using eminent domain to force people to sell their land so that interstates can be built. These examples are more closely related to SNP than those involving war or racial trauma, and they involve similar processes of rhetorical renderings of humans as displaceable. Individuals are constructed as "better off" in their displacement, or the displacement itself is "for the good of the country," state, or region. What tends to be left out of the histories of these developments are the voices of the people affected. And even if their voices are included, they often make no difference to policy and law.

Identity, Place, and (Dis)place(ment)

Recent postcolonial studies in anthropology, geography, and history have questioned the "inseparability of identity from place." These studies say that the "notion of culture based on the transmutation of race into cultural relativism, a notion that immutably ties a culture to a fixed terrain, has become increasingly problematic" as large, forced migrations have occurred.[42] Massive migrations and forced displacements have called into question the ways that culture, identity, and place have traditionally been inextricably linked. This postmodern view of identity recognizes the ways that the violence of forced displacement can shatter an individual's sense of identity and the role of place within that identity. Furthermore, "Displacement, we learn, is not experienced in precisely the same way across time and space, and does not unfold in a uniform fashion. Rather, there is a range of positionings of Others in relation to the forces of domination and vis-à-vis other Others."[43] This "paradigm shift from self/other to historically grounded multiple subject positions" is what makes further study about internal displacement in this country so important.[44] For those internally displaced in the United States in order to build roads, parks, and shopping centers, while not victims of war or necessarily systemic racism (although this certainly happens as rulings are made about which lands and property will be condemned), the processes by which people are rhetorically displaced are jarringly similar.[45] The value systems steeped in race, class, and gender are resoundingly clear in the decision-making processes of those in power as decisions are made about *who* is displaceable: whose identity counts as one who can be forced from her or his home?[46] And what have been the cultural, economical, and educational effects of such a displacement? Is their alienation in any way similar to the crossing of transnational borders? How do postmodern notions of nation, identity, and the "realm in between" inform our understanding of the internally displaced of the United States?[47] The cultural third time-spaces Lavie and Swedenburg describe are certainly different than those created by the displacement of white families from their mountain homes to (in many cases) the lowlands of those mountains. But the communities were equally diverse in their reception to the mountaineers. Some were sympathetic, some were ambivalent, some were suspicious. The studies in Lavie and Swedenburg's collection examine the multiple subject positions of those displaced, while also recognizing dominant forces of power, and the ways that displacements have affected and been affected by their "new" cultures. Similar questions need to be addressed as those in the United States continue to be displaced for economic development. Lavie and Swedenburg urge for ways to rethink "global political economy," looking at the cultural productions of "hybrid" cultures and their cultural, economic, and political value in societies. Concern for hybrid cultures is similar to the ways conservationists have been rethinking how to co-manage the environment with indigenous cultures. And finally, New Literacy Studies researchers examine the "hybrid literacy practices" that are the result of cultures and power relationships coming in contact with each other.[48]

Displacement in this country, however, has tended to exclude the voices of the displaced. The implication, Gaventa argues, is that "research that replicates land-tenure patterns (e.g., findings concentrated in a few hands and not accessible to the people directly affected by the land) will do little to alter the patterns of power and powerlessness that landownership patterns have helped to create."[49] Rather than working with the concept of hybrid cultures, processes in the United States have tended toward the easier approach of assessing the whole, not piece-by-piece, thereby making the relocations of families and communities easier (that is, more cost-effective) for economic developers.

In order for a rhetorics of displacement to be reconceived, not only must the approach to economic development research change but also, as Gaventa urges, that research must be "accessible to the communities affected" by these issues. Individual stories, regional identities, and community participation become crucial for land and economic development to occur as equitably as possible.

Identity, Eminent Domain, and a New Rhetorics of Displacement

The very use of the word *displacement* to describe the forced removal of people from their homes is a conscious choice steeped in politics and ideology. When the issue of mountain residents was initially discussed, their removal was discussed as "relocation." It was only in 1960s and 1970s when researchers began studying the effects of relocation, that the term displacement was used. Displacement has a powerful resonance and highlights the violent nature of forcing people to leave their homes and the consequent psychological effects. Using the notion of displacement is a "tactic" in asserting individual stories within discourses of power.

For instance, Malea Powell situates part of her analysis of Native American rhetoric in Michel de Certeau's notion of the particular "uses" of discursive texts. She highlights the ways that Winnemucca and Eastman, for example, use a rhetoric of survivance that "insinuate[s] itself" into the white man's dominant discourses about Native Americans.[50] In this way, survivance is a tactic, in de Certeau's sense, because it resists dominant discourse yet is always already controlled by it. The notion of de Certeau's "tactic," then, is seen as "the space of the other."[51] The tactic I suggest, with regard to reconceiving a new rhetorics of displacement, is to theorize displacement through the philosopher Jacques Derrida's notion of displacement. By examining Derrida's notion of displacement as a tactic, we begin to see displacement as a means by which to undermine hegemonic discourses.

Derrida's notion of displacement "involves a violent intervention: turbulence, irruptions, explosion: 'the deviance of meaning, its reflection-effect in writing, sets something off.'" While displacing people may be for the public good, it will also be violent—and in recognizing that violence (as Stuckey argues about literacy practices), more inclusive decision-making processes can occur. However, Derrida's concept of displacement does not mean replacing one theory of thought for another. Rather, Derrida's method of deconstruction, as it involves displacement, examines a hierarchy that is "not eliminated; rather, it is displaced, cut loose from its metaphysical grounding when it is inverted, so that speech comes to be seen as a special case of an archi-writing. With this displacement, speech can no longer function in the same way."[52] The "irruptive emergence" of new societies and new ways of thinking could not exist without the knowledge and definition of the old, but it is the unique use of rhetoric that changes societal definitions of particular identities.[53] Derrida's reference to marginalized thought as displacing and disrupting the dominant ideology emphasizes that this assertion is violent but that discourses of power always come back to establish order, even if the order has been disrupted. In order to disrupt the established order, then, individual narratives must be inserted into the metanarratives told about particular events.

Until now and across several kinds of events, rhetorics of displacement have traditionally included:

1. *Degrading remarks.* These remarks, if not outright racist or classist or full of disdain, are paternalistic and condescending. In either case, one group is deciding that it knows best over another.

2. *Assumption of illiteracy,* with literacy narrowly defined. Some of the degrading remarks include that people are "stupid" or illiterate or not capable of making decisions for themselves because of some sort of lack in terms of language skill. The assumption is a lack of literacy, based on narrow views of literacy and linked to specific ideologies, rendering some groups displaceable.

3. *Disregard for the voice of the displaced.* Together with the assumption of knowing what is best for a group of people, this is the perceived ability to also be able to define what constitutes the "common good." In many historical instances, the people being displaced are not allowed a voice in determining the common good.

Rhetorics of displacement, as they have traditionally been defined, have not included the rhetoric of the marginalized or dispossessed. By including discourses of identity and having them come in contact with discourses of power, hegemonic discourses can then be disrupted. This theoretical and conceptual change can then affect the actual processes of displacement that have historically had devastating and long-term effects for communities. These revised processes of displacement would include formal policies whereby potential displacees have a voice *during* the process, not later when historians or rhetoricians decide to examine their texts and participation. Ideally, this process would include a concurrent merging of voices where there is not a dichotomy of displacer and displacee, but rather a reciprocal relationship where procedures and policies are set by the diversity of involved parties. This rhetorics of displacement would recognize the notion of what I call "moving literacies." As I concluded in chapter 5, people who are being displaced are moving, and with them their individual and community identities are moving. As New Literacy Studies scholars continue to examine literacy by taking into account texts, context, power, and "identities in practice," I suggest doing so through the lens of processes of displacement.[54] In this way we link moving identities with moving bodies, and define a situated literacy event as one that recognizes that literacy is never stagnant—it is always, already moving.[55]

As controversy continues to surround the recent Supreme Court decision on eminent domain, issues of displacement, identity, condemnation, and landowner rights continue to dominate citizens' concerns as they discuss the appropriate use of land, public use, and eminent domain.[56] The legacy of decision making in the past affects the decisions made in the future. Therefore when only those in power are part of the decision-making processes, future actions based on those decisions usually result in resistance from the communities affected. As Justice Kennedy noted in his concurring decision, it is up to local communities to decide whether and to what use certain land will be deemed. However, as the mountain and surrounding residents of Shenandoah National Park suggest, communities consist of those with power, those with means, those with the social and political position (or at least the appearance of such) to make decisions that affect the futures of others, those whose access to literacy and power has been diminished in some way.

The prevalence of documentaries about Appalachia, literacy centers in Kentucky, West Virginia, and other states, Appalachian cultural centers, and the interdisciplinary academic field called Appalachian studies suggests the relevance and importance of studying the area, its peoples, its various uses of language, and its ways of living to understand the country and the ways that the country has gone about its political, economic, and social business. As this study has suggested, the letters written by the small portion of residents left in Shenandoah National Park during its development in the 1930s complicate definitions of the mountaineer, southern identity, and literacy. This previously unnarrated history accounts for the literacy and illiteracy of mountain families, the poor and wealthy park residents, and published and unpublished representations of the folk that inhabited this landscape during the early part of the twentieth century. Their letters, their determination to participate in a discourse from which they were largely excluded, serve as cautionary tales to contemporary decision makers as they wield the power given them and attend to the people with rights over the land, while making important community decisions about how that land will serve the "greater good." In the words of Rockingham County resident Lillie Coleman Herring, "You all had no right to give a way the buildings. and I say if you all were a going to give them a way wouldent it be more nicer to give it to the one who awned the property." Herring's ideas, together with those of her neighbors, about fairness, justice, and decency have a legitimate place alongside economic development and land conservation. A new rhetorics of displacement would document residents' concerns, include them in the processes of planning and development, and ultimately include their concerns in the decision-making process rather than dismiss them.

Appendix

Time Line of the Development of Shenandoah National Park

1907
Congress considers national park in the eastern United States; bill not authorized (President Theodore Roosevelt)

1916
25 August President Woodrow Wilson approves legislation creating the National Park Service; Stephen T. Mather appointed first NPS director (1917–29)

1924
January Shenandoah Valley, Inc. (SVI), founded in Virginia to advocate for Shenandoah National Park; 1,100 people attend first meeting
February Secretary of the Interior Hubert Work (1923–28) creates the Southern Appalachian National Park Commission (SANPC); George Pollock, owner of Skyland, hosts SANPC there to promote SNP

1925
January SVI lobbies Congress for park in Virginia; Shenandoah National Park Association founded

1926
Harry F. Byrd governor of Virginia (to 1930)
March Virginia assembly approves State Commission on Conservation and Development (SCCD); William E. Carson appointed chair
May President Coolidge signs bill authorizing 521,000 acres for SNP; also approves acreage for Great Smoky Mountains and Mammoth Cave National Parks
SCCD begins two-year tract-by-tract survey of property and census of landowners

1927
NSP director resurveys land for SNP

1928
Roy O. West secretary of the Interior (to 1929)
February SCCD Chair Carson persuades Congress to reduce SNP to 321,000 acres
March Virginia legislature passes Public Park Condemnation Act

1929

Ray L. Wilbur secretary of the Interior (to 1933); Horace M. Albright National Park
Service director (to 1933)

Landowner Lewis Willis organizes the Landowners' Protective Association

April President and Mrs. Hoover purchase Rapidan Camp in Madison County, and
establish Hoover School with teacher Christine Vest

October Public Park Condemnation Act passes into law after Warren County Circuit
Court rejects Thomas J. Rudacille's lawsuit challenging its constitutionality

U.S. Stock Market Crash

1930

November SCCD Chair Carson tries to persuade President Hoover and Congress to
pass bill to use drought relief funds to pay area residents to build first segment of
Skyline Drive

1931

Congress approves bill in January; contractors, who hired some area residents, begin
construction of Skyline Drive using emergency relief funds

1932

Social worker Miriam Sizer conducts survey of park residents

SCCD Chair Carson persuades Congress to further reduce SNP to 160,000 acres

Congress passes the Emergency Construction and Relief Act; funds given to Bureau
of Public Roads to continue construction of Skyline Drive

1933

President Franklin Delano Roosevelt takes office 4 March; CCC, WPA, TVA formed

Harold Ickes secretary of the Interior (to 1946); Arno B. Cammerer NPS director (to
1940); Harry F. Byrd U.S. senator (to 1965)

May "CCC Boys" arrive to continue construction on Skyline Drive, funded through
the recently passed Federal Emergency Relief Act (FERA)

James Ralph Lassiter named engineer-in-charge of Skyline Drive

1934

February Federal government purchases land for resettlement homesteads; Ferdinand Zerkel (park booster) employed by the Federal Homestead Corporation (of
the Department of the Interior New Deal Agency); FHC purchases 343 acres in
Ida Valley (Page County) for resettlement homes

"Secretary's List" formed for aged or infirmed—including Matilda Breeden, John
Russell Nicholson, Annie Shenk, and Lewis Willis—to live their lives in the park

Prominent Albemarle County landowner Robert Via sues Commonwealth of Virginia over constitutionality of Public Park Condemnation Act; district court rules
against him

FDR revives homestead project through the Department of Agriculture's Resettlement Administration

1935

October FSA photographer Arthur Rothstein documents rural life in SNP

November U.S. Supreme Court refuses to hear Robert Via's case against the Commonwealth of Virginia

December Federal government accepts title to 176,429.8 acres from Commonwealth of Virginia; remaining residents sign special use permits

Virginia Assembly Delegate Wilbur C. Hall becomes SCCD Chair

Bureau of Reclamation completes Hoover Dam; Park Service takes over building and recreation

1936

March James R. Lassiter named SNP superintendent

July FDR dedicates SNP at ceremony at Skyland

A. E. Demaray serves as acting director of NPS

Home economist Mozelle Cowden begins work with Shenandoah Homesteads Project in Luray, Virginia

R. Taylor Hoskins appointed SNP chief park ranger

1937

USDA's Farm Security Administration takes over Homestead Project; 172 families moved into homesteads

October First residents moved to Ida Valley Resettlement Homesteads

1938

Last SNP family moved into Homestead

Chief Ranger Taylor Hoskins leaves SNP to become superintendent at Mammoth Cave National Park in Kentucky

1939

World War II begins

1940

Newton B. Drury NPS director (to 1951)

1947

James R. Lassiter leaves SNP as superintendent

1958

Taylor Hoskins returns to SNP to serve as superintendent (to 1972)

Notes

Introduction

1. Once the land became official federal property late in 1935, the Civilian Conservation Corps began dismantling vacated homes for materials for the Resettlement Administration, the agency charged with providing eligible residents with homesteads.

2. I use the term *rhetorics* here to imply that there is not a single rhetoric of displacement but rather multiple dimensions of rhetorical constructs of displacement. Similarly, I use the term *literacies* to imply that language use is complex and comprises several literacies, rather than one clearly defined literacy.

3. Chapter 6 will discuss the events surrounding the development of the Tennessee Valley Authority and the ways in which displacement in forming a reservoir was similar to and different from displacement in forming the park.

4. Jacqueline Jones Royster defines literacy as social action, saying that the use of literacy by its very nature functions as an action. Her theories about literacy reflect accepted thinking in rhetorical studies—for example, Carolyn Miller's definition of genre as social action. Kenneth Burke's conception of "symbolic action" serves as the basis for contemporary rhetorical and literacy studies' thinking about the action-inducing nature of language. In "Language as Symbolic Action," Burke explains that humans' ability to use language comes from the ability to distinguish symbols and to use symbols in order to induce some sort of action. Humans' ability to "filter" certain events in order to produce language that persuades establishes the nature of language as symbolic. In *Rhetoric of Motives*, Burke says that rhetoric is "rooted in an essential function of language itself, a function that is wholly realistic, and is continually born anew; the use of language as a symbolic means of inducing cooperation in beings that by nature respond to symbols" (qtd. in *The Rhetorical Tradition*, p. 1032).

5. From Aristotle's *Rhetoric*, book 1, chapter 2.

6. See the work of Deborah Brandt, J. Elsbeth Stuckey, Ellen Cushman, David Schaafsma, Shirley Brice Heath, Jacqueline Jones Royster, Brian Street, and David Barton and Mary Hamilton.

7. Susan Miller, "X-files in the Archive," p. 3.

8. See James Paul Gee's "The New Literacy Studies" and Brian Street's "What's 'New' in New Literacy Studies?"

9. Barton and Hamilton, "Literacy Practices," p. 9.

10. See Heath, *Ways with Words*. See also Street's "Literacy Events and Literacy Practices."

11. Royster, *Traces of a Stream*, p. 6.

12. Keith Jenkins's concept of historiography accounts for the ways in which the past and history are distinctive and are "always already" stories and narratives. He says that historians (and other researchers) "interpret the same phenomenon differently through discourses that are always on the move, that are always being de-composed and re-composed; are always positioned and positioning, and which thus need constant self-examination as discourses by those who use them" (*Re-thinking History*, pp. 11–12).

13. Barton and Hall, introd. to *Letter Writing*, p. 1.

14. Ibid. Barton and Hall assert that artifacts in social context can divulge "the role of literate activity in society" (1).

15. See the work of Charles Perdue and Nancy Martin-Perdue, Audrey Horning, Darwin Lambert, Richard Drake, Dwight Billings, John Gaventa, Stephen Foster, Stephen Fisher, and David Whisnant, among others.

16. According to Deborah Brandt, "Literate abilities originate in social postures and social knowledge that begin well before and extend well beyond words on a page" (*Literacy in American Lives*, p. 4). Further, Brandt theorizes "sponsors of literacy," suggesting that larger social, political, and economic systems influence what kind of literacy is acquired and how it is consequently used. To address issues of literacy acquisition and the "economic transformations" of America as a whole, Brandt analyzes literacy histories from "ordinary" people and the ways in which their literacy learning is enacted within systems of institutional power. Similarly, Barton and Hamilton conclude that "literacy practices are patterned by social institutions and power relationships, and some literacies are more dominant, visible and influential than others" ("Literacy Practices," p. 12).

17. On one occasion, Superintendent Lassiter wrote to several residents who were having a dispute about land cultivation and who had rights to it. He said to the residents, "I sincerely trust that you people can arrange this matter satisfactorily to all concerned and not be bothering us with all of your petty quarrels and scraps." See Lassiter's letter to Alex Morris, March 23, 1935.

18. Today's Park Service is quite sensitive not only to the cultural heritage of its preservation areas but also to the people involved in making those sites possible. Chapter 6 will discuss current conservation efforts through which working *with* residents and indigenous people is a priority.

19. Several park exhibits and historical projects quote from excerpts of the letters to augment other research, but none of them focuses on the letters as a collection.

20. Katherine Sohn suggests in her work that countering past representations and consequent attitudes is an ongoing struggle for contemporary Appalachian communities. Historical constructions that can be ascribed to authorities long dead continue to affect life and education in these communities; see Sohn's *Whistlin' and Crowin'*. Peter Mortensen similarly recommends the importance in tracing conduits of power that link the region's past identity; see his "Representations of Literacy and Region."

21. See Julia Kristeva's link between discourse and identity in her essay "Women's Time."

22. Stuckey, *Violence of Literacy*, p. 64.

23. Other means of recourse included starting fires, stealing CCC supplies, and poaching.

24. In her important work, Brandt focuses on individual literacy development together with large-scale economic development. Similarly, studies such as Stuckey's, Barton and Hamilton's, and Heath's examine the literate events and texts in an individual's life (or a small group).

25. See Heath's *Ways with Words* for a discussion of the "protean shapes" of literacy, and Brandt's *Literacy in American Lives* for a discussion of the ways that literacy is not constant.

26. See the work by Sylvia Scribner, "Literacy in Three Metaphors," and Kim Donehower, "Reconsidering Power." See also Royster, *Traces of a Stream;* Stuckey, *Violence of Literacy;* and Street, "What's 'New,'" p. 80.

1. Literacy, Status, and Narrative Representation

1. See Shapiro, *Appalachia on Our Minds;* Pudup, Billings, and Waller, *Appalachia in the Making;* Drake, *A History of Appalachia;* Fisher, *Fighting Back in Appalachia;* Foster, *The Past is Another Country;* Gaventa, *Power and Powerlessness;* Horning, *In the Shadow of Ragged Mountain;* Perdue and Martin-Perdue, "'To Build a Wall Around These Mountains'"; and Whisnant, *All That Is Native and Fine.*

2. See Henninger, *Ordering the Façade,* p. 5. Henninger's work traces historical and cultural implications of visual representations of southerners. See also Wendy Ewald's *Appalachia: A Self-Portrait,* and James Agee and Walker Evans's *Let Us Now Praise Famous Men.*

3. Written materials were examples of one way park officials and local developers (mis)represented mountain residents. The Farm Security Administration also commissioned photographs through the Federal Writers Project (available at the Library of Congress) of mountaineers, which largely depicted them as poor and despondent. These pictures were commissioned to show the effects of the Great Depression and were purposeful in their depictions of the poor and dispossessed. In addition, this process of displacement is discernible across different kinds of displacement. See chapter 6 for an in-depth discussion of rhetorical patterns of displacement rhetoric.

4. Drake, *History of Appalachia,* p. 4.

5. Lambert, *Undying Past,* p. 14.

6. In-depth histories about the archeological and geological past of the area are discussed by Darwin Lambert and Audrey Horning. Generally, the area was rich in plant and animal life and its resources have long been fought over.

7. Drake, *History of Appalachia,* p. 12.

8. Ibid., p. 33.

9. Lambert, *Undying Past,* p. 34, and Drake, *History of Appalachia,* p. 35.

10. Horning, *In the Shadow,* p. 16.

11. Lambert, *Undying Past,* p. 44.

12. See Horning, *In the Shadow,* for further historical detail about these disputes. See also Hofstra, "Land Policy and Settlement in the Northern Shenandoah Valley." Per-

due and Martin-Perdue conducted some foundational archival and records research built on by subsequent scholars of the region.

13. Thanks to Reed Engle for making this distinction.

14. Horning's historical archaeological research suggests "the pervasive nature of the institution of slavery and serve as a stark reminder that the story of the historic Nicholson Hollow community today belongs not only to the descendents of farming families but equally to those African Americans whose contributions to mountain life have seldom been acknowledged" (*In the Shadow*, p. 39).

15. Drake, "Slavery and Antislavery," p. 17. Drake cites *Freedom of Thought in the Old South*, by Clement Eaton, who discusses the Quakers' participation in antislavery rhetoric in the Shenandoah Valley. Both Drake and John Inscoe (*Appalachians and Race*) have described the historical disputes over the ways Appalachians contributed to southern society and slavery.

16. See Inscoe's "Race and Racism" for a detailed account of the various kinds of racism present in Appalachia.

17. Ibid., p. 123.

18. Cultural resource specialist Reed Engle is currently writing a book about the history of Lewis Mountain, a resort originally designated for African Americans in the park's boundaries, and which caused controversy within the National Park Service as issues of desegregation were discussed.

19. See the *Fifteenth Census . . . : Population*, vol. 3, pt. 2, p. 1141.

20. Ibid., p. 1166.

21. Ibid., p. 1380.

22. The names of the African American landowners who were surveyed, but whose property did not end up becoming part of the park include Mary Barber, K. B. Blair, W. D. Blair, Bawd Blakey, Tom Jones, and Sallie Simmons.

23. See Anita Puckett's "Identity, Hybridity, and Linguistic Ideologies" and "The Melungeon Identity Movement," where she discusses her linguistic and anthropological research on the construction of "whiteness" in Appalachia. See also Barbara Ellen Smith's "De-gradations of Whiteness."

24. That is not to say, however, that wealth was an indicator of slave ownership. Saving money to purchase a slave was one of the ways yeoman farmers spent their extra money. Thanks to Dr. Caroline E. Janney for pointing out this fact.

25. Link, *Hard Country*, p. 6.

26. The *McGuffey Reader*, which has recently seen a significant resurgence in sales by Christian home-schooling families, was steeped in Victorian and Christian values. Lucille Schultz's conclusions about the values implicit in letter-writing instruction during the turn of the century parallel the overall rhetoric contained in this popular reader used throughout much of Virginia.

27. Link, *Hard Country*, p. 7. Race also played a factor in resistance to government control over education as some whites resisted "mixed" schools. Furthermore, the tradition of "honor" was then being contested, as Progressives and the middle class sought social reform. According to Randall Hall in "A Courtroom Massacre," which is

based on Bertram Wyatt-Brown's *The Shaping of Southern Culture: Honor, Grace and War*, "In a society based upon honor, external standing in the community determined an individual's self-worth, and recognition by others of one's strength and independence underlay the ability to be influential and successful. Challenges to honor had to be answered immediately and decisively, or the recipient of the challenge risked shame in the eyes of the community. . . . Standards of honor grew more difficult to define, . . . [and t]he violence implicitly accepted by the doctrine [of honor] inhibited the growth of the orderly, businesslike, and evangelical society south by Progressives" (p. 277).

28. Link, *Hard Country*, p. 88. Inscoe, in "Race and Racism," also addresses this issue in terms of race. He refers to James Klotter, who has "argued convincingly that it was the region's perceived 'whiteness' that so appealed to northern interests at the time and inspired them to divert their mission impulses toward deserving highlanders after their disillusionment with similar efforts on behalf of southern blacks during Reconstruction" (p. 106).

29. In *Sex, Race, and the Role of Women in the South*, Joanne Hawks and Sheila Skemp call for further studies of women that attend to the education of the working classes and suggest that history tends to exclude those not living in the urban upper classes. In addition, according to Barton and Hall, everyday letter writing was often self-taught (introd. to *Letter Writing*, p. 8), and "complete command of reading and writing skills is not necessary for the effective forms of letter-writing" (p. 9).

30. The President's School (the Hoover School), built by President Herbert Hoover and his wife, Lou Hoover, opened February 1930 and remained open until 1933. The school was located within Hoover's mountain retreat property in Madison County. Mrs. Hoover was very interested in the local children and secured a school and its teacher, Christine Vest. Vest donated her papers and correspondence to the National Archives. Her papers serve as important resources about education in this area at the time. Visitors today can visit Rapidan Camp, nestled among the park's trails and the Rapidan River.

31. Chapter 5 discusses the significance of this in terms of contemporary education practices. Information from local school board offices, the Virginia Department of Education (in Richmond), and oral histories indicates that the very founding of SNP had an impact on education and literacy.

32. Nellie Haney Sims, oral history interview, March 24, 2005.

33. See Brandt, *Literacy in American Lives*. Brandt says that "individual literacy exists only as part of larger material systems, systems that on the one hand enable acts of reading or writing and on the other hand confer their value" (p. 1). In this way, broader political and economic climates have direct impact on the education and literacy of individual persons.

34. Ibid. Brandt also suggests that "literacy is a valued commodity in the U.S. economy, a key resource in gaining profit and edge. This value helps to explain, of course, the length people will go to secure literacy for themselves or their children. But it also explains why the powerful work so persistently to conscript and ration the resource of literacy. The competition to harness literacy, to manage, teach, and exploit it, intensi-

fied throughout the twentieth century. It is vital to pay attention to this development because it largely sets the terms for individuals' encounters with literacy" (p. 21).

35. Senator Byrd, who was Virginia's governor from 1926 to 1928, was an early supporter of the park's promotion. As senator, he was very concerned about the displacement of mountain families and worked to obtain assistance for them through the Resettlement Administration.

36. Billings, Pudup, and Waller, introd. to *Confronting Appalachian Stereotypes*, p. 3. This collection, edited by Billings, Norman, and Ledford, is one such set of works that confronts the historical and economic factors contributing to the dominant discourses about Appalachia. It, together with another collection, *Appalachia in the Making*, edited by Pudup, Billings, and Waller, seeks to tell a broader story of Appalachia through "community studies," in-depth examinations of Appalachian communities that complicate the narratives of homogeneity and highlight the diversity of the region. In their introduction to *Appalachia in the Making*, the editors cite Altina Waller's *Feud* and Durwood Dunn's *Cades Cove* as two of the first community studies that "undercut the traditional assumption of Appalachian exceptionalism and demonstrated that historical records existed for a social science history of Appalachian communities that could supplement, if not supplant, existing folk and oral history" (p. 12).

37. The introduction to *Appalachia in the Making* outlines the historical studies that have examined the attitudes about Appalachians. Here I provide only a very brief summary of the main attitudes about Appalachians.

38. See, for instance, John Fox Jr.'s *The Trail of the Lonesome Pine* (1908), Harry Caudill's *Night Comes to the Cumberlands* (1963), Sherman and Mandel's *Hollow Folk* (1933), Horace Kephart's *Our Southern Highlanders* (1912), John C. Campbell's *The Southern Highlander and His Homeland* (1921), and James Agee and Walker Evans's *Let Us Now Praise Famous Men* (1941).

39. The development of these theories is discussed in detail in Billings, Pudup, and Waller, "Taking Exception with Exceptionalism," the introduction to *Appalachia in the Making*.

40. Ibid., p. 8.

41. See Baghban, "Application of Culturally Relevant Factors," which discusses funding issues for contemporary literacy programs; and Merrifield, Bingman, Hemphill, and deMarrais, *Life at the Margins*, which emphasizes current trends in literacy education in Appalachia.

42. See Billings, Pudup, and Waller, introd. to *Appalachia in the Making*, pp. 6 and 3.

43. See Susan Miller, *Assuming the Positions*, p. 141, where she suggests that ordinary writing (e.g., letter writing) "demonstrate[s] how education was figured in ways . . . as *identical to* subject formation" (emphasis in original).

44. According to Brandt, "The sheer acceleration of economic and technological changes that courses through American lives" affects the "major formations of literacy" (*Literacy in American Lives*, p. 187). Brandt's study examines specifically how these changes affected the value placed on literacy.

45. Relatively speaking, the National Park Service at this time was a small entity

within the Department of the Interior. Once the CCC was established in 1933 and Roosevelt used construction of Skyline Drive as promotion of a WPA project, the NPS grew in size and power.

46. For instance, there is a current AIDS activist movement in Appalachia. See Anglin, *Women, Power, and Dissent.* Several working-class women's labor movements have been organized recently and have traditions in Appalachia. See Maggard's "Gender, Race, and Place." The 1922 national coal strike is one such instance where Appalachians took a definitive stance against powerful businesses. However, according to Dwight Billings, there are other countless anonymous actions that resist the stereotypes of Appalachia (see Billings, Pudup, and Waller, introd. to *Confronting Appalachian Stereotypes*, p. 15).

47. In Brandt's *Literacy in American Lives,* she studies "ordinary citizens," and states that she began her study with the assumption that individual context was important in understanding literacy learning. As she attended to individual contexts and, "As the analysis proceeded, additional elements of context—especially economics and history—surged into view and became vital for explaining what I found" (p. 4).

48. Dabney, *Virginia: The New Dominion,* and Link, *Hard Country.*

49. The issues of industrialization and reconstruction in Virginia were similar to other southern states recovering from the Civil War.

50. Two related movements occurred in the late nineteenth century, the conservation movement and the tourism movement. See Cindy S. Aron's *Working at Play.*

51. Virginia has a tradition of "honor," e.g., Robert E. Lee's sense of being Virginian first and American second. See Bertram Wyatt-Brown's discussion of honor, grace, and war in *The Shaping of Southern Culture.*

52. See Ted Olson's "In the Public Interest?" where he discusses the Blue Ridge Parkway and the various political and economics motivations for constructing a scenic highway in the mountains.

53. See Unrau and Willis, *Administrative History,* at http://www.cr.nps.gov/history/online_books/unrau-williss/adhi.htm, where there is a complete description of the cast of characters involved in promoting, founding, and developing Shenandoah National Park.

54. See Pollock, "Answer to Government Questionnaire."

55. See SNPA's "A National Park Near the Nation's Capital," pp. 5–6.

56. See *National Parks Bulletin,* December 25, 1924, p. 2.

57. Ibid., p. 5.

58. See www.nps.gov/shen/, www.vahistory.org/shenandoah.html, which provides general information and history about the NPS and the park; Engle, *Greatest Single Feature;* Horning, *In the Shadow;* and Lambert, *Undying Past,* for more detailed histories of the park.

59. E-mail correspondence, January 2006.

60. The SCCD was also charged with establishing Virginia state parks. At the same time that SNP was being developed, Virginia's first six state parks were also being

developed: Seashore, Westmoreland, Staunton River, Douthat, Fairy Stone, and Hungry Mother.

61. These land tract surveys, which include ownership information, land values, and the amounts paid to landowners, are currently housed in the SNP's Archives.

62. Engle, "Shenandoah National Park," p. 9.

63. Horning, *In the Shadow*, p. 100.

64. See oral history interview with Estelle Nicholson Dodson, November 23, 1977.

65. Recent newspaper accounts describe contemporary disputes regarding access to information, building of new parking lots, and representation.

66. Engle's *The Greatest Single Feature* provides many more details surrounding the history of Skyline Drive.

67. Correspondence with Reed Engle, February 2006.

68. Horning's work, including *In the Shadow*, provides comprehensive discussion and analysis of the representations of park residents and the historical, material, and archaeological evidence that disputes those representations.

69. Sizer, "Suggestions," p. 2.

70. Ibid., p. 1.

71. See also Sizer, "Tabulations."

72. See Horning's *In the Shadow*, where she describes Sizer's relationship with mountain residents.

73. "U.S. Will Move Village Where Soap Is Unknown and Chaucer English Is Spoken," *Washington Herald*, May 2, 1932, B2. More recently, several linguists have done extensive research on the links (or lack thereof) between Appalachian Englishes and Elizabethan English. See Montgomery, "In the Appalachians They Speak Like Shakespeare." In addition, linguists are currently studying the diversity in Appalachian Englishes. See Wolfram and Christian, *Appalachian Speech*; Hazen and Fluharty, "Defining Appalachian English"; and Puckett, "Let the Girls Do the Spelling."

74. Elsie Weil, "'Lost' Communities in Blue Ridge Hills: Centres Where Intelligence Practically Is Missing Reported by Psychologists," *New York Times*, October 19, 1930, p. A1.

75. See Audrey Horning's conclusions about social and economic life in this area based on her historical archaeological evidence in "Archeological Considerations" and "Beyond the Shenandoah Valley."

76. Pollock, *Skyland*, p. 135.

77. See Katrina Powell, "Writing the Geography of the Blue Ridge Mountains," which discusses the ways that these images are embedded in our cultural memories.

78. Sherman and Henry, *Hollow Folk*, p. 1.

79. Many of the photographs of park residents, their homes, and their lands were taken by C. Arthur Rothstein, a Farm Security Administration photographer commissioned to take photographs as part of the Federal Writers Project to document rural life and the effects of the Great Depression. The photographs are now located in the Library of Congress, http://memory.loc.gov/ammem/. Two of these photographs, one of Teeny Florence Corbin Nicholson and one of John R. Nicholson, are included in this book.

80. Engle, "Shenandoah National Park," p. 8.

81. Reed Engle, e-mail correspondence.

82. See Engle's *Everything Was Wonderful*, a historical account of the CCC and the young men who built the Skyline Drive and other park structures in the 1930s.

83. In fact, Dark Hollow had its own church and school.

84. See Ted Olson's "In the Public Interest?" where he says, "The New Deal provided much of the funding for depression-era parkways," although the Skyline Drive "was a legacy of President Herbert Hoover," who believed "that a scenic highway project in the newly created Shenandoah National Park would generate jobs for some Americans" (p. 101).

85. Ibid., p. 102.

86. Ibid., p. 112.

87. See Elna C. Green's introduction to *The New Deal and Beyond*, where she states that "New Deal agencies compelled southern states to create statewide welfare programs for the first time. Under pressure from such agencies as the Federal Emergency Relief Administration, the states had to hire professional staff, establish systematic reporting procedures, and learn how to calculate family budgets" (p. x). In addition, the work of the women employed by the Resettlement Administration "paralleled [that] of social workers" (p. xi).

88. Within the Department of Public Welfare, all correspondence regarding clients and their assistance or relief matters were confidential and therefore remain sealed. However, within the park's archives, these documents are available for public access.

89. While the resident and her son are named in Humrickhouse's letter, in the interest of confidentiality I have not included the names of the residents discussed. While the letters in the SNP Archives are of public record, correspondence written today by social workers about their clients is carefully guarded in the interest of client privacy.

90. See Green's *This Business of Relief*, in which she discusses the ways that public relief and assistance programs developed in Richmond, Virginia. See also Skocpol's *Protecting Soldiers and Mothers*, where she discusses the origins of relief programs with widows' pensions during the Civil War.

91. Green, *This Business of Relief*, p. 112.

2. Representation, Advocacy, and Identification

1. See *Shenandoah National Park: Official Pictorial Book*. This booklet notes on the title pages that it was "Published Under the Approval of: Southern Appalachian National Park Commission, Virginia State Conservation and Development Commission, Shenandoah National Park Association, State and Local Officials, And Leading Educational and Business Institutions of Virginia."

2. There were some instances in which families were able to influence the park's boundaries. Reed Engle describes one such instance involving a wealthy landowner who was able to influence boundary lines. See "Skyline Drive: A Road to Nowhere?"

3. See Perdue and Martin-Perdue, *Talk about Trouble*; Horning, *In the Shadow*; and Engle, "Shenandoah National Park," for more detailed histories of the region.

4. St. Luke's Mission on Tanner's Ridge was one of several Episcopal missions in the area that were part of the archdeaconry of the Blue Ridge, which was headed by Archdeacon (later bishop) Wiley Roy Mason in Charlottesville.

5. As mentioned previously, whenever letters were sent directly to the director, senators, members of Congress, or the president, their offices usually forwarded the letters to the NPS or SNP for Cammerer or Lassiter to respond to.

6. Under the Organic Act, the NPS was required to preserve buildings of "historic value." The survey of homes and buildings recommended that over forty buildings be preserved and restored. According to Engle, "There was legal imperative in this mass confusion" (personal correspondence).

7. As Reed Engle has pointed out to me, other residents may have been assisted by missionaries, social workers, or local postmasters in various rhetorical strategies, including the rhetoric of apology.

8. This property was referred to as the Mims Cottage by park residents. The Mimses sold two tracts to the park, one two-acre tract for $2,000 and one thirty-acre tract for $2,035.

9. The NPS had specific guidelines about how the landscapes should look. As "federalized spaces," the national parks were formed under the direction of landscape architects, who adhered to a "combination of careful site locations of road cuts and tunnels, revegetation, . . . and color coordination of the road and tunnels with the natural shades . . . all basic Park Service landscaping practices implemented throughout the country." See Barber, "Local Places, National Spaces," p. 53.

10. It is important to make a distinction here. Many of the mountain residents living in the area that would become the park were not poor. There was a wide variety of socioeconomic backgrounds among those people who lived in the mountains that became Shenandoah National Park, as is evidenced by the Mims family. However, by the time Arthur Rothstein came to take photographs for the FSA in 1935, most of the wealthier residents had sold their property and left the area. Those left in the park during this time were those with the least means; either they could not afford to leave on their own or the money provided through the sale of their meager homes was not enough to buy or build new homes in the more expensive lowlands. Therefore, those writing letters at this time tended to be less educated and were viewed by officials as a certain "class of people."

11. Matilda "Aunt Cassie" Breeden was one of the residents granted life tenure.

12. The letters written by Daisy Nicholson are primarily signed "Mrs. Haywood Nicholson." In addition, the letters signed "Haywood Nicholson" appear to have the same handwriting. One letter signed as "Haywood" refers to "my husband," indicating that Daisy Nicholson likely wrote the letters for her husband. Haywood and Daisy Nicholson moved to a Madison County RA homestead in 1937.

13. I do not quote directly from Daisy and Haywood Nicholson's letters because I was not granted permission from their descendents to do so. Their letters, however, are some of the most poignant in the collection, advocating for their neighbors and calling the park's attention to its responsibilities.

14. Many of the businesses within the park's boundaries were closed, although several remained open under SUP. Mercantiles, post offices, and service stations were halted once the NPS took control of the land. See Caroline Janney's research in "Why Not Panorama?"

15. Foss and Foss, "New Context," p. 11.

16. Ibid., p. 15.

3. Genre Knowledge and Assumptions about Class and Education

1. This discussion mirrors the form/content debates in the field of rhetoric and composition and approaches to teaching writing. See genre theory scholars such as Charles Bazerman, Amy Devitt, and Anis Bawarshi among others, who argue for a rhetorical theory approach to genre whereby emphasis is placed less on the features of a text and much more on the text's social context, rhetorical purposes, and themes. In this way, the users of genres are key in defining those genres. This implies, then, that inexperienced writers do know about rules, even if they are not practiced in them. The mountain residents' adherence to the form of the letter shows that genre knowledge, and consequently discursive knowledge, was not unknown to them.

2. See the *Fifteenth Census... Population*, Enumeration District No. 83–23, Sheet No. 8B.

3. Roosevelt's initiative, the Civilian Conservation Corps (CCC), resulted in most of the labor performed in establishing the park. Primarily young men from other areas, these "boys" built the overlooks, walls, and gutters of the Skyline Drive, planted vegetation, and razed those houses deemed of "no value" to the park.

4. See Theda Skocpol's *Protecting Soldiers and Mothers* for a discussion of appeals for government aid based on status as wives/widows of veterans.

5. Meadows meant "raised," stating, "I have not never raised no hell at all," implying that because he had been cooperative, he should be granted his request.

6. I was not able to locate the descendents of John Jewell and was therefore not able to quote directly from his letter. I include a description of it here because of its poignancy in demanding justice.

7. Lillard presumably did not name her neighbor for fear of her safety. There were instances where Park officials revealed who had "reported" violators, who in turn threatened the reporters.

8. The intended word is "sod." Some of Dyer's *s*'s are printed backward and thus look like *z*'s.

9. See Skocpol's *Protecting Soldiers and Mothers*, where she discusses the ways in which women were constructed as widows, beginning with the Civil War.

10. See Schultz, "Letter-Writing Instruction."

11. Maybin, "New Literacy Studies," p. 197.

12. Janet Maybin discusses the processes "involved in the mediation of texts through language, and the implications of these processes for the participants

involved" (ibid., p. 207). Like the studies she discusses, this project takes on a "Fou-cauldian notion of discourse . . . to show how people's subjectivity is shaped through their insertion, via local events, into the broader institutional discourses" (pp. 207–8). In this way, Maybin argues, "institutional power is diffused" (p. 208). The analysis here, however, contributes further to this discussion by deconstructing these processes, identifying them *and* making them visible to those who have not had access to them (like some student writers, for instance).

13. Katrina Powell, "Participant and Institutional Identity."

4. Resistance, Negotiation, and Social Action

1. By "uphold," I mean that park officials looked favorably on those residents who reported violations of others in the park. In this way, some residents self-regulated, in the Foucauldian sense, thereby enforcing the boundaries that contained them.

2. Foucault, *Power/Knowledge*, p. 142.

3. Ibid., pp. 77 and 73.

4. Here I refer to the letters written by members of the organization Children of Shenandoah to their congressional district representatives. Though this organization has since disbanded, their work advocating for their ancestors remains.

5. In this way I refer to Judith Butler's notion of gesturing, as it can pertain to per-formance of generic conventions. See Butler, *Gender Trouble*.

6. The nonstandard syntax and spelling and the responses of those in power to res-idents' form of literacy foreshadow the assumptions about language use discussed in contemporary composition studies: that is, how students are viewed when they come to college with certain sets of skills.

7. Archaeologist Audrey Horning has done an extensive study on the Nicholson family and the multiple identities they exhibited through their actions and written documents. See *In the Shadow of Ragged Mountain*.

8. Park officials, and NPS director Arno Cammerer in particular, wanted evidence of human habitat to be done away with. Therefore, all houses within one to two miles of the proposed Skyline Drive were to be destroyed or moved.

9. Of the five letters written by the Campbells, one letter is signed "James R Camp-bell" with different handwriting. The other four, with similar handwriting, are signed "Mrs. James R. Campbell," "JR Campbell," and "Mr. and Mrs. Jas R. Campbell." I assume these four to be written by Lilly Pearl Nicholson Campbell.

10. Street, *Literacy in Theory and Practice*, p. 15.

11. Most residents wrote letters only once. Rebecca Baugher (chapter 3), Lilly Pearl Campbell, John T. Nicholson, and Reverend Gird Cave were among the few people who wrote letters multiple times to park officials.

12. Park officials' attitudes toward the physical presence of mountain residents res-onate theories of the body as a social category. The bodies that acted "appropriately" were found in favor, but the beggars on Skyline Drive were deemed as behavior prob-lems. Their bodies occupied a space that the genteel, the tourists, did not want to see and often complained about. According to Sherryl Vint's discussion of Foucault, "Reg-

ulation of the body is a way of regulating social subjects, or, as Judith Butler describes it, social norms govern the particular material features of bodies that are allowed to materialize as part of our social order, each with its predictable place in this order" ("Burden of Survival," p. 143). In other words, by begging on Skyline Drive, residents disrupted the accepted social order.

13. According to Lois Cave Hurt, Gird and Click's children made paper flowers out of crepe paper and were able to sell them to the tourists driving across Skyline Drive. She said her mother, Gertie Cave, Click's daughter, could make them beautifully, and that the children were able to sell many to the tourists.

14. Richard Nicholson's letter is an example of the importance of today's conservation efforts, which seek to work with people living in areas designated for preservation. See chapter 6 for further discussion of these recent efforts both in the United States and internationally.

15. See chapter 6 for a comparative discussion of Great Smoky Mountains National Park.

16. Schultz, "Letter-Writing Instruction," p. 110.

17. Ibid., p. 111.

18. Scholars writing about the people living in Shenandoah National Park are careful not to be too nostalgic in telling their story. While some residents were misled, and some were naïve, they were not completely inexperienced in fending for their rights as humans.

19. Barton and Hall, introd. to *Letter Writing*, p. 11.

20. See Althusser, "Ideology and Ideological State Apparatuses."

21. See Leef Smith, "Anger in Appalachia: Researchers Fighting to Open Records on 1930s Shenandoah Park Settlement," *Washington Post*, March 6, 2000, p. B01.

22. See Liesel Nowak, "Exhibit Explores Displaced Lives," *Daily Progress* (Charlottesville, VA), August 2, 2004, p. A1.

23. See Peter A. Hornbostel, "Old Rag Mountain Parking Lot Project Questioned" (letter to the editor), *Madison County Eagle*, July 4, 2002, p. A4+.

24. Although this group has since been dismantled, the Web site of the Children of Shenandoah is available at www.usgennet.org/usa/va/shenan/index.htm.

5. Social Participation and Resisting Cultural Codes

1. Royster, *Traces of a Stream*, p. 125.

2. Ibid., p. 161.

3. According to Susan Miller, "*Education* thus preserves an unstable subjectivity that is partially anchored by acquiring and deploying, digesting and recirculating, commonplace cultural goods" (*Assuming the Positions*, p. 141).

4. Bourdieu, "Economics of Linguistic Exchanges," p. 131.

5. Cushman, "Rhetorician as Agent," p. 80. Cushman's work in an inner-city community is crucial to understanding the park residents' encounter with and negotiation of government documents. Based on her ethnographic research, including extensive interviews, Cushman concludes that "even though residents understood all too well

how odious gatekeepers were, adults pressured each other to *act* like they were 'respectable,' to *appear* to gatekeepers to uphold prevailing values, to scheme in whatever ways necessary in order to take care of kids, kin, and community. In short, residents pressed each other into playing up to, but not necessarily into, the ideologies of gatekeepers. To do this, they gathered, selected, and deployed a range of rhetorical tools in order to linguistically represent themselves, over the phone, in person, and on paper in ways they believed landlords would deem appropriate" (p. 80). In Appalachian studies, John Gaventa describes this relationship as "an instilled conception of the appropriate relationship between the leaders and the led." See Gaventa, *Power*, p. 200.

6. Lu, "Essay on the Work," pp. 22 and 23.

7. Hazen and Fluharty, "Defining Appalachian English," pp. 50 and 62. See also Wolfram and Christian, *Appalachian Speech*, and Dannenberg and Wolfram, "Ethnic Identity."

8. Lu, "Essay on the Work," p. 36.

9. Trimbur, "Linguistic Memory," p. 587.

10. Matsuda, "Myth of Linguistic Homogeneity," p. 638.

11. Schultz, "Letter-Writing Instruction," p. 111.

12. Gumperz, "On Interactional Sociolinguistic Method," p. 461.

13. Fisher, *Fighting Back in Appalachia*, p. 4.

14. See McDonald and Muldowny's *TVA and the Dispossessed*. Elia Kazan's film *Wild River* dramatically depicts a family resisting the TVA.

15. From e-mail correspondence, July 7, 2005.

16. General Assembly of Virginia, Public Park Condemnation Act, March 22, 1928, pp. 1–7 (National Archives, Washington DC).

17. Fisher, *Fighting Back in Appalachia*, p. 4.

18. Foucault, "Intellectuals and Power," p. 210.

19. Barton and Hamilton, *Local Literacies*, p. 4.

20. The SNP Archives contain many letters written by social workers to Zerkel and Lassiter, describing residents and their actions and the workers' recommendations for financial aid, housing, and assistance from the government. The National Archives in College Park, Maryland, contain many more, though some are not available to the public due to privacy issues. Letters located at the SNP Archives are protected by privacy as well, especially when officials discuss issues of sex and disease.

21. Taylor, *Toxic Literacies*, p. 9 (emphasis in original).

22. Historian Elna C. Green has written extensively on the history of social work in Richmond, Virginia, and the ways in which social values of "worthiness" played into the ways services were determined. See her chapter "The End of the Poor Laws: The New Deal and Social Welare," in *This Business of Relief*.

23. Taylor, *Toxic Literacies*, p. 243 (emphasis in original).

24. See Daniell, "Narratives of Literacy."

25. See Taylor's foreword to Barton, Hamilton, and Ivanič's *Situated Literacies*, p. 5, in which Taylor is summarizing James Paul Gee's conclusions in "The New Literacy Studies."

26. Barton and Hall, introd. to *Letter Writing*, p. 1.

27. See Mary Louise Pratt, Alessandro Portelli, Michael Frisch, Ronald Grele, Sylvia Salvatici, Peter Burke, and Linda Shopes for theoretical discussions about oral history as a crucial aspect of historical narrative.

28. Salvatici, "Memory Telling," pp. 21 and 23.

29. Webster, "Border Crossings," p. 826.

30. Ibid.

31. Interview with Lois Cave Hurt, personal interview, December 2005.

32. Phone conversation with Larry Baugher, December 3, 2005.

33. Webster, "Border Crossings," p. 826.

34. Ibid.

35. Teachers of writing might also connect this argument to understanding the literacy contexts of students' lives. By using literacy narrative pedagogy, connecting past experience with future inquiry, teachers of writing can assist students in their pursuits of college and workplace literacy.

36. Daniell, "Narratives of Literacy," p. 403.

37. Taylor, foreword to *Situated Literacies*, p. xi.

38. In his foreword to Collins and Blot's *Literacy and Literacies*, Brian Street points to the recent criticism of New Literacy studies, citing Collins and Blot as well as Brandt and Clinton. While situated studies are important, "critics of NLS, then, accuse it of 'relativism' and argue that its attention to the local will exclude children from varying backgrounds from access to the language and literacy of power" (p. xii). Linking texts, power, and identity, according to Street, answers this concern about specificity. This book links these important issues, as the letter writers' engagement in discursive practices is examined through the lens of the power structures of the National Park Service.

39. There is a concurrent conversation in the United States about reciprocity and ethnographic research. See Powell and Takayoshi, "Accepting Roles Created for Us."

40. Brandt, *American Lives*, p. 1.

41. Barton, Hamilton, and Ivanič, *Situated Literacies*, p. 1.

42. Brandt, "Sponsors of Literacy," p. 166.

43. Theobald, *Teaching the Commons*, p. 62.

44. Daniell, "Narratives of Literacy," p. 404.

45. Similarly, if teachers of writing ask their students to engage in literacy narrative, teachers and students must be aware of the implications implicit in exploring and documenting individual literacy history.

46. Including the rhetoric of the dispossessed does not, however, guarantee satisfaction for those displaced. A recent article in the *Atlanta Journal-Constitution* described the oral history project about the residents being displaced from their Powder Springs neighborhood in Atlanta so that a major overpass could be built. The Georgia Department of Transportation "conducted an oral history project to ease the disruption that can accompany construction." The DOT spent $30,000 collecting oral histories to "offset the overpass's impact on the community." While many residents appreciate the effort

of preserving their community's stories, some said the effort does not make up for their losses. According to resident Essie Young, who has lived in the neighborhood since the 1940s, "An oral history won't cover uprooting people from their homes" (McQueen, "Bittersweet Preservation," p. A6).

47. Exhibits at the Byrd Visitor Center display many photographs and narratives by mountain families in order to tell the story of how the park was formed. A revised, interactive exhibit is expected to be open to the public in March 2007.

6. Rhetorics of Displacement and the Politics of Eminent Domain

1. See Stacey Stowe, "Rell Seeks Legislative Review of Ruling on Eminent Domain," *New York Times*, June 25, 2005, p. A1.

2. Justice John Paul Stevens, opinion of the Court, *Kelo v. City of New London*, pp. 8, 10, 12–13.

3. See Meltz, *When the United States Takes Property*, p. 2.

4. Justice John Paul Stevens, opinion of the Court, *Berman v. Parker*, p. 35.

5. See Freeman and Braconi, "Gentrification and Displacement." This recent work on urban revitalization and gentrification concludes that race, class, and gender influence local city planners' decisions.

6. See "3 US Judges Hear Park Case: Validity of Land Condemnation Act will be Argued in Federal Court," *Daily News-Record* (Harrisonburg, VA), December 10, 1934. See also Reed Engle's *The Greatest Single Feature*, in which he discusses Via's and similar lawsuits.

7. Gaventa, "Political Economy," p. 227.

8. See Linda Greenhouse, "Justices Rule Cities Can Take Property for Private Development," *New York Times*, June 23, 2005, p. A1.

9. See David Bloome's foreword to *Local Literacies* which states, "literacy needs to be understood locally and historically (both in terms of the histories of individuals and in terms of the histories of the places and the social relationships in which they find themselves," p. xiv.

10. Malea Powell, "Down by the River," pp. 56 and 57.

11. Malea Powell, "Rhetorics of Survivance," p. 398.

12. Malea Powell, "Down by the River," p. 57.

13. See Margaret Bender, *Linguistic Diversity in the South*, and *Signs of Cherokee Culture*. This linguistic anthropologist's work on Cherokee literacy makes similar arguments about documenting the language use of individuals within a culture.

14. Chandler, *Myth of TVA*, p. 16.

15. Ibid., p. 1.

16. McDonald and Muldowney, *TVA and the Dispossessed*, p. 4.

17. See David Lilienthal, "Democracy on the March," qtd. in Chandler, *Myth of TVA*, p. 56.

18. Chandler, *Myth of TVA*, p. 58.

19. Lilienthal, qtd. in ibid., p. 99.

20. Chandler, *Myth of TVA*, p. 100.

21. Ibid., pp. 1, 2, 8, 11–12.

22. According to economist Allan Pulsipher, a past chief economist with the TVA in the 1980s and current professor and executive director of the Energy Center at Louisiana State University, issues of "inter generational equity" have never been discussed. The implication of the TVA's buying more land than it needed and now selling it "for high end residential developments that included things like golf courses" further confirms the necessity of closely examining so-called economic benefits of condemning land for the purpose of economic development (e-mail correspondence).

23. Chandler, *Myth of TVA*, p. 11.

24. Dunn, *Cades Cove*, pp. 249 and 252.

25. Stan Stevens, "Legacy of Yellowstone," pp. 30, 33, 38.

26. See Sneed, "National Parklands." Sneed discusses one example in Stevens's collection of a new U.S. park that has been established in conjunction with the Canadian government on the Alaska border.

27. See the IUCN Commission on National Parks and Protected Areas, qtd. in Stevens, "New Alliances for Conservation," p. 40 (emphasis mine).

28. See Olson, "In the Public Interest?"

29. Roe, "Use of Conservation Elements," p. 228.

30. Gaventa, "Political Economy of Land Tenure," p. 233.

31. Ibid., p. 240.

32. Similar issues in the United States include housing development displacement, worker displacement due to factory closings, and natural disaster displacement. See Marie Howland, *Plant Closings*; Margo Percival Koss, *Forced to Move*; and Peter Kuhn, *Losing Work, Moving On*, for examples.

33. See displacement.net, a resource operated by the International Network on Displacement and Resettlement (INDR) and maintained by University of Arizona anthropology professor Ted Downing. The INDR consists of researchers and practitioners who formulate "policies and mitigation methods, conducting research and developing theoretical models to mitigate damages to [displacement] victims."

34. See Holtzman and Nezam, *Living in Limbo*, p. 91.

35. Ibid., p. 92.

36. See Edward Newman and Joanne van Selm's *Refugees and Forced Displacement*. This recent collection also examines the particular vulnerabilities faced by individuals and communities as a result of displacement. Also see N. Shanmugaratnam, Ragnhild Lund, and Kristi Anne Stolen's *In the Maze of Displacement*, and Art Hansen and Anthony Oliver-Smith's *Involuntary Migration and Resettlement*.

37. Holtzman and Nezam, *Living in Limbo*, pp. 91, 90.

38. Ibid., p. xv.

39. Ellen Cushman, among others, urges researchers to be careful of seeing themselves as missionaries when researching literacy and literate practices among communities. At the same time, she engages in reciprocal and participatory research, whereby participants gain something out of the research done by academics. Similarly, Gaventa concludes, "Though the results were controversial and were never completely pub-

lished by the Appalachian Regional Commission (which funded the study), the project helps demonstrate the power of participatory, land research led by those most affected by land issues" ("Political Economy," p. 232).

40. Gaventa, "Political Economy," p. 241.

41. See Engle's "Skyline Drive," which describes how SNP's boundaries were influenced by some with social standing.

42. Lavie and Swedenburg, "Introduction," p. 2.

43. Ibid., p. 4.

44. Ibid., p. 5.

45. In the wake of natural disasters such as hurricanes Rita and Katrina in the United States in 2005, discussions of the complexities of displacement have recently resurged and have had global implications. These discussions mirror the long-standing discussions of displacements caused by forced migration, urban renewal, and relocation. At the time this manuscript went to press, those displaced by these natural disasters continued to wait for federal aid and insurance settlements. As they wait for assistance, they too face similar narratives by those holding the power over those funds, narratives of victimization, worth, racism, and merit. In a work in progress titled "Public and Private Memories of Displacement: Narrating Removal and Relocation" (in the forthcoming *Narrative Knowledge/Narrative Action*, edited by Debra Journet and Beth Boehm), I further elucidate the ways in which narratives across displacement events are similar and the ways in which personal or oral history narratives can counter the dominant representations of the dispossessed.

46. Shettima's work on government irrigation projects and the Maiatsine rising of the 1980s in Nigeria links the importance of ecology, identity, and displacement. Furthermore, the ways that threats of displacement and government-instituted ecology can incite resistance, and violent government retaliation, are also examined.

47. Minh-ha Trinh, qtd. in Lavie and Swedenburg, "Introduction," p. 16. Lavie and Swedenburg base their discussion on Trinh's work in *When the Moon Waxed Red* (New York: Routledge, 1991).

48. Street, "What's 'New,'" p. 80.

49. Gaventa, "Political Economy," p. 242.

50. Malea Powell, "Rhetorics of Survivance," p. 405.

51. See Michel de Certeau, *Practice of Everyday Life*, p. 37.

52. Krupnick, introd. to Derrida, *Displacement*, pp. 11 and 12. Krupnick discusses Derrida's use of the concept of displacement throughout his work.

53. See Malea Powell, "Down by the River" and "Rhetorics of Survivance."

54. Bartlett and Holland, "Theorizing the Space," p. 6.

55. Shirley Brice Heath (*Ways with Words*) theorizes about the "protean" shapes of literacy and the ways it fluctuates based on context. Similarly, Deborah Brandt says that examining literacy through "political and economic changes" "emphasizes the instability of literacy" (*Literacy in American Lives*, p. 7). "Moving" literacies, as I've defined it, adds a dimension to literacy that includes the lens of displacement.

56. At the time this book went to press, the Virginia General Assembly was wait-

ing for Governor Tim Kaine to sign House Bill No. 2954, a bill that would limit eminent domain in Virginia. However, Kaine is under enormous pressure from powerful Virginia lobbyists, mostly from northern Virginia, where transportation and development issues are influenced by large corporations, to maintain the current Virginia eminent domain laws, which offer little protection to property owners. On February 24, 2007, the Virginia General Assembly passed the new bill, which would repeal a portion of the current Code of Virginia by defining limits of the power of eminent domain and more explicitly defining the concept of "public use." In passing this bill, Virginia joined thirty-seven other states that have followed Justice Kennedy's warnings to be mindful of the potential of favoritism and to closely examine their eminent domain laws so that takings such as those in the Kelo case are less likely to occur. The new bill limits the transferring of lands to *individuals* purely for economic gain and ensures that a "well cared for property" cannot be condemned or considered blighted just because it is not deemed as economically feasible as new development.

Bibliography

Published Sources

Althusser, Louis. "Ideology and Ideological State Apparatuses (Notes towards an Investigation)." In *Lenin and Philosophy and Other Essays*, 123–73. London: NLB, 1971.

Anglin, Mary K. *Women, Power, and Dissent in the Hills of Carolina*. Urbana: University of Illinois Press, 2002.

Appalachian Land Ownership Task Force. *Who Owns Appalachia? Landownership and Its Impact*. Lexington: University Press of Kentucky, 1983.

Aron, Cindy S. *Working at Play: A History of Vacations in the United States*. Oxford: Oxford University Press, 1999.

Baghban, Marcia. "The Application of Culturally Relevant Factors to Literacy Programs in Appalachia." *Reading-Horizons* 24.2 (Winter 1984): 75–82.

Bakhtin, Mikhail. "Discourse in the Novel." In *The Dialogic Imagination: Four Essays by M. M. Bakhtin*, edited by Michael Holquist, 259–422. Austin: University of Texas Press, 1981.

Barber, Alicia. "Local Places, National Spaces: Public Memory, Community Identity, and Landscape at Scotts Bluff National Monument." *American Studies* 45.2 (Summer 2004): 35–64.

Bartholomae, David. "Inventing the University." In *When a Writer Can't Write*, edited by Mike Rose, 134–65. New York: Guilford, 1985.

Bartlett, Lesley, and Dorothy Holland. "Theorizing the Space of Literacy Practices." *Ways of Knowing Journal* 2.1 (2002): 10–22.

Barton, David, and Nigel Hall, eds. *Letter Writing as Social Practice*. Amsterdam: John Benjamins, 1999.

Barton, David, and Mary Hamilton. "Literacy Practices." In Barton, Hamilton, and Ivanič, *Situated Literacies*, 7–15.

———. *Local Literacies: Reading and Writing in One Community*. London: Routledge, 1998.

Barton, David, Mary Hamilton, and Roz Ivanič, eds. *Situated Literacies: Reading and Writing in Context*. London: Routledge, 2000.

Bawarshi, Anis. "The Genre Function." *College English* 62.3 (January 2000): 335–60.

Bazerman, Charles. "Systems of Genres and the Enactment of Social Intentions." In *Genre and the New Rhetoric*, edited by Aviva Freedman and Peter Medway, 79–104. Portsmouth, NH: Boynton / Cook-Heinemann, 1994.

Beaver, Patricia Duane. *Rural Community in the Appalachian South.* Lexington: University Press of Kentucky, 1986.

Becker, Jane S. *Selling Tradition: Appalachia and the Construction of an American Folk, 1930–1940.* Chapel Hill: University of North Carolina Press, 1998.

Bender, Margaret, ed. *Linguistic Diversity in the South: Changing Codes, Practices, and Ideology.* Athens: University of Georgia Press, 2004.

———. *Signs of Cherokee Culture: Sequoyah's Syllabary in Eastern Cherokee Life.* Chapel Hill: University of North Carolina Press, 2006.

Benjamin, Walter. *Illuminations.* New York: Schocken Books, 1978.

Berman v. Parker, 348 U.S. 26, No. 22. November 22, 1954.

Billings, Dwight B. Introduction to Billings, Norman, and Ledford, *Confronting Appalachian Stereotypes,* 3–20.

Billings, Dwight B., and Kathleen Blee. *The Road to Poverty: The Making of Wealth and Hardship in Appalachia.* Cambridge: Cambridge University Press, 2000.

Billings, Dwight B., Gurney Norman, and Katherine Ledford, eds. *Confronting Appalachian Stereotypes: Back Talk from an American Region.* Lexington: University Press of Kentucky, 1999.

Billings, Dwight B., MaryBeth Pudup, and Altina Waller. "Taking Exception with Exceptionalism: The Emergence and Transformation of Historical Studies of Appalachia." Introduction to Pudup, Billings, and Waller, eds., *Appalachia in the Making,* 1–24.

Blight, David W. *Race and Reunion: The Civil War in American Memory.* Cambridge: Belknap Press of Harvard University Press, 2001.

Bloome, David. Foreword to Barton and Hamilton, *Local Literacies,* xii–xv.

Bourdieu, Pierre. "The Economics of Linguistic Exchanges." *Social Science Information* 16.6 (1984): 645–68.

Bradshaw, Michael. *The Appalachian Regional Commission: Twenty-Five Years of Government Policy.* Lexington: University Press of Kentucky, 1992.

Brandt, Deborah. *Literacy in American Lives.* Cambridge: Cambridge University Press, 2001.

———. "Sponsors of Literacy." *College Composition and Communication* 49.2 (1998): 165–85.

Brandt, Deborah, and Kate Clinton. "Limits of the Local: Expanding Perspectives on Literacy as Social Practice." *Journal of Literacy Research* 34.3 (2002): 337–56.

Brooke, Robert. E-mail correspondence. June 2004.

———, ed. *Rural Voices: Place-Conscious Education and the Teaching of Writing.* New York: Teachers College Press, 2003.

Burke, Kenneth. "From *Language as Symbolic Action.*" In *The Rhetorical Tradition: Readings from Classical Times to the Present,* edited by Bruce Herzberg and Patricia Bizzell, 1034–41. Boston: Bedford Books of St. Martin's Press, 1990.

———. *A Rhetoric of Motives.* Berkeley: University of California Press, 1969.

Burke, Peter. "History as Social Memory." In *Varieties of Cultural History,* 43–59. Cambridge: Polity Press, 1997.

Butler, Judith. *Gender Trouble: Feminism and the Subversion of Identity.* New York: Routledge, 1990.

Campbell, John C. *The Southern Highlander and His Homeland.* New York: Russell Sage Foundation, 1921.

Campbell, Karlyn Kohrs, and Kathleen Hall Jamieson. "Form and Genre in Rhetorical Criticism: An Introduction." In *Form and Genre: Shaping Rhetorical Action,* 9–32. Falls Church, VA: Speech Communication Association, 1978.

Certeau, Michel de. *The Practice of Everyday Life.* Los Angeles: University of California Press, 2002.

Chandler, William U. *The Myth of TVA: Conservation and Development in the Tennessee Valley, 1933–1983.* Cambridge: Ballinger, 1984.

Chatty, Dawn, and Marcus Colchester, eds. *Conservation and Mobile Indigenous Peoples: Displacement, Forced Settlement, and Sustainable Development.* New York: Berghahn Books, 2002.

Chiseri-Strater, Elizabeth. "World Travelling: Enlarging Our Understanding of Nonmainstream Literacies." In *Literacy Across Communities,* edited by Beverly J. Moss, 179–86. Cresskill, NJ: Hampton Press, 1994.

Cody, Sherwin. *Success in Letter Writing: Business and Social.* Chicago: A. C. McClurg, 1908.

Collins, James, and Richard K. Blot. *Literacy and Literacies: Texts, Power, and Identity.* Cambridge: Cambridge University Press, 2003.

Cope, Bill, and Mary Kalantzis. *Multiliteracies: Literacy Learning and the Design of Social Futures.* London: Routledge, 2000.

Crane, Suzanne. "Teaching Advanced Research Techniques to Community College Students: Examining the Eviction of Mountain Residents from the Shenandoah National Park." *Inquiry* 1.2 (Fall 1997): 40–43.

Cushman, Ellen. "The Rhetorician as an Agent of Social Change." *College Composition and Communication* 47.1 (1996): 29–41.

———. *The Struggle and the Tools: Oral and Literate Strategies in an Inner City Community.* Albany: State University of New York Press, 1998.

Dabney, Virginius. *Virginia: The New Dominion: A History from 1607 to the Present.* Charlottesville: University Press of Virginia, 1971.

Daniell, Beth. "Narratives of Literacy: Connecting Composition to Culture." *College Composition and Communication* 50.3 (February 1999): 393–410.

Dannenberg, Clare, and Walt Wolfram. "Ethnic Identity and Grammatical Restructuring: Be(s) in Lumbee English." *American Speech* 73 (1999): 139–59.

Devitt, Amy. "Generalizing about Genre: New Conceptions of an Old Concept." *College Composition and Communication* 44.4 (December 1993): 573–86.

Donehower, Kim. "Reconsidering Power, Privilege, and the Public/Private Distinction in the Literacy of Rural Women." In *Women and Literacy: Local and Global Inquiries for a New Century,* edited by Beth Daniell and Peter Mortensen. NCTE-LEA Research Series in Literacy and Composition. Mahwah, NJ: Lawrence Erlbaum Associates, 2007.

Drake, Richard B. *A History of Appalachia*. Lexington: University Press of Kentucky, 2001.

———. "Slavery and Antislavery in Appalachia." In *Appalachians and Race: The Mountain South from Slavery to Segregation*, edited by John C. Inscoe, 16–26. Lexington: University Press of Kentucky, 2001.

Dunn, Durwood. *Cades Cove: The Life and Death of a Southern Appalachian Community, 1918–1937*. Knoxville: University of Tennessee Press, 1988.

Eldred, Janet Carey, and Peter Mortensen. "Reading Literacy Narratives." *College English* 54 (1992): 512–39.

Eller, Ronald D. *Miners, Millhands, and Mountaineers: Industrialization of the Appalachian South, 1880–1930*. Knoxville: University of Tennessee Press, 1982.

Engle, Reed. E-mail correspondence. January 2006.

———. *Everything Was Wonderful: A Pictorial History of the Civilian Conservation Corps in Shenandoah National Park*. Luray, VA: Shenandoah Natural History Association, 1999.

———. *The Greatest Single Feature . . . A Skyline Drive*. Luray, VA: Shenandoah National Park Association Press, 2006.

———. "Shenandoah National Park: A Historical Overview." *Cultural Resource Management* 21.1 (1998): 9.

———. "Skyline Drive: A Road to Nowhere?" October 6, 2004. Shenandoah National Park Web site: www.nps.gov/shen/3b2a2.htm (accessed July 7, 2005).

Ewald, Wendy. *Portraits and Dreams and Appalachia: A Self-Portrait*. Frankfort, KY: Gnomon, 1979.

Faulkner, William. *Requiem for a Nun*. 1950; New York: Vintage Books, 1975.

Fifteenth Census of the United States: 1930: Population, vol. 3, pt. 2. Washington DC: U.S. Department of Commerce, Bureau of the Census, 1932.

Findley, Warren. "Musicians and Mountaineers: The Resettlement Administration in Appalachia." *Appalachian Journal* (1979): 105–23.

Fisher, Stephen L., ed. *Fighting Back in Appalachia: Traditions of Resistance and Change*. Philadelphia: Temple University Press, 1993.

Fordney, Chris. "Boundary Wars." *National Parks* 70.1–2 (January 1996): 24–34.

Foss, Karen A., and Sonja K. Foss. "A New Context for the Study of Women as Communicators: Re-visioning Public Address." In *Women Speak: The Eloquence of Women's Lives*, 1–22. Prospect Heights, IL: Waveland Press, 1991.

Foster, Stephen. *The Past Is Another Country: Representation, Historical Consciousness, and Resistance in the Blue Ridge*. Berkeley: University of California Press, 1988.

Foucault, Michel. *The Archaeology of Knowledge and The Discourse on Language*. Translated by A. M. Sheridan Smith. New York: Pantheon Books, 1972.

———. *The History of Sexuality: An Introduction*. New York: Vintage Books, 1990.

———. "Intellectuals and Power." In *Language, Counter-Memory, Practice*, edited by Donald F. Bouchard, 205–17. Ithaca, NY: Cornell University Press, 1977.

———. "The Order of Discourse." In *Untying the Text: A Poststructuralist Reader*, edited and introduced by Robert Young, 48–78. London: Routledge & Kegan Paul, 1981.

———. *Power/Knowledge—Selected Interviews and Other Writings, 1972–1977.* Edited by Colin Gordon. Brighton, UK: Harvester Press, 1980.

———. "The Subject and Power." In *Power*, edited by J. Faubion, translated by Robert Hurley, 160–61. New York: New Press, 2000.

Freeman, Lance, and Frank Braconi. "Gentrification and Displacement in New York City." *Journal of the American Planning Association* 70.1 (2004): 39–52.

Freire, Paulo. *Pedagogy of the Oppressed.* 30th anniversary ed. Translated by Myra Bergman Ramos. New York: Continuum, 2003.

Frisch, Michael. "Oral History and Hard Times: A Review Essay." In *A Shared Authority: Essays on the Craft and Meaning of Oral and Public History*, 5–13. Albany: State University of New York Press, 1990.

Gaventa, John. "The Political Economy of Land Tenure: Appalachia and the Southeast." In *Who Owns America? Social Conflict Over Property Rights*, edited by Harvey M. Jacobs, 227–44. Madison: University of Wisconsin Press, 1998.

———. *Power and Powerlessness: Quiescence and Rebellion in an Appalachian Valley.* Oxford: Clarendon Press, 1980.

Gaventa, John, Barbara Ellen Smith, and Alex Willingham, eds. *Communities in Economic Crisis: Appalachia and the South.* Philadelphia: Temple University Press, 1990.

Gee, James Paul. "The New Literacy Studies: From 'Socially Situated' to the Work of the Social." In Barton, Hamilton, and Ivanič, *Situated Literacies*, 180–96.

———. *Social Linguistics and Literacies: Ideology in Discourses*, 2nd ed. New York: Routledge, 1996.

Geertz, Clifford. "Blurred Genres: The Refiguration of Social Thought." In *Local Knowledge: Further Essays in Interpretive Anthropology*, edited by Clifford Geertz, 19–35. New York: Basic Books, 1983.

Goffman, Erving. *Frame Analysis: An Essay on the Organisation of Experience.* Harmondsworth, UK: Penguin, 1974.

———. *The Presentation of Self in Everyday Life.* New York: Doubleday Anchor, 1959.

Green, Elna C. *This Business of Relief: Confronting Poverty in a Southern City, 1740–1940.* Athens: University of Georgia Press, 2003.

———. Introduction to *The New Deal and Beyond: Social Welfare in the South since 1930*, edited by Elna C. Green, vii–xix. Athens: University of Georgia Press, 2003.

Grele, Ronald J. "Movement without Aim: Methodological and Theoretical Problems in Oral History." In *Envelopes of Sound: The Art of Oral History*, 2nd ed., 123–54. Westport, CT: Praeger, 1991.

Gumperz, John. "On Interactional Sociolinguistic Method." In *Talk, Work and Institutional Order: Discourse in Medical, Mediation and Management Settings*, edited by C. Roberts and S. Sarangi, 453–71. Berlin: Moutonde Gruyter, 1999.

Gustanski, Julie Ann, and Roderick H. Squires, eds. *Protecting the Land: Conservation Easements Past, Present, and Future.* Washington DC: Island Press, 2000.

Hall, Randall L. "A Courtroom Massacre: Politics and Public Sentiment in Progressive-Era Virginia." *Journal of Southern History* 70.2 (May 2004): 249–92.

Hansen, Art, and Anthony Oliver-Smith. *Involuntary Migration and Resettlement: The Problems and Responses of Dislocated People.* Boulder, CO: Westview Press, 1982.

Hawks, Joanne V., and Sheila L. Skemp, eds. *Sex, Race, and the Role of Women in the South.* Jackson: University Press of Mississippi, 1983.

Hazen, Kirk, and Ellen Fluharty. "Defining Appalachian English." In *Linguistic Diversity in the South: Changing Codes, Practices, and Ideology,* edited by Margaret Bender, 50–65. Athens: University of Georgia Press, 2004.

Heath, Shirley Brice. *Ways with Words: Language, Life and Work in Communities and Classrooms.* Cambridge: Cambridge University Press, 1983.

Henninger, Katherine R. *Ordering the Façade: Photography and Contemporary Southern Women's Writing.* Chapel Hill: University of North Carolina Press, 2007.

Hofstra, Warren R. "Land Policy and Settlement in the Northern Shenandoah Valley." In *Appalachian Frontiers: Settlement, Society and Development in the Preindustrial Era,* edited by Robert D. Mitchell, 109–10. Lexington: University Press of Kentucky, 1991.

Holtzman, Steven B., and Taies Nezam. *Living in Limbo: Conflict-Induced Displacement in Europe and Central Asia.* Washington DC: World Bank, 2004.

Horning, Audrey. "Archeological Considerations of 'Appalachian' Identity." In *The Archeology of Communities: A New World Perspective,* edited by Marcello A. Canuto and Jason Yaeger, 210–30. London: Routledge, 2000.

———. "Beyond the Shenandoah Valley: Interaction, Image, and Identity in the Blue Ridge." In *After the Backcountry: Rural Life in the Great Valley of Virginia, 1800–1900,* edited by Kenneth E. Koons and Warren R. Hofstra, 145–66. Knoxville: University of Tennessee Press, 2000.

———. *In the Shadow of Ragged Mountain: Historical Archaeology of Nicholson, Corbin, and Weakley Hollows.* Luray, VA: Shenandoah National Park Association, 2004.

Howland, Marie. *Plant Closings and Worker Displacement: The Regional Issues.* Kalamazoo, MI: W. E. Upjohn Institute for Employment Research, 1988.

Hymes, Dell. "Models of the Interaction of Language and Social Life." In *Directions in Sociolinguistics: The Ethnography of Communication,* edited by John Gumperz and Dell Hymes, 35–71. New York: Holt, Rinehart & Winston, 1972.

Inscoe, John, ed. *Appalachians and Race: The Mountain South from Slavery to Segregation.* Lexington: University of Kentucky Press, 2001.

———. "Race and Racism in Nineteenth-Century Southern Appalachia: Myths, Realities, and Ambiguities." In Pudup, Billings, and Waller, *Appalachia in the Making,* 103–31.

Ivanič, Roz. *Writing and Identity: The Discoursal Construction of Identity in Academic Writing.* Amsterdam: John Benjamins, 1998.

Janney, Caroline E. "Why Not Panorama?" July 2, 2004. Shenandoah National Park
    Web site: www.nps.gov/shen/whynotpanorama.htm (accessed July 7, 2005).
Jenkins, Keith. *Re-thinking History.* London: Routledge, 1991.
Jolley, Harley E. *The Blue Ridge Parkway.* Knoxville: University of Tennessee Press,
    1969.Kahn, Kathy. *Hillbilly Women.* Garden City, NY: Doubleday, 1972.
Susette Kelo, et al., Petitioners v. City of New London, Connecticut, 545 U.S., No. 04–108.
    June 23, 2005.
Kephart, Horace. *Our Southern Highlanders.* New York: Outing, 1913.
Koss, Margo Percival. *Forced to Move: Housing Displacement in the United States.* New
    York: Garland, 1993.
Kristeva, Julia. *Desire in Language: A Semiotic Approach to Literature and Art.* New
    York: Columbia University Press, 1980.
———. "Women's Time." In *The Rhetorical Tradition: Readings from Classical Times to
    the Present,* edited by Bruce Herzberg and Patricia Bizzell, 1251–66. Boston: Bed-
    ford Books of St. Martin's Press, 1990.
Krupnick, Mark, ed. Introduction to *Displacement: Derrida and After,* 1–17. Blooming-
    ton: Indiana University Press, 1983.
Kuhn, Peter J., ed. *Losing Work, Moving On: International Perspectives on Worker Dis-
    placement.* Kalamazoo, MI: W. E. Upjohn Institute for Employment Research,
    2002.
Lambert, Darwin. *The Undying Past of Shenandoah National Park.* Boulder, CO:
    Roberts Rienhart, 1989.
Lassiter, James R. *Shenandoah National Park.* Richmond: The Commonwealth, 1936.
Lavie, Smadar, and Ted Swedenburg, eds. "Introduction: Displacement, Diaspora,
    and Geographies of Identity." In *Displacement, Diaspora, and Geographies of Identity,*
    1–26. Durham, NC: Duke University Press, 2001.
Lewis, Ronald L. *Transforming the Appalachian Countryside: Railroads, Deforestation, and
    Social Change in West Virginia, 1880–1920.* Chapel Hill: University of North Car-
    olina Press, 1998.
Link, William A. *A Hard Country and a Lonely Place: Schooling, Society, and Reform in
    Rural Virginia, 1870–1920.* Chapel Hill: University of North Carolina Press, 1986.
Lu, Min-Zahn. "An Essay on the Work of Composition: Composing English against
    the Order of Fast Capitalism." *College Composition and Communication* 56.1 (Sep-
    tember 2004): 16–50.
Macedo, Donaldo. Introduction to *Pedagogy of the Oppressed,* by Paulo Freire, 30th
    anniversary ed., translated by Myra Bergman Ramos. New York: Continuum,
    2003.
Maggard, Sally Ward. "Coalfield Women Making History." In Billings, Norman, and
    Ledford, *Confronting Stereotypes in Appalachia,* 228–50.
Martin-Perdue, Nancy J., and Charles L. Perdue Jr., eds. *Talk about Trouble: A New
    Deal Portrait of Virginians in the Great Depression.* Chapel Hill: University of North
    Carolina Press, 1996.

Matsuda, Paul Kei. "The Myth of Linguistic Homogeneity in U.S. College Composition." *College English* 68.6 (July 2006): 637–51.

Maybin, Janet. "The New Literacy Studies: Context, Intertextuality and Discourse." In Barton, Hamilton, and Ivanič, *Situated Literacies*, 197–209.

McDonald, Michael J., and John Muldowney. *TVA and the Dispossessed*. Knoxville: University of Tennessee Press, 1982.

McGuffey, William H. *The McGuffey Reader: McGuffey's Rhetorical Guide; Fifth Reader; The Eclectic Series containing elegant extracts in prose and poetry with copious rules and rhetorical exercises*. New York: Clark, Austin, & Smith, 1844.

McNeil, W. K., ed. *Appalachian Images in Folk and Popular Culture*. Knoxville: University of Tennessee Press, 1995.

Meltz, Robert. *When the United States Takes Property: Legal Principles*. Washington DC: Congressional Research Service Report, 1991.

Merrifield, Juliet, Mary Beth Bingham, David Hemphill, and Kathleen Bennett deMarrais. *Life at the Margins: Literacy, Language, and Technology in Everyday Life*. Vermont: Teachers College Press, 1997.

Miller, Carolyn. "Genre as Social Action." *Quarterly Journal of Speech* 70 (1984): 151–67.

Miller, Susan. *Assuming the Positions: Cultural Pedagogy and the Politics of Commonplace Writing*. Pittsburgh: University of Pittsburgh Press, 1998.

———. "X-Files in the Archive." *Peitho* [newsletter of the Coalition of Women Scholars in the History of Rhetoric and Composition] 8.1 (Fall 2003): 1–4.

Mills, Henry E. *A Treatise upon the Law of Eminent Domain*. St. Louis: F. H. Thomas, 1879.

Montell, William Lynwood. *The Saga of Coe Ridge: A Study in Oral History*. Knoxville: University of Tennessee Press, 1970.

Montgomery, Michael. "In the Appalachians They Speak Like Shakespeare." In *Language Myths*, edited by Laurie Bauer and Peter Trudgill, 66–76. New York: Penguin, 1998.

———. "The Scotch-Irish Element in Appalachian English: How Broad? How Deep?" In *Ulster and North America: Transatlantic Perspectives on the Scotch-Irish*, edited by H. Blethen and C. Wood, 189–212. Tuscaloosa: University of Alabama Press, 1997.

Mortensen, Peter. "Representations of Literacy and Region: Narrating 'Another America.'" In *Pedagogy in the Age of Politics: Writing and Reading (in) the Academy*, edited by Patricia A. Sullivan and Donna J. Qualley, 100–120. Urbana, IL: National Council of Teachers of English, 1994.

Newkirk, Thomas. *The Performance of Self in Student Writing*. Portsmouth: Heinemann, 1997.

Newman, Edward, and Joanne van Selm, eds. *Refugees and Forced Displacement: International Security, Human Vulnerability, and the State*. Tokyo: United Nations University Press, 2003.

Nicholson, John T. "The Old Mountain Home." *Madison County Eagle*. June 1, 1934.

Olson, Ted. *Blue Ridge Folklife.* Jackson: University Press of Mississippi. 1998.

———. "In the Public Interest? The Social and Cultural Impact of the Blue Ridge Parkway, a Depression-Era Appalachian 'Public Works' Project." In *The New Deal and Beyond: Social Welfare in the South since 1930,* edited by Elna C. Green, 100–115. Athens: University of Georgia Press, 2003.

Pasternak, Donna L. "Learning Tolerant Practice in Appalachia." In *Profession.* New York: Modern Language Association, 2003. 94–104.

Perdue, Charles L., Jr., and Nancy J. Martin-Perdue. "Appalachian Fables and Facts." *Appalachian Journal* (Autumn/Winter 1979–80): 84–104.

———. "'To Build a Wall around These Mountains': The Displaced People of Shenandoah." *Magazine of Albemarle County History* 49 (1991): 48–71.

Pluckett, John. *Foxfire Reconsidered: A Twenty-Year Experiment in Progressive Education.* Urbana: University of Illinois Press, 1989.

Pollock, George Freeman. *Skyland: The Heart of the Shenandoah National Park.* Edited by Stuart E. Brown Jr. Berryville: Chesapeake, 1960.

Portelli, Alessandro. "Oral History as Genre." In *The Battle of Valle Giulia: Oral History and the Art of Dialogue.* Madison: University of Wisconsin Press, 1997. 3–39.

Powell, Katrina M. "Participant and Institutional Identity: Self-representation Across Multiple Genres at a Catholic College." In *Writing Selves/Writing Society: Research from Activity Perspectives,* edited by Charles Bazerman and David Russell, 280–306. Fort Collins, Colo.: The WAC Clearinghouse and Mind, Culture, and Activity, 2003. http://wac.colostate.edu/books/selves_societies/powell/powell.pdf.

———. "Virginia Women Writing to Government Officials: Letters of Request as Social Participation." In *Women and Literacy: Local and Global Inquiries for a New Century,* edited by Beth Daniell and Peter Mortensen, 71–90. NCTE-LEA Research Series in Literacy and Composition. Mahwah, NJ: Lawrence Erlbaum Associates, 2007.

———. "Writing the Geography of the Blue Ridge Mountains: How Displacement Recorded the Land." *Biography: An Interdisciplinary Journal* 25.1 (Winter 2002): 73–94.

Powell, Katrina M., and Pamela Takayoshi. "Accepting Roles Created for Us: Reciprocity, *Kairos,* and Feminist Research Methodology." *College Composition and Communication* 54.3 (February 2003): 394–422.

———. "*CCC* Interchanges (A Response to Ellen Cushman)." *College Composition and Communication* 56.1 (September 2004): 150–156.

Powell, Malea D. "Down by the River, or How Susan La Flesche Picotte Can Teach Us about Alliance as a Practice of Survivance." *College English* 67.1 (September 2004): 38–60.

———. "Rhetorics of Survivance: How American Indians Use Writing." *College Composition and Communication* 53 (2002): 396–434.

Pratt, Mary Louise. "*I, Rigoberta Menchu* and the 'Culture Wars.'" In *The Rigoberta Menchu Controversy,* edited by Artura Arias, 29–48. Minneapolis: University of Minnesota Press, 2001.

Puckett, Anita. "Identity, Hybridity, and Linguistic Ideologies of Racial Language in the Upper South." In *Linguistic Diversity in the South: Changing Codes, Practices, and Ideology*, edited by Margaret Bender, 120–37. Athens: University of Georgia Press, 2004.

———. "'Let the Girls Do the Spelling and Dan Will Do the Shooting': Literacy, the Division of Labor, and Identity in a Rural Appalachian Community." *Anthropological Quarterly* 65.3 (July 1992): 137–47.

———. "The Melungeon Identity Movement and the Construction of Appalachian Whiteness." *Journal of Linguistic Anthropology* 11.1 (2001): 131–46.

Pudup, Mary Beth, Dwight B. Billings, and Altina L. Waller, eds. *Appalachia in the Making: The Mountain South in the Nineteenth Century*. Chapel Hill: University of North Carolina Press, 1995.

Pulsipher, Alan. Personal correspondence, 2005.

Reeder, Carolyn, and Jack Reeder. *Shenandoah Heritage: The Story of the People before the Park*. Washington DC: Potomac Appalachian Trail Club, 1978.

———. *Shenandoah Secrets: The Story of the Park's Hidden Past*. Washington DC: Potomac Appalachian Trail Club, 1991.

———. *Shenandoah Vestiges: What the Mountain People Left Behind*. Washington DC: Potomac Appalachian Trail Club, 1980.

Reynolds, George P. "The CCC: The Road to Recovery." In *Foxfire 10*. New York: Anchor, 1993. 240–302.

Roberts, William. *The History of Letter Writing*. New York: William Pickering, 1843.

Roe, Charles E. "Use of Conservation Easements to Protect the Scenic and Natural Character of the Blue Ridge Parkway: A Case Study." In *Protecting the Land: Conservation Easements Past, Present, and Future*, edited by Julie Ann Gustanski and Roderick H. Squires, 221–29. Washington DC: Island Press, 2000.

Royster, Jacqueline Jones. *Traces of a Stream: Literacy and Social Change among African American Women*. Pittsburgh: University of Pittsburgh Press, 2000.

Salstrom, Paul. *Appalachia's Path to Dependency: Rethinking a Region's Economic History, 1730–1940*. Lexington: University Press of Kentucky, 1994.

Salvatici, Sylvia. "Memory Telling: Individual and Collective Identities in Post-War Kosovo: The Archives of Memory." In *Archives of Memory: Supporting Traumatized Communities through Narration and Remembrance*, edited by Natale Losi, Luisa Passerini, and Silvia Salvatici, 15–52. Psychosocial Notebook II, Geneva, IOM (October 2001).

Schultz, Lucille M. "Letter-Writing Instruction in 19th Century Schools in the United States." In Barton and Hall, *Letter Writing as Social Practice*, 109–130.

———. *The Young Composers: Composition's Beginnings in Nineteenth Century Schools*. Carbondale: Southern Illinois University Press, 1999.

Scribner, Sylvia. "Literacy in Three Metaphors." *American Journal of Education* 93.1 (November 1984): 6–21.

Sexton, Roy. "The Forgotten People of the Shenandoah." *America Civic Annual* 2 (1930): 19–22.

Shands, William E. *The Subdivision of Virginia's Mountains: The Environmental Impact of Recreation Subdivision in the Massanutten Mountain—Blue Ridge Area, Virginia: A Survey and Report.* Washington DC: Central Atlantic Environment Center, 1974.

Shanmugaratnam, N., Ragnhild Lund, and Kristi Anne Stolen. *In the Maze of Displacement: Conflict, Migration and Change.* Norway: Norwegian Academic Press, 2003.

Shapiro, Henry D. *Appalachia on Our Minds: The Southern Mountains and Mountaineer in the American Consciousness, 1870–1920.* Chapel Hill: University of North Carolina Press, 1978.

Shenandoah National Park: Official Pictorial Book. Edited by Daniel P. Wine and Harold E. Phillips. Harrisonburg, VA: Shenandoah National Park Tourist Bureau, 1929.

Sherman, Mandel, and Thomas Henry. *Hollow Folk.* New York: Thomas Crowell, 1933.

Shettima, Kole Ahmed. "Ecology, Identity, Developmentalism and Displacement in Northern Nigeria." In *Displacement and the Politics of Violence in Nigeria,* edited by Paul E. Lovejoy and Pat A. T. Williams, 66–80. Leiden: Brill, 1997.

Shopes, Linda. "Oral History and the Study of Communities: Problems, Paradoxes, and Possibilities." *Journal of American History* 89.2 (September 2002): 588–98.

Simmons, Dennis E. "Conservation, Cooperation, and Controversy: The Establishment of Shenandoah National Park, 1924–1936." *Virginia Magazine of History and Biography,* 89.4 (October 1981): 115–35.

Simmons, Dennis Elwood. "The Creation of the Shenandoah National Park and the Skyline Drive." PhD diss., University of Virginia, 1978.

Sizer, Miriam. "Tabulations." Shenandoah National Park Papers, National Archives Satellite, College Park, Maryland, 1932. No page numbers.

———. "Suggestions Concerning Some Types of Mountain People in the Proposed Shenandoah National Park." Shenandoah National Park Papers, National Archives Satellite, College Park, Maryland. No date.

Skocpol, Theda. *Protecting Soldiers and Mothers: The Political Origins of Social Policy in the United States.* Cambridge: Belknap Press of Harvard University Press, 1992.

Smith, Barbara Ellen. "'Beyond the Mountains': The Paradox of Women's Place in Appalachian History." *National Women's Studies Association Journal* 11.3 (1999): 1–17.

———. "De-gradations of Whiteness: Appalachia and the Complexities of Race." *Journal of Appalachian Studies* 10.1–2 (2004): 38–57.

Sneed, Paul G. "National Parklands and Northern Homelands: Toward Co-management of National Parks in Alaska and the Yukon." In *Conservation through Cultural Survival: Indigenous Peoples and Protected Areas,* edited by Stan Stevens, 135–54. Washington DC: Island Press, 1997.

Sohn, Katherine Kelleher. "Whistlin' and Crowin' Women of Appalachia: Literacy Practices since College." *College Composition and Communication* 54 (2003): 423–52.

Sommers, Nancy, and Laura Saltz. "The Novice as Expert: Writing the Freshman Year." *College Composition and Communication* 56.1 (September 2004): 124–49.

Stevens, Stan, ed. *Conservation through Cultural Survival: Indigenous Peoples and Protected Areas.* Washington DC: Island Press, 1997.

———. "The Legacy of Yellowstone." In Stevens, *Conservation through Cultural Survival,* 13–32.

———. "New Alliances for Conservation." In Stevens, *Conservation through Cultural Survival,* 33–62.

Street, Brian. Foreword to *Literacy and Literacies: Texts, Power, and Identity,* edited by James Collins and Richard K. Blot, xi–xv. Cambridge: Cambridge University Press, 2003.

———. *Literacy in Theory and Practice.* New York: Cambridge University Press, 1984.

———. "What's 'New' in New Literacy Studies? Critical Approaches to Literacy in Theory and Practice." *Current Issues in Comparative Education* 5.2 (2003): 77–91.

Stuckey, J. Elsbeth. *The Violence of Literacy.* Portsmouth, NH: Heinemann, 1991.

Taylor, Denny. Foreword to Barton, Hamilton, and Ivanič, *Situated Literacies,* xi–xv.

———. *Toxic Literacies: Exposing the Injustice of Bureaucratic Texts.* Portsmouth, NH: Heinemann, 1996.

Theobold, Paul. *Teaching the Commons: Place, Pride, and the Renewal of Community.* Boulder, CO: Westview, 1997.

Trimbur, John. "Linguistic Memory and the Politics of U.S. English." *College English* 68.6 (July 2006): 575–88.

Turner, William H., and Edward J. Cabbell, eds. *Blacks in Appalachia.* Lexington: University Press of Kentucky, 1985.

Unrau, Harlan D., and G. Frank Williss. *Administrative History: Expansion of the National Park Service in the 1930s.* Denver: National Park Service, 1983. Available at: http://www.cr.nps.gov/history/online books/unrau-williss/adhi.htm.

Vint, Sherryl. "The Burden of Survival: The Ambiguous Body in Dorothy Allison's Fiction." In *Critical Perspectives on Dorothy Allison,* edited by Christine Blouch and Laurie Vickroy, 129–57. Lewiston, NY: Edwin Mellen Press, 2004.

Webster, Wendy. "Border Crossings: Enforced Displacement and Twentieth-Century History." *Women's History Review* 9.4 (2000): 825–33.

Whisnant, David. *All That Is Native and Fine: The Politics of Culture in an American Region.* Chapel Hill: University of North Carolina Press, 1983.

Wilhelm, Gene. "Folk Culture History of the Blue Ridge Mountains." *Appalachian Journal* (Spring 1975): 192–222.

———. "Shenandoah Resettlements." *Pioneer American* (March 1982): 15–40.

Wolfram, Walt, and Donna Christian. *Appalachian Speech.* Washington DC: Center for Applied Linguistics, 1976.

Wyatt-Brown, Bertram. *The Shaping of Southern Culture: Honor, Grace and War, 1760's-1880's.* Chapel Hill: University of North Carolina Press, 2001.

Archival Material: Manuscript Letters and Other Documents Located in Resource Management Records, Shenandoah National Park Archives, Luray, Virginia

"A National Park Near the Nation's Capital: Information Bulletin." Northern Virginia Park Association. Page, VA: 1924. Zerkel Collection, Box 2, Folder 10.

Baugher, Joseph Wilson. (Rockingham County landowner). Letter to A. E. Cammerer. February 14, 1936. Box 96, Folder 12.

Baugher, Lloyd. (Rockingham County resident). Letter to "Dear Sir." May 8, 1935. Box 96, Folder 12. Note: This letter is signed "Lloyd Baugher" but the handwriting is very similar to the letters signed by "Mrs. Lloyd Baugher" and "Mrs. Rebecca Baugher."

Baugher, Rebecca Jane Powell (wife of Lloyd Baugher). (Rockingham County resident). Letter to James R. Lassiter. March 31, 1936. Box 96, Folder 12.

———. Letter to Charles H. Taylor. February 19, 1936. Box 96, Folder 12.

Bert, C. V. Letter to Elsie Baugher. December 9, 1935. Box 96, Folder 12.

———. Letter to James R. Lassiter. November 3, 1938. Box 96, Folder 23.

Breeden, Matilda. (Greene County life-tenure resident). Letter to "Dear Sir." No month or day, 1938. Box 96, Folder 23.

Buracker, James R. (Page County landowner). Letter to "Dear Sir." February 27, 1935. Box 96, Folder 28.

Cammerer, Arno. Letter to William C. Hall. December 1935. Box 97, Folder 46.

———. Letter to James R. Lassiter. June 1934. Box 97, Folder 50.

———. Letter to James R. Lassiter (regarding Marvin Mundy). December 14, 1935. Box 97, Folder 55.

———. Letter to local resident. October 10, 1936. Box 96, Folder 28.

———. Letter to Marvin Mundy. 1935. Box 97, Folder 55.

———. Letter to Janet C. Walton. December 11, 1935. Box 97, Folder 46.

Campbell, James R. (Rappahannock landowner). Letter to James R. Lassiter. November 30, 1937. Box 96, Folder 32.

Campbell, Lilly Pearl Nicholson (wife of James R. Campbell). Letter to James R. Lassiter. November 6, 1936. Box 96, Folder 32.

———. Letter to James R. Lassiter. February 14, 1938. Box 96, Folder 32.

Cave, G. A. (Gordon A. "Gird"). (Madison County landowner). Letter to James R. Lassiter. March 26, 1937. Box 96, Folder 34.

———. Letter to James R. Lassiter. December 1937. Box 96, Folder 34.

———. Letter to Taylor Hoskins. November 3, 1937. Box 96, Folder 34.

———. Letter to Taylor Hoskins. Undated. Box 96, Folder 34.

Cave, Walter Lee. (Madison County resident). Letter to ? March 24, 1937. Box 96, Folder 34.

Cochran, Marian. (Social worker). Letter to Resettlement Administration. December 23, 1938. Box 97, Folder 51.

Comer, Fannie Baugher. (Page County resident and wife of Frank P. Comer). Letter to James R. Lassiter. December 16, 1935. Box 96, Folder 42.

———. Letter to James R. Lassiter. December 24, 1935. Box 96, Folder 42.

Cowden, Mozelle. (Social worker). Letter to Ranger Taylor Hoskins. November 16, 1937. Box 96, Folder 34.

Demaray, A. E. (Acting director, National Park Service, 1936). Letter to Rebecca Baugher. March 6, 1936. Box 96, Folder 12.

Dodson, Buck. (Madison County landowner). Letter to James R. Lassiter. March 24, 1936. Box 96, Folder 54.

Dyer, Lizzie Nicholson (wife of Charley Dyer). (Madison County landowner). Letter to Ranger Taylor. May 8, 1936. Box 96, Folder 61.

Gray, Mrs. Elbert C. (Page County resident). Letter to James R. Lassiter. October 25, 1937. Box 97, Folder 7.

Hall, William C. (Chairman, State Commission on Conservation and Development). Letter to Janet C. Walton. December 1935. Box 97, Folder 46.

Haney, Lula A. (Greene County landowner). Letter to President Franklin D. Roosevelt. Date Box, Folder.

Hensley, Clarence Elmer. (Rockingham County resident). Letter to James R. Lassiter. December 5, 1936. Box 97, Folder 16.

Hensley, Columbia Frances. (Wife of Rockingham County landowner Nicholas Wysong Hensley). Letter to James R. Lassiter. March 26, 1936. Box 97, Folder 16.

Hensley, Victoria Sullivan Meadows. (Second wife of Thomas N. Hensley, Rockingham and Page counties landowner). Letter to James R. Lassiter. March 9, 1936. Box 97, Folder 16.

Herring, Lillie Coleman. (Wife of George R. Herring, Greene County landowner). Letter to Ferdinand Zerkel. March 17, 1935. Box 97, Folder 17.

———. Letter to Ferdinand Zerkel. November 26, 1935. Box 97, Folder 17.

Hoskins, Taylor. Letter to Daisy Nicholson (Mrs. Haywood Nicholson). September 1936. Box 97, Folder 61.

Humrickhouse, Mable. Letter to Taylor Hoskins. October 27, 1937. Box 97, Folder 59.

———. Letter to James R. Lassiter. February 3, 1938. Box 96, Folder 23.

Ickes, Harold. Letter to Harry F. Byrd. August 25, 1945. Box 98, Folder 1.

Jeffries, Helen. Letter to James R. Lassiter. November 28, 1939. Box 96, Folder 4.

Jewell, John. Letter to James R. Lassiter. March 23, 1936. Box 97, Folder 27.

Lam, Bluford. H. Letter to "Dear Sirs." December 10, 1936. Box 97, Folder 33.

Lam, James. Letter to James R. Lassiter. April 27, 1936. Box 97, Folder 33.

Lam, William Zebedee. (Page County landowner). Letter to Ferdinand Zerkel. April 17, 1936. Box 97, Folder 33.

Lassiter, James R. Letter to Charles F. Bailey. March 5, 1938. Box 96, Folder 1.

———. Letter to G. W. Baugher. March 20, 1935. Box 96, Folder 12.

———. Letter to Tom Breeden. February 2, 1938. Box 96, Folder 23.

————. Letter to Tom Breeden. February 7, 1938. Box 96, Folder 23.

————. Letter to Harry F. Byrd. October 4, 1937. Box 96, Folder 34.

————. Letter to Walter L. Cave. April 16, 1935. Box 96, Folder 34.

————. Letter to Marian Cochran. January 3, 1939. Box 97, Folder 51.

————. Letter to Otis Davis. July 8, 1935. Box 96, Folder 49.

————. Letter to William C. Hall. June 29, 1935. Box 96, Folder 4.

————. Letter to Charles G. Leavell. March 11, 1936. Box 97, Folder 54.

————. Letter to Charles Melton. December 7, 1937. Box 97, Folder 48.

————. Letter to Alex Morris. March 23, 1935. Box 96, Folder 12.

————. Letter to Boss Morris. January 1935. Box 97, Folder 51.

————. Letter to Daisy Nicholson (Mrs. Haywood Nicholson). April 1936. Box 97, Folder 61.

————. Letter to Charles Ross. October 1936. Box 96, Folder 17.

————. Letter to Janet E. Walton. June 12, 1935. Box 96, Folder 23.

Leavell, Charles G. Letter to James R. Lassiter. March 9, 1936. Box 97, Folder 54.

Lillard, Ida. Letter to James R. Lassiter. July 18, 1936. Box 97, Folder 37.

Mason, Wiley Roy. (Archdeacon, Blue Ridge Episcopal Mission). Letter to James R. Lassiter. March 19, 1935. Box 97, Folder 44.

Meadows, Ben. Letter to James R. Lassiter. February 7, 1938. Box 97, Folder 46.

Meadows, Lilla. Letter to James R. Lassiter. November 19, 1938. Box 97, Folder 46.

Melton, Charles. Letter to James R. Lassiter. December 1937. Box 97, Folder 48.

Morris, Boss. Letter to Ferdinand Zerkel. March 10, 1935. Box 97, Folder 17.

National Parks Bulletin. Washington DC: December 25, 1926.

Nicholson, Daisy (signed Mrs. Haywood Nicholson). Letter to James R. Lassiter. April 1, 1936. Box 97, Folder 61.

————. Letter to James R. Lassiter. August 29, 1936. Box 97, Folder 61.

Nicholson, Haywood. Letter to James R. Lassiter. December 14, 1936. Box 97, Folder 61.

————. Letter to James R. Lassiter. November 1, 1937. Box 97, Folder 61.

Nicholson, John T. Letter to Taylor Hoskins. January 28, 1937. Box 98, Folder 1.

————. Letter to James R. Lassiter. April 10, 1935. Box 97, Folder 66.

————. Letter to James R. Lassiter. September 20, 1937. Box 98, Folder 1.

Nicholson, Richard (son of Teeny Nicholson). Letter to Virginia senator Harry S. Byrd. 1945. Box 98, Folder 1.

Nicholson, Teeny Florence Corbin (wife of Reverend George Bailey Nicholson, mother of Richard Nicholson). Letter to Ranger Taylor Hoskins. March 13, 1937. Box 98, Folder 1.

————. Letter to Ranger Taylor Hoskins. March 8, 1938. Box 98, Folder 1.

————. Letter to Ranger Taylor Hoskins. March 13, 1938. Box 98, Folder 1.

Onslow, Walter. Letter to Secretary of the Interior Ickes. May 28, 1934. Box 97, Folder 50.

Pollock, George. "Answer to Government Questionnaire Concerning Proposed Southern Appalachian National Park." Ferdinand Zerkel Papers, Box 6, Folder 1.

Ross, Charles. Letter to James R. Lassiter. October 28, 1936. Box 96, Folder 17.

Strother, Botts. Letter to Lassiter. February 19, 1938. Box 96, Folder 4.

Taliaferro, June. Letter to Taylor Hoskins. November 18, 1937. Box 97, Folder 60.

Walton, Janet C. Letter to William Hall. December 4, 1935. Box 97, Folder 46.

———. Letter to James R. Lassiter. December 12, 1935. Box 96, Folder 23.

Zerkel, Ferdinand. Letter to William C. Armstrong. January 19, 1935. Box 96. Folder 34.

———. Letter to William C. Armstrong. February 1, 1935. Box 97, Folder 51.

———. Letter to B. F. Atkins. December 19, 1935. Box 96, Folder 4.

———. Letter to Doc Breeden. April 21, 1934. Box 96, Folder 23.

———. Letter to Marcellus Breeden. January 21, 1935. Box 96, Folder 23.

———. Letter to Amos Hoffman. September 2, 1936. Box 96, Folder 1.

———. Letter to local resident. April 3, 1937. Box 96, Folder 34.

———. Letter to G. A. Moskey. April 20, 1935. Box 96, Folder 34.

Oral History Interviews

Baugher, Larry. Telephone conversation. December 3, 2005.

Dodson, Estelle Nicholson. Oral history interview, November 23, 1977. Shenandoah National Park Oral History Collection, SC #4030, Special Collections, Carrier Library, James Madison University, Harrisonburg, VA.

Hurt, Lois Cave. Oral history interview conducted by the author, December 2005. Criglersville, VA. Meadows, Ora. Oral history interview conducted by the author, November 2005. Stanley, VA.

Sims, Nellie Haney. Oral history interview conducted by the author, March 24, 2005. Stanardsville, VA.

Index